A WORLD OF VIOLENCE

Corrections in America

CONTEMPORARY ISSUES IN CRIME AND JUSTICE SERIES

Roy Roberg, Consulting Editor

The Myth of a Racist Criminal Justice System (1987)
William Wilbanks, Florida International University

Gambling Without Guilt: The Legitimation of an American Pastime (1988)
John Rosecrance, University of Nevada at Reno

Death Work: A Study of the Modern Execution Process (1990)
Robert Johnson, The American University

Lawlessness and Reform: The FBI in Transition (1990)
Tony G. Poveda, State University of New York at Plattsburgh

Women, Prison, and Crime (1990)
Joycelyn M. Pollock-Byrne, University of Houston–Downtown

Perspectives on Terrorism (1991)
Harold J. Vetter, Portland State University
Gary R. Perlstein, Portland State University

Serial Murderers and Their Victims (1991)
Eric W. Hickey, California State University, Fresno

Girls, Delinquency, and the Juvenile Justice System (1992)
Meda Chesney-Lind, University of Hawaii, Manoa
Randall G. Sheldon, University of Nevada at Las Vegas

Juries and Politics (1992)
James P. Levine, Brooklyn College

Media, Crime, and Criminal Justice: Images and Realities (1992)
Ray Surette, Florida International University

Street Kids, Street Drugs, Street Crime: An Examination of Drug Use and Serious Delinquency in Miami (1993)
James A. Inciardi, University of Delaware
Ruth Horowitz, University of Delaware
Anne E. Pottieger, University of Delaware

Ethics in Crime and Justice: Dilemmas and Decisions, Second Edition (1994)
Joycelyn M. Pollock, Southwest Texas State University

It's About Time: America's Imprisonment Binge (1994)
John Irwin, Professor Emeritus, San Francisco State University
James Austin, National Council on Crime and Delinquency

Sense and Nonsense about Crime and Drugs: A Policy Guide, Third Edition (1994)
Samuel Walker, University of Nebraska at Omaha

Crime Victims: An Introduction to Victimology, Third Edition (1995)
Andrew Karmen, John Jay College of Criminal Justice

Hard Time: Understanding and Reforming the Prison, Second Edition (1995)
Robert Johnson, The American University

Morality in Criminal Justice: An Introduction to Ethics (1995)
Daryl Close, Tiffin University
Nicholas Meier, Kalamazoo Valley Community College

Renegade Kids: Suburban Outlaws (1995)
Wayne S. Wooden, California State Polytechnic University, Pomona

A World of Violence: Corrections in America (1995)
Matthew Silberman, Bucknell University

✳

A World of Violence
Corrections in America

MATTHEW SILBERMAN
Bucknell University

Wadsworth Publishing Company
Belmont, California
A Division of Wadsworth, Inc.

Criminal Justice Editor: *Brian K. Gore*
Editorial Assistant: *Jennifer Dunning*
Production Services Coordinator: *Gary Mcdonald*
Production: *Rogue Valley Publications*
Print Buyer: *Diana Spence*
Permissions Editor: *Jeanne Bosschart*
Designer: *Andrew H. Ogus*
Copy Editor: *Sheryl Rose*
Cover Designer: *William Reuter Design*
Cover Photograph: *Len Rubenstein*
Compositor: *Scratchgravel Publishing Services*
Printer: *Malloy Lithographing, Inc.*

The pseudonym "Central Prison" is entirely fictitious. Any resemblance to the name of a real prison is purely coincidental. Portions of this book are based on material previously published by the author in the following publications: "Dispute Mediation in the American Prison: A New Approach to the Reduction of Violence," pp. 522–532 in *Policy Studies Journal,* Vol. 16, No. 3 (Spring, 1988), used with permission; "Dispute Resolution in a Maximum Security Penitentiary: Alternatives to Violence," pp. 104–120, in Miriam K. Mills, editor, *Alternative Dispute Resolution in the Public Sector* (1991), Nelson-Hall Inc., Publishers, used with permission; "The Production of Violence in the American Prison: Historical, Structural, and Cultural Contexts," pp. 3–20 in *Legal Studies Forum, Vol.* 16, No. 1 (1992), used with permission; and "Violence as Social Control in Prison," pp. 77–97, in James Tucker, editor, *Law and Conflict Management* (*Virginia Review of Sociology,* Vol. 1, 1992), JAI Press, used with permission.

This book is printed on acid-free recycled paper.

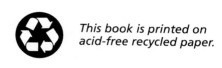

International Thomson Publishing
The trademark ITP is used under license.

Printed in the United States of America

1 2 3 4 5 6 7 8 9 10—99 98 97 96 95

Library of Congress Cataloging-in-Publication Data

Silberman, Matthew.
    A world of violence : corrections in America / Matthew Silberman.
      p. cm.
    Includes bibliographical references (p.   ) and index.
    ISBN 0-534-24540-4 (acid-free recycled paper)
    1. Prison violence—United States.   2. Prison administration-
-United States. 3. Prison gangs—United States. I. Title.
HV9025.S55 1995
365'.64—dc20
                                        94-10573

Contents

*

Foreword

The Contemporary Issues in Crime and Justice Series introduces important topics that until now have been neglected or inadequately covered for students and professionals in criminal justice, criminology, and related fields including law, psychology, public administration, social work, and sociology. The volumes cover philosophical and theoretical issues and analyze the most recent research findings and their implications for practice. Consequently, each volume will stimulate further thinking and debate on the issues it covers and will provide direction for policy formulation and implementation.

In *A World of Violence,* Matthew Silberman expands the boundaries of knowledge regarding the causes, consequences, and possible solutions to the violence in our nation's prison system. He begins with the premise that the contemporary goal of corrections, "humane incapacitation," is an unrealistic one in most prisons today. Due to a convict code which dominates the cultural life of the prison and emphasizes strength and toughness, inmates must become "hardened" in order to survive. In this provocative work, we are provided with a sense of what it is like to live and function in a coercive prison environment. Through survey research, anecdotal stories, and quotes from prisoners, the violence associated with the convict code and its impact

on both prisoners and prison staff become frighteningly apparent. It further
becomes evident that not only racial discord, but racial discrimination as
well, play significant roles in exacerbating an increased level of violence in
our correctional institutions.

Not too surprisingly, this culture of violence produces violent inmates.
This violence is then exported back into society since well over 90 percent
of inmates are released at some point in time. Violence, however, is a two-
way street. Just as it is exported from the correctional system, it is also imported from society—especially from a "frontier culture" which has led to
the legitimation of self-righteous acts of violence when one's values or sense
of worth are violated and where social inequalities are common. Silberman
takes a sobering look at what can be done to make prisons more humane
and less violent. He suggests that if we can understand that we are caught in
a vicious cycle of interaction between societal and state violence, we can
begin to break the cycle with public policies designed to civilize the nation
in general and the prison system in particular.

Finally, it is suggested that because it is unlikely that American society is
going to become more civilized in the near future, the reduction of prison
violence will most likely be limited to changes in policy that affect both
whom we send to prison and what we do with them once they are there.
To this end, Silberman puts forth some innovative recommendations regarding ways to minimize the effects of a frontier culture on prison violence, including some critical pitfalls to avoid when administering prison
systems. Overall, this work makes a significant contribution to the literature
on prison violence and policy regarding the reduction of such violence.
Hopefully, *A World of Violence* will influence policy makers to seriously consider the alternative approaches to reducing prison violence that have been
presented in this text.

                                                              Roy Roberg

Preface

This book represents the culmination of twenty years of research and writing on the punishment of crime. As a sociologist, I am interested in mechanisms of social control, the social devices designed to produce order in society. In my research on correctional institutions, I discovered that acts of violence, both legitimate and illegitimate, are the inevitable consequences of the reliance on force as a mechanism of social control. The contemporary state, it seems, relies primarily on coercion—the use or threatened use of force—to produce order through the deterrence of criminal activity and the incapacitation of convicted offenders. Consequently, those who are incarcerated for long periods of time learn to survive by becoming more violent in a world in which violence becomes a way of life.

Even in organizations intended to rehabilitate juvenile delinquents and youthful drug offenders, the central controlling mechanism is the threatened use of force. Although infrequent in most community-based programs, occasional assaults on residents by staff nevertheless become important symbolic events which make it clear who is in a position of authority. Residents are always aware of the potential for violence, even when it does not occur regularly. In some cases, the informal inmate social structure is based on physical intimidation and dominance. In one therapeutic community for drug offenders, psychological coercion or "mind control" was reinforced by the constant threat of incarceration for residents who failed to accept the therapeutic ideology of the community.

The essence of criminal punishment is the denial of liberty. No matter what sort of euphemisms we attach to punishment or its settings—rehabilitation, therapeutic community, or "group home"—the reality experienced by the subjects of criminal punishment is the loss of liberty. The modern penitentiary makes no pretense regarding its central purpose as the coercive agent of the community. As the purest form of state-mandated violence, except perhaps for the death penalty, the reality of living in a violent world has a dramatic impact on those who live and work there. The denial of liberty and the loss of control over one's own fate alter the consciousness of the subjects of such coercive regimes. Violence begets violence, and the modern convict, predisposed to respond aggressively when threatened, is a product of the modern penitentiary system.

The main purpose of this book is to contribute to our understanding of the social, legal, and institutional causes of violence in corrections. Only then will we be able to do something about the violence that pervades the system. In studying the causes of prison violence, this book attempts to contribute to the official goal of the professionally managed prison of the 1990s, the "humane incapacitation" of the incarcerated.

The study of prison violence leads to the inevitable conclusion that the production of violence in prison and the production of violent men by the prison system have consequences for society as a whole. The violent world of corrections reinforces the violence that is already endemic in our culture and adds a new layer to that violence. These violent men return to their home communities and become role models to those who have little hope of success through conventional paths in today's economy. Thus, the creation of a less violent correctional system can only benefit society as a whole.

To give students a more realistic account of what the world of corrections is like "from the inside," much of the book is based on original research on maximum security prisons, group homes, and a therapeutic community. In addition, illustrations from both academic scholarship and journalistic accounts of life behind bars supplement and broaden the scope of the work. The media, both print and visual, have also proven to be invaluable sources of material on contemporary American life.

This book is primarily intended to be a supplement for courses in criminology, criminal justice, and corrections. Students of corrections will find illustrations of life within both minimum and maximum security facilities as well as core theoretical constructs such as the deprivation and importation models of imprisonment. The book also evaluates the core theories of crime and deviance, especially as they relate to the production of violence: compliance, labeling, and control theories. For this reason, students of social control and social deviance will find this book a useful supplement to more standard texts. This book is also an excellent supplement for courses on law and society. Chapter 6, for example, examines the role of the courts in regulating correctional institutions and the impact of judicial oversight on how correctional institutions function. And, finally, introductory sociology students can benefit from a text that examines issues as broad as stratification and racism, life inside prisons, and the mutual interaction between prison and society.

Acknowledgments

Funding for the research presented in this book was provided, in part, by the Pennsylvania Governor's Justice Commission, the United States Bureau of Prisons, and Bucknell University. The analysis and interpretation of these data are solely the responsibility of the author and not those who provided the resources to conduct the research.

I am grateful to the residents and inmates of the different institutions for their participation in this study and to the numerous staff members without whose assistance and advice this research would not have been possible. To protect the identities of those who participated in this study, I have used pseudonyms for the names of both the institutions and the participants. Where feasible, I avoided using names altogether. Any resemblance to the names of existing institutions, their staff, inmates or residents, past or present, is purely coincidental.

I am also grateful to those undergraduate research assistants who assisted in some aspect of the data collection and analysis. Adam Bouloukos did bibliographic research on alternative dispute resolution, which was useful in examining mediation as a strategy for reducing prison violence. Aubrey Schneggenburger received a Knight Foundation summer grant to analyze official transcripts of Pennsylvania House and Senate Judiciary Committee Hearings on the Camp Hill Prison riot. I am especially indebted to David Wood whose assistance in collecting data from official documents and coding the questionnaire data for computer analysis was invaluable.

Professor Deborah Abowitz, sociologist and associate dean at Bucknell University, has been an important resource over the years in reading portions of this work in its earlier versions, parts of which have been published in article form. Her comments on matters of style and methodology have been extremely constructive and productive. I would like to thank Professor Leslie Patrick-Stamp, Department of History, Bucknell University, for her comments on an earlier version of Chapter 4. I am also grateful to the anonymous reviewers who commented on portions of this work when in article form. I especially thank the reviewers of this book: Steven Egger, Sangamon State University; Eric Hickey, California State University,

Fresno; Vince Hoffman, Michigan State University; Kevin Minor, Eastern Kentucky University; and Robert Regoli, University of Colorado, whose comments on an earlier draft of this manuscript were extremely helpful. I found the reviewers' comments to be thoughtful and have taken them seriously. I have agreed with many of them and disagreed with some. But, even in the latter case, the comments helped to clarify many of the issues addressed in the book.

Matthew Silberman

To Sharon

✳

A WORLD OF VIOLENCE

Corrections in America

1

*

Exploring Corrections
from the Inside

DEFINING THE PROBLEM

This is a book about the quality of life inside prisons in America today. Overcrowded conditions, racial tensions, and the demise of the rehabilitation ideal have contributed to conditions that are dangerous and inhumane. The danger is twofold. First, many prisons create an environment that encourages predators in the prison population to terrorize and exploit the majority of inmates who might otherwise do their time with little difficulty. Second, danger to the public results from the production of violent individuals learning to survive in a violent world. In other words, the American prison system both reflects and contributes to the high level of violence in contemporary society.

With few exceptions, there are more offenders incarcerated per capita in the United States than in any other advanced industrial nation.[1] Appellate courts have found most state prison systems to be in violation of the Eighth Amendment prohibition against cruel and unusual treatment due to "overcrowding and other prison conditions" (Young and Brown, 1993:2–3). Overcrowding, by itself, is not inhumane if it does not lead to other harms. The courts have found that double bunks and other inconveniences are reasonable products of the consequences of a criminal conviction

(Skovron, 1988:188). But prisoners are not put in prison to be further at risk for murder and mayhem. Visible consequences of the "totality of conditions" that do harm to the individual are increased blood pressure and higher assault rates (Skovron, 1988:190).

The most professionally run institutions today adhere to the philosophy that the purpose of the institution is the "humane incapacitation" of the convicted offender. No longer is rehabilitation held as an ideal. The prison system has become a human warehouse.

But the goal of humane incapacitation is an unrealistic one in most prisons today. A vicious cycle is in place. At one time, the most unpredictable and aggressive prisoners were kept in line by a prisoner social structure that has all but disappeared. Today, the convict world dominates the cultural life of the prison inmate. It is a world of violence in which weakness is shunned and strength is worshiped. Consequently, inmates are shaped by their experience and become "hardened" by it in order to survive in this world. The production of violent convicts reinforces the violence in the institution in general. And this leads to more violence.

During the 1970s and early 1980s, prison officials lost control of many of their institutions. Prison gangs took over in a number of cases. Finally, in order to regain control of these institutions, prison officials reinstituted the "Big House" philosophy of the past. But unlike past procedures in which institutional control was maintained by delegating authority to inmate leadership, the current practice is to use highly trained, aggressive correctional officers who have the ability to contain inmates with little harm to themselves or to others. Working in specially trained teams, these officers use disciplined force to control the inmate population. Gang leaders have been separated from others and placed in special housing units. Prison systems have developed specialized maximum security penitentiaries modeled after the federal prison at Marion in which the most dangerous prisoners are tightly monitored (DiIulio, 1990:15).

Rather than eliminating violence, the state is taking control of that violence and regularizing it. Nevertheless, the reality of prison is such that whether it is a gang leader threatening rape or murder or an official threatening solitary confinement, the threat of violence is part of the day-to-day reality of life for the convict.

One illustration of the impact of living in a world of violence on individuals is provided by the example of "state-raised youth" (Irwin, 1980:53; Abbott, 1981:3–22). These are individuals who have been exposed to institutional life from early childhood or adolescence. Many were orphaned or abandoned by parents and became institutionalized at an early age. Orphanages, sometimes euphemistically called "children's homes," house many neglected, dependent, and delinquent children. Here, these would-be criminals describe feelings of abandonment and personal failure. In this environment, their vulnerable identities are quickly shaped by what they consider the most brutal experiences of their lives, sometimes at the hands of other children and sometimes at the hands of their controllers.

Where does all this violence come from? First, there is the system of punishment itself. Relying on the state and its institutions to control criminal conduct, modern society depends on an instrument of domination that is coercive (violent) in its essence. The modern state is defined in terms of its monopoly of the legitimate means of coercion. A bureaucratic structure has been created for the enforcement of those regulations. A formal set of substantive rules, the criminal law, governs the behavior of citizens, and a formal set of procedural law, concerning arrests, trials, and sentencing, governs officials in their determination of who has violated the law and what shall be done. The prison system is the purest form of state coercion in that it monitors and controls the behavior of social "outcasts" on a continuous basis.

The first experience of being locked up is unsettling for most people. The clanging of the bars symbolizes the ultimate loss of control over a person's fate and body. Over time, there may be a loss of control over the individual's mind as well. To avoid going "stir crazy," inmates use a variety of adaptive strategies designed to preserve their sense of who they are. But these very strategies alter their consciousness and being. The violation of the self, as we know from rape victims, hostages, and others, fundamentally alters one's self-perception and the perception of others. Imprisonment, like rape, violates one's personhood. In the interests of security, prisoners are subject to strip searches, and their cells are shaken down by correctional officers looking for contraband drugs or weapons. On many occasions, the right to privacy that we as citizens take for granted as essential to the preservation of our individual dignity is routinely violated in the prison world.

THE PURPOSE OF THE BOOK

The purpose of the book is to contribute to our understanding of the causes of violence in correctional institutions and through this understanding make it possible to make them safer for both inmates and staff. In addition, by understanding the interaction between prison and society, we can address those societal conditions that produce violence both inside and outside the prison world.

It is also essential for the public to understand that what goes on in corrections is of direct interest to them, for conditions that contribute to violence in prison ultimately affect society as well. To the extent that conditions in maximum security prisons make it necessary for prisoners to become more violent in order to survive, individuals who are eventually released from prison are often more dangerous to society than when they went in.

Finally, this book presents a sociological analysis of relationships between prison and society as well as the internal dynamics of life within correctional institutions. The purpose of such an analysis is to identify the *structural* and *cultural* bases of social behavior. Such an analysis is not designed to affix praise or blame on any individual or group for processes that are rooted in the nature of society itself.

DOING RESEARCH IN CORRECTIONS

Conducting research in corrections is difficult for a variety of reasons. Prison inmates and residents of therapeutic communities fear that personal disclosures of misconduct may find their way to administration ears, despite assurances of confidentiality. Some of the more sophisticated maximum security prisoners express concerns that research findings will be used to justify more restrictive policies. Maximum security prisoners also express concern that participation in research projects, even those conducted by outside university researchers such as the author, will be seen by fellow convicts as a sign of "weakness" and increase their vulnerability to assault.

For the university researcher, there is the added difficulty of entering a different world, one whose cultural values and norms are very different from the researcher's accustomed environment. To gain familiarity with each new setting, group homes, therapeutic communities, or maximum security prisons, it is necessary to spend some time as an observer in each setting before attempting to construct scales designed to measure the experiences of those who spend a significant portion of their lives in these worlds. It is also essential to establish a neutral role to avoid being perceived by inmates as a tool of the administration. In doing research at Central Prison, the author used a vacant human services office adjacent to the prisoners' living quarters. Completed questionnaires and field notes were removed from the institution before the end of each day. To gain the trust of inmates and avoid identification with the administration, the author did not wear a body alarm worn by staff to summon assistance in an emergency.

In all three research settings, group homes, the therapeutic community, and the maximum security prison, the author was able to administer questionnaires to inmates, conduct interviews with staff and inmates, and examine official statistics. The author was free to walk freely through the institutions, including the maximum security penitentiary, but not without some official and self-imposed limitations. There were no areas that were "off limits," including disciplinary segregation or disciplinary hearings. In all three settings, the best time to "drop by" was in the evening, when residents or prisoners are more apt to talk about their experiences. In the prison setting, the author spent most of his time in the education unit where classes and club meetings took place. This was a major area for inmate groups to congregate and use prison resources.

Sampling Problems in Corrections Research

There are fewer problems conducting research in minimum security facilities. Once staff approval has been obtained, residents are usually cooperative participants in the research effort. The results reported in Chapter 8 are based on a 100 percent sample of the residents of the therapeutic community.

In the maximum security prison, however, it quickly became evident that an attempt to conduct a random sample from among the more than 1000 incarcerated prisoners was not feasible. Consequently, a quota sampling framework was used. Sample clusters were selected by work unit and living quarters in order to represent inmates in all sectors of the prison population. Working with staff who had rapport with the prisoners under their supervision, especially correctional counselors, helped to overcome the natural distrust of the inmates.

According to inmate "informants,"[2] the mass administration of questionnaires in ways that appear to be imposed from outside or above encourages systematic deception in responses. For some, the biggest obstacle to participation was the appearance of "weakness" created by cooperating with a study designed to make prisons "safer." These inmates would participate in the research only if the questionnaire were administered individually and in confidence. It was necessary, therefore, to administer questionnaires, which took on the average about 90 minutes to complete, on an individual basis or in small groups. Thus, sample size was sacrificed in the interest of enhancing the accuracy of the data.

Questionnaires were administered to a representative sample of 96 inmates. Of these, 86 consented to an examination of their official records or "jackets." Due to transfers of prisoners within and between institutions, 81 (94.2 percent) of the files were complete at the time they were examined. A comparison of ethnic backgrounds, age, criminal offense, sentences, and security levels in the sample and in the prison population as a whole reveals similar distributions, validating the representativeness of the sample.[3] A comparison of the sample and population characteristics suggests that nonparticipants tended to be younger, white inmates with relatively short prison terms, that is, those most likely to avoid the appearance of "weakness."

Measurement Issues in Corrections Research

Numerous scales have been constructed by social scientists to measure adaptation to correctional institutions. But the therapeutic community and the contemporary prison create their own language and culture to express their distinctive ways of life. Thus, it may become necessary to adapt these scales to the social context of the institution being studied. To accomplish this, the author has found over the years that it is necessary to use a complex mix of methodologies to describe the experiences of residents or prisoners accurately.

The first step is to enter the field as a participant observer without any preconceptions whatsoever. Jacobs (1974) describes the difficulty of maintaining a neutral observer role when doing research in a maximum security prison. But doing so is essential to gain the trust of both staff and inmates in order to develop an accurate assessment of the difficulties both face. The research proposal to study violence at Central Prison described the goal of the research: "to make the prison environment safer for inmates and staff alike." Posted at various locations throughout the institution was a notice that stated the purpose of the research was "to understand [prison] life, especially the kinds of situations that lead to personal conflicts between inmates and between inmates and staff. I am interested in your experiences and your opinions as inmates at [Central]. With your help, I would like to be able to make suggestions that would make this institution (and others) safer."

The next step in the research process is to systematically analyze field observations and interviews in order to construct a meaningful picture of the research setting (see Glaser and Strauss, 1967; Lofland, 1984). From these observations and interviews, it is possible to construct questionnaires to systematically test the hypotheses generated by the observations. The scales that are constructed may be derived from standardized scales in the research literature or they may be modified to reflect the unique understandings of the participants in each research site. For example, a general measure of alienation did not have any predictive value in a maximum security prison, whereas an institutional alienation scale designed to reflect the particular conditions of powerlessness experienced by inmates strongly predicted assaultive conduct. The points of reference for prison inmates concerning powerlessness are other inmates or staff members who exert control over their daily lives, not society at large, which is the focus of the standard alienation scale.

Similarly, self-rating scales that describe the self-images of the residents and prisoners in their respective settings must be tailored to identities constructed by the settings themselves. For example, becoming a "member of the family" was an important part of the experience of the resident of the therapeutic community. Similarly, the distinction between "inmate" and "convict" is important to those who live in the prison world.

In the therapeutic community, senior staff, many of whom were ex-addicts and former residents of this or some other therapeutic community, were able to provide feedback regarding the accuracy of the self-rating scales. Similarly, staff members at Central were helpful in making suggestions about the most tactful ways to ask sensitive questions to inmates and the terminology most likely to be meaningful to them. The questionnaire was also pretested by three inmates, one white, one black, and one Hispanic, to make certain that it made sense to all three groups. Where appropriate, scales were evaluated for their internal consistency and construct validity (Cronbach and Meehl, 1955; Selltiz, Jahoda, Deutsch and Cook, 1965:158–163; Carmines and Zeller, 1979; McIver and Carmines, 1981).[4]

THE SETTINGS: GROUP HOMES, A THERAPEUTIC COMMUNITY, AND A MAXIMUM SECURITY PRISON

Research was conducted in three types of settings: group homes for juvenile delinquents, a therapeutic community for youthful offenders ages 17 through 25, and a maximum security prison. Research on the community-based programs was conducted in the 1970s when support for alternatives to incarceration for juveniles and young adults was at its peak. Research on the maximum security prison was conducted during a 14-month period from mid-1984 to mid-1985, following a decade in which incarceration had become the primary response to criminal conduct, leading to overcrowded conditions in many of our prisons.

Pseudonyms are used for all the settings in order to protect the identities of those who participated. To further protect participants in the study, pseudonyms are used for individuals as well or, in some cases, no names are used at all. In addition, the use of identifying information is avoided. It is not the intention of the author to praise or blame individuals for their conduct, but rather to come to an understanding of how the cultural values and social structures of society as a whole shape what goes on in corrections and to further understand how the realities of prison life have their own consequences for individuals who reside in this world and for the society that they must return to some day.

The author conducted two in-depth studies of group homes, one in 1972 and the second in 1975. The first study was on Fellowship House, a program run by a religious ministry to convicted criminals. The second was a comparative study of three group homes run by professional youth workers in juvenile probation departments and youth service bureaus in rural and small-town settings. All four group homes were located in different counties. The purpose of the youth service bureaus was to divert delinquent youth from the criminal justice system into alternative placements such as individual foster homes and group homes run by professionals and volunteers (often college students). Providing more structure than a single-family foster home, group homes were typically run by a married couple or single person who lived in the home and were assisted by caseworkers and/or volunteer counselors. All the group homes in these studies were small, housing about six residents each.

The study of the therapeutic community, Rainbow Village, was conducted from the middle of 1973 through March 1974. In 1971, Rainbow Village had been converted from a prerelease facility for prisoners from a nearby prison into a full-time alternative therapeutic community. Many of the staff were ex-cons and ex-addicts from other therapeutic communities. Unlike its predecessors, which stressed voluntary commitment, Rainbow Village was intended as a direct sentencing alternative for drug-dependent offenders ages 17–25 who had been convicted of drug-related felonies. Located in a small city, Rainbow Village consisted of two large mansions, a few miles from one another, one on the edge of the city and one in a deteriorating residential area. The number of residents varied considerably during the ten-month research period from approximately 50 residents at its peak to as few as 30 to 35 at its lowest level.

The study of Central Prison was conducted a decade later during a fourteen-month period from mid-1984 to mid-1985 in a maximum security prison. The institution is characterized by a relatively high degree of professionalism among its employees, who are both well educated and well trained, less overcrowding than most similar institutions at the time, and relatively little gang activity. The official stance of the institution was expressed by one of its senior staff who described its primary goal as the "humane incapacitation" of the inmate population.

Systematic comparative data for assault rates in different prisons are not generally available. But to the observer, the incidence of assaults at Central appeared to be relatively low. During the five-year period prior to this research for which the data were available, 1978–82, the average number of reported assaults per annum was an estimated 32.64 per 1000 inmates.[5] This compares favorably with Crouch and Marquart's (1989:201) findings after the Texas Department of Corrections had regained control over its prison system. In 1987, the annual assault rate had dropped to 32.31 per 1000 inmates in eight Texas prisons, down from between 112.56 and 139.26 per 1000 inmates between 1983 and 1986 when gang activity was at its worst.

Although not as overcrowded as other prisons, Central is typical of contemporary prisons in a number of ways. It is typical in terms of the seriousness of the offenses of those incarcerated, its isolation from the community, and the "pains of imprisonment," the deprivations of taken-for-granted privileges of the free citizen (see Sykes, 1958:65–78). Roughly 10 percent of the prisoners were doing life sentences, primarily for homicide, including many who had committed homicides while incarcerated. About half the prisoners were convicted of armed robberies and 11 percent for drug-related offenses (this is just before the launching of the "drug wars"). The remainder had committed felonies such as assaults, weapons charges, larceny, and fraud.

Unlike many prisoners elsewhere who see themselves as doing "gang time" (see Jacobs, 1977:157; Irwin, 1980:186–195), Central prisoners still try to "do their own time" in the traditional sense (Irwin, 1980:34). Nevertheless, shared ethnicity was the primary basis for group affiliation at Central. There were over 1000 inmates incarcerated at Central at the beginning of the study, in addition to almost 200 who were in temporary custody awaiting trial or transfer to another institution.

OVERVIEW OF THE BOOK

Chapter 2 gives the reader a sense of what life is like in the contemporary prison. Relying on both the author's field observations and studies by social scientists and others, the reader is exposed to a view of prison life from the inside. Some inmates report living in a state of fear, yet others have adapted to this violent world by becoming overtly aggressive in order to survive. Correctional officers, too, must be tough and aggressive as they face prisoners who may be unwilling to comply with regulations. This chapter describes the convict code as a source of violent confrontation, including homicide, and the effects of administrative policies on convict norms and behavior.

Chapter 3 describes the importance of ethnic affiliation as a basis for group life in prison and the emergence of prison gangs. It also examines the effect of race on the enforcement of regulations by correctional officers, attitudes toward religious expression, and staff–inmate relations. Finally, the basis of so many disputes in prison, including many with lethal outcomes, centers on control over the distribution of drugs and the sexual exploitation of weaker inmates.

Beginning with a history of violence in American prisons in response to policy change in prison administration, Chapter 4 turns to a discussion of the cultural origins of violence in American society as a whole. The chapter explores the role of the frontier cultural tradition as a source of legitimation for the use of violence in confrontations that threaten a man's integrity, family, or property. In the prison world, this is translated into a focal concern with the maintenance of "respect."

Chapter 4 focuses on the dynamics of prison life from the perspective of the *importation* model, which argues that prison violence is a product of external societal conditions outside the control of prison officials. Chapter 5 examines prison from the perspective of the *deprivation* model, which argues that prison violence is a product of the inevitable consequences of confinement in a "total institution" (see Goffman, 1961). Relying on official statistics and questionnaires administered to inmates at Central Prison, this chapter evaluates three major theories of social organization and social control: *compliance, labeling,* and *control* theories. These three theories describe how institutional life produces alienation, the convict identity, and the weakening of bonds to conventional society, respectively, as sources of violence in prison.

Chapter 6 traces the history of legal reform concerning prisoners' rights and prison administration over the past 30 years. The chapter examines the effects of court decisions on prison conditions. Some of the earlier reforms are seen as contributing to increases in the level of violence in prisons. More recently, court decisions have provided a framework for the emergence of a new professionalism in prison administration. Inmate violence has begun to decline along with the number of complaints by inmates concerning violations of their civil rights.

Chapter 7 examines the impact of alternatives to imprisonment on society. Historically, these alternatives, such as group homes for delinquent youth and therapeutic communities for youthful drug offenders, have widened the net of social control, increasing the number of citizens who are subject to the coercive mechanisms of social control of the modern state. This chapter also examines the impact of contemporary alternatives to incarceration, such as intensive probation and electronic monitoring, on levels of violence in society.

Chapter 8 provides an in-depth account of life inside a therapeutic community and how psychological coercion replaces physical coercion as a mechanism of social control. Similarities to other forms of mind control or "brainwashing" are described. "Dropping out" takes the place of violence in response to coercion by those in authority. Those who do not drop out become converts to the therapeutic ideology and dependent on the therapeutic community as a way of life that is drug free and crime free.

The purpose of Chapter 9 is to identify the social origins of violence in society and to describe the mechanisms by which that violence is transmitted to the prison world. Racial inequality and economic instability contribute to the production of violence in society and the form that it takes in prison. The chapter also explores the impact of racial conflict and violence inside prisons on violence in the inner cities and racial ideologies that further divide Americans.

Chapter 10 asks the question: In the face of growing violence in society at large, how is it possible to reduce violence in a prison system that merely reflects the societal problems that create the need for prisons in the first place? In the short run, we need public policies that limit incarceration to those who really need to be there and institutions that are safe and humane in order to minimize the amount of harm done to those who must be imprisoned. The chapter also explores ways to minimize the effects of structural inequalities and the culture of violence on the internal management of prisons. Using the least restrictive environment necessary to accomplish the goals of incarceration would go a long way to reducing the production of violence in prison and in society at large. The chapter examines different approaches to separating the most dangerous prisoners from the general prison population and methods for empowering inmates without threatening the authority of correctional officers in order to reduce conflict within the prison population. Increasing professionalism in prison administration is seen as a short-term solution to the reduction of violence in prisons. A long-term solution awaits the transformation of society itself.

NOTES

1. Young and Brown (1993:4–5) report that, on December 31, 1989, the U.S. incarceration rate, including local jails as well as state and federal prisons, was 398 per 100,000 population. This rate was higher than the incarceration rates in either Eastern European or Western European countries (Young and Brown, 1993:4–5). The Polish incarceration rate was the closest to the American rate at 265 per 100,000, and the Netherlands was the lowest at 44 per 100,000. Writing in 1985, Currie (1985:28) reports that only the former Soviet Union and South Africa had higher incarceration rates than the U.S., but many prisoners were political prisoners rather than " 'street' criminals." Currie reports

that Japan's incarceration rate was only 44 per 100,000 at the time.

2. The term "informant" in sociological research simply describes someone who provides information, no matter how harmless, about the organization. Informants are distinguished from respondents who provide information about their own experiences in interviews or questionnaires. The term "informant" is a loaded one in the prison world and connotes a sense of betrayal, as in "snitch" or "rat." I use the term here in the more neutral sociological sense.

3. Black prisoners were slightly over-represented in the sample. In the total prison population, 58.4% were black and 40.4% were white; 12.4% of the prisoners were Hispanic (some of whom were classified as white and some black). In the sample, 62% identified themselves as black, 24% white, 11% Hispanic, and the remainder Native American. In what follows, the population parameters were taken from an official brochure published by the institution. The mean age for the sample was 36 compared with 34 in the total population. Except for a slight underrepresentation of those with sentences of five years or less, the sentences were almost identical in the two groups. The percent distributions for the population and sample (in parentheses) were: life = 10.6% (11.8%); over 25 years = 26.5% (28.0%); 11–25 years = 34.5% (35.5%); 6–10 years = 17.4% (18.3%); 1–5 years = 11.0% (4.3%); (missing data = 2.2%). The percentage in the 1–5 year group may be inflated because of the inclusion of inmates from a nearby minimum security camp; but these inmates were not included in the sample. A check of the actual distribution of inmates who were classified as maximum security (categories 5 and 6 on a 6-point scale) in the population was 39.1% compared with 37.3% of the sample. This institution houses inmates in both maximum security cell blocks and in dormitories. Prisoners who were classified as maximum custody and/or maximum security were usually housed in the cell blocks.

4. Each of the scales is described more fully in Chapters 5 and 8. Item analysis was used in Likert scales such as the alienation and prisonization scales to eliminate items that did not correlate with the overall index variable, increasing the internal consistency of each measure. The self-reported assaultiveness scale was validated through the construction of two subscales, one measuring assaultiveness directed at staff and the other at inmates. The percentage of inmates who report committing at least one assault on another inmate while at this institution is 88.9%, 62.5%, and 40.0%, for those who score 2–3, 1, and 0, respectively, on the staff hostility subscale ($\chi^2 = 8.42$, df = 2, $p < .01$). A strong association between the self-report and official measures of assaultiveness provides evidence of the construct validity of the self-report measure. The proportion of inmates with assault records increased systematically with increases in self-reported assaultiveness. None of those who score 0 on the self-report assaultiveness scale have an assault record; 28.2% of those who score 1–2 have an assault record; and 57.1% of those who score 3–5 have an assault record ($\chi^2 = 15.28$, df = 2, $p < .001$). There were no instances in which an inmate who did *not* report committing an assault was charged with an assault; that is, there were *no false*

positives in the official assault statistics! In other words, in the sample, *there were no instances in a which an innocent person was accused of committing an assault.* Finally, a strong correlation between two independent measures of adherence to the convict code provided evidence for the validity of each. Highly prisonized inmates (scoring at or above the median ≥ 28) were three times more likely to define themselves as convicts than those who were less prisonized (74.3% vs. 27.5%, $\chi^2 = 16.35, p < .001$).

5. This estimate is based on the assumption of an average daily population of 1250 inmates, the population in mid-1984.

REFERENCES

Abbott, Jack Henry (1981). *In the Belly of the Beast.* New York: Random House.

Carmines, Edward G. and Richard A. Zeller (1979). *Reliability and Validity Assessment.* Newbury Park, CA: Sage.

Cronbach, Lee J. and Paul E. Meehl (1955). "Construct Validity in Psychological Tests," *Psychological Bulletin* 52:281–302.

Crouch, Ben M. and James W. Marquart (1989). *An Appeal to Justice: Litigated Reforms of Texas Prisons.* Austin, TX: University of Texas Press.

Currie, Elliot (1985). *Confronting Crime: An American Challenge.* New York: Pantheon Books.

DiIulio, John J. (1990). "Prisons That Work," *Federal Prisons Journal* 1 (4): 7–15.

Glaser, Barney G. and Anselm L. Strauss (1967). *The Discovery of Grounded Theory: Strategies for Qualitative Research.* Chicago, IL: Aldine.

Goffman, Erving (1961). *Asylums.* Garden City, NY: Anchor Books.

Irwin, John (1980). *Prisons in Turmoil.* Boston: Little, Brown.

Jacobs, James B. (1974). "Participant Observation in Prison," *Urban Life and Culture* 3:221–240.

Jacobs, James B. (1977). *Stateville: Penitentiary in Mass Society.* Chicago, IL: University of Chicago Press.

Lofland, John (1984). *Analyzing Social Settings: A Guide to Qualitative Observation and Analysis.* Belmont, CA: Wadsworth.

McIver, John P. and Edward G. Carmines (1981). *Unidimensional Scaling.* Newbury Park, CA: Sage.

Selltiz, Claire, Marie Jahoda, Morton Deutsch, and Stuart W. Cook (1965). *Research Methods in Social Relations.* New York: Holt, Rinehart, Winston.

Skovron, Sandra Evans (1988). "Prison Crowding: The Dimensions of the Problem and Strategies of Population Control." Pp. 183–198 in *Controversial Issues in Crime and Justice,* edited by J. E. Scott and T. Hirschi. Newbury Park, CA: Sage.

Sykes, Gresham M. (1958). *The Society of Captives: A Study of a Maximum Security Prison.* Princeton, NJ: Princeton University Press.

Young, Warren and Mark Brown (1993). "Cross-National Comparisons of Imprisonment." Pp. 1–49, in *Crime and Justice: A Review of Research* (Volume 17), edited by Michael Tonry. Chicago, IL: University of Chicago Press.

2

✳

Violence in a Violent World

This chapter is intended to give the reader a sense of what life is like in the violent world of the contemporary prison. For those who are doing time, reactions vary from terror to bravado in a world that is threatening to one's well-being, both physical and mental. Of course, those who have been in secure institutions since adolescence, or even earlier in some cases, tend to see prison as a way of life. These "state-raised youth" identify with a set of values in which defense of one's manhood is essential and life is cheap. John Irwin's (1980:53) estimate that roughly 10 percent of today's prison population is state-raised is not unreasonable. These inmates constitute a core of dangerous people who contribute to the violent atmosphere in the most secure penitentiaries. They have a "propensity to form cliques, a willingness to threaten and actually engage in violence for protection or for increases in power, prestige, and privilege, . . . [and join] gangs in adult prisons" (Irwin, 1980:53–4).

Prison guards, too, enter a violent world in which their own ability to defend themselves physically is essential to their role as an officer (Crouch and Marquart, 1989:57). The dangers are real and made clear by occasional assaults on officers, including sexual assaults and murders of correctional officers, which are more likely to occur during prison disturbances (Jacobs, 1977:159–172; Useem and Kimball, 1987).

14

At Central Prison, fully one-third of all assault charges are for assaults against staff members. This underrepresents assaults on inmates since many of these remain undetected, whereas assaults on staff members are almost always reported. Some places within maximum security institutions are more dangerous than others. In some institutions, certain cell blocks are considered so dangerous that officers are reluctant to enter them. This was not the case at Central. Paradoxically, the vast majority of assaults on staff at Central occur in the disciplinary segregation unit, the jail within the jail.

THE VIOLENCE EXPERIENCE: INMATES

Fear

Under normal circumstances, the threat of violence is frightening. From combat soldiers to police officers, the fear of harm is a normal reaction, even to the most heroic of individuals. For the uninitiated, this fear is real. The person who is in prison for the first time experiences high levels of anxiety, unsure of what might happen to him.

Schmid and Jones (1991) report that first-time inmates undergo a radical assault on their conventional identities. The loss of control is especially unnerving, leading to uncertainty and anxiety regarding future expectations. As one new inmate expressed it, "Will I end up fighting for my life?" (Schmid and Jones, 1991:418). At Central, an older first offender, whose crimes had been nonviolent, described his first night behind bars as the most frightening event in his life. He resolved then and there never to violate the law again. Slightly built offenders often face threats of gang rape the moment they enter county jails while awaiting trial (Earley, 1992:55). At Leavenworth, a maximum security federal penitentiary, "There is a saying that . . . 'Every convict has three choices. He can fight [kill someone], he can hit the fence [escape], or he can fuck [submit]' " (Earley, 1992:55–56).

The visitor to a maximum security prison may find the clang of the bars behind him or her unnerving. The feeling of loss of control is present, even though you know that you are coming out again, aren't you? But after a while, you get used to it, and this is precisely the situation for the vast majority of inmates. Most prisoners at Central have been incarcerated before. As one prisoner who has been in and out of jail since he was an adolescent put it, "Prison is reality, [the world] out there is illusion."

The "honors quarters" house mostly nonviolent, professional criminals, including those affiliated with organized crime syndicates. These prisoners are offenders who do not have a history of violence in prison and for whom there is little evidence that they were directly involved in violent activity on the street. Thus, from the point of view of prison administrators, they are nonviolent because they do not present an immediate threat to the safety of other prisoners or to the officers. Nevertheless, one prisoner in this unit described his constant state of terror. He slept with his back to the wall, facing a barricaded door (these rooms have doors rather than cell bars) every night for fear that some convict might find his way in to "rip him off" or assault him. Many assaults at this prison take place in the early morning hours, when cells, dorms, and rooms are unlocked for wake-up call and breakfast. Potential victims are most susceptible at this time.

Both white and black unaffiliated prisoners expressed fear of organized "gangs" in this prison (more on this in Chapter 3). These "independents" were typically individuals who had committed crimes as lone bandits and had few ties to organized groups in the prison. Black independents seemed to be especially vulnerable, receiving "pressure" from black groups and feeling threatened by the presence of tough white convicts. "Pressure" in prison can mean anything from the need to affiliate for protection to providing a valuable resource for the group such as sex or drugs.

Fighting Back

In one way or another, survival in prison depends on adapting to violence as either perpetrator or victim. In his best-selling book, *In the Belly of the Beast*, Jack Abbott (1981:79) wrote that, as a young inmate, he had learned that "you must either kill or turn the tables on anyone who propositions you with threats of force." When an older inmate tried to rape him, Abbott took a knife to his throat and forced him to perform fellatio on him. Abbott adds (1981:121), "Many times you have to 'prey' on someone, or you will be 'preyed' on yourself." Jack Abbott had been imprisoned at the federal penitentiary in Marion, Illinois, considered at the time to be the most secure prison in the country, when Norman Mailer, the well-known author, lobbied to secure his release because of his talent as a writer (see Mailer, 1981:xvi).

While doing research on a community-based therapeutic community for drug offenders called Rainbow Village (see Chapter 8), the author encountered an inmate in a local county jail who had recently been the intended victim of a sexual assault. A slightly built, 130-pound youth convicted of burglary, he was doing time for the first time. A quick study, he had learned the key to survival in the prison world and decided to defend himself with all his might—to try to kill his assailant was his only defense. If not, he was destined to become someone's "punk," subject to continued sexual exploitation. He did not kill his assailant but was able to put up a credible defense. As a result, he was placed in maximum security detention. Over the next several months he added about 30 or 40 pounds of muscle and was prepared to defend himself in any future altercation.

Private and Public Worlds

It may help the reader to get a sense of the transforming effect that the threat of violence has on those who do time in today's prisons by looking at the world through the eyes of the hard-core convict at Central. Some convicts, with bandanas around their heads and covered with tattoos such as "one percenter" and "born to lose," project a tough "biker" image to those around them. Still others are feared by other inmates because of their reputations as ruthless killers on the street or in prison. Yet in private, these same convicts may express their desire to be left alone, to do their time with a minimum of interference from those in authority or fellow prisoners. In other words, we see here a sharp division between the private and public selves of the convict who has learned to survive in prison by his willingness to be violent. His reputation for violence enables him to control his world in ways that would be impossible otherwise.

These convicts express a strong division between their private and public selves. Nacci and Kane (1982:140), citing Keen (1970) on the notion that prison is "time out from personal identity" for the convicted felon, describe homosexuality in prison as a suspension of conventional heterosexual identities while in prison. But if we recognize that homosexuality in prison occurs in a context of actual or threatened violence in most cases and is as much an expression of power as it is sexuality, the heterosexual/homosexual dichotomy reflects not a time out but the ability of the person to segment his private and public selves. Privately, each person wishes for peace, but publicly each is prepared for war. Privately, most inmates prefer heterosexual relations, yet publicly many participate in aggressive homosexual activity as part of the struggle for power among and between groups and individuals. To preserve a heterosexual identity while engaging in homosexual behavior, the dominant partner or aggressor " 'feminizes' his object of interest . . . [placing] men who play female roles in submissive positions" (Lockwood, 1980:117).

But it is important to note that, over time, the private self may be transformed by the publicly expressed self-identity. In other words, eventually we become what we do. We are "taken in" by our own performance as we come to believe in the role we are playing (Goffman, 1961:17–21). Jack Abbott's murderous response to a waiter who, in his words, showed him "disrespect" is one symptom of this phenomenon (Sullivan, 1990). Abbott

(1981:75), who killed another prisoner when he was 21 years old, explains that "you are not killing in physical self-defense . . . [but] in order to live respectably in prison." Abbott then took this survival strategy with him into the streets and stabbed the waiter to death within six weeks of his release from prison.

Even the short-term inmate may incorporate some of the convict world in his view of himself when he is isolated from the support networks that validate his preprison identity (Schmid and Jones, 1991). One of the major distinctions between those who fully identify themselves as *convicts* and those who do not is the extent to which they maintain ties to the outside world.

Paradoxically, the biker and the mafioso are least likely to lose their preprison identities because of these ties to the outside world. In other words, the prison experience is unlikely to change their sense of who they are. On the other hand, prisoners who join prison gangs are likely to develop a single coherent convict identity that they then bring with them to the streets. For example, many prison gangs that originated in the California prison system, such as the Aryan Brotherhood and the Mexican Mafia, have chapters on the outside and the expectation of lifelong membership. Similarly, by the 1970s, street gangs from Chicago such as the Devil's Disciples and the Black P Stone Nation (formerly the Blackstone Rangers) had become prison gangs in the Illinois state prisons, providing members little opportunity to develop distinct nonprison private selves (Jacobs, 1977:138–174). The group that is least likely to maintain a distinct nonprison identity are state-raised youth. These are individuals who have lived in state-run institutions for most of their lives, beginning in childhood or early adolescence, and have never really developed coherent ties to the outside world (Irwin, 1980:53–54; Abbott, 1981:3).

Professional thieves and members of organized crime groups are most likely to have frequent visitors (at least once a month) from family and friends (see Silberman, 1992:88). Some of the more aggressive prisoners, many of whom identify themselves as convicts such as bikers and members of street gangs, have strong ties to family and friends on the outside that insulate them from identifying exclusively with life in prison, although geographical distance and isolation often makes it difficult for friends and family to visit. According to Wheeler (1961), there is a curvilinear relationship between identification with the convict code, which he calls "prisonization," and the amount of time served. In other words, over time inmates identify more and more with the values and beliefs that are part of the convict world, but as they get closer to release they return to their preprison identities. But this is not the case for at least one-third of prisoners doing time at Central. These inmates rarely (less than once a year) receive visits from anyone on the outside and have little incentive to retain their commitment to conventional society.

Asked to distinguish between the kind of person the inmate is in prison and on the street, here are some of their responses:

"On the street, I am/was somewhat more sociable, whereas here I let very few [get] close to me in a friendly manner."

"In the streets, I can turn my back on people, here I can't."

"[In prison], observant of all those around me."

"Introvert in prison, outgoing outside prison."

"In prison, I might react more violently, whereas on the street I might walk away."

"More antisocial [in prison]. I like to meet people on the streets, but here it's best to have as few friends as possible."

"I've become sort of a racist."

"I show a tough side in prison."

THE VIOLENCE EXPERIENCE: CORRECTIONAL OFFICERS

Not only do inmates justify violence in the name of self-defense, but correctional officers frequently lend support to such aggressive responses. For example, young male prisoners may be advised to defend themselves should other prisoners try to take advantage of them sexually; these officers make it clear that they can do nothing to stop these attacks and the prisoner must stand up like a man or he will eventually be taken advantage of (Bowker, 1980:13).

Correctional officers themselves have a similar code of conduct in which the respected officer is one who demonstrates that he can successfully take it and "dish it out" to inmates (see Crouch and Marquart, 1989:83). He must be as "tough" as the convict (Crouch, 1986:194; Crouch and Marquart, 1989:52–54). In general, violence is expected in confrontations that occur with and among inmates. Marquart and Crouch (1985:568) describe the "willingness to use force" as "rite of passage" for correctional officers in a Texas prison. This is a logical extension of the cultural legitimation of the use of violence in defense of personal masculine integrity. In prison, violence is legitimated by staff and prisoners alike.

At Central, disturbance control officers took pride in their work, physical ability, and courage. Sometimes referred to as "goon squads," officers who have physical ability and street fighting skills are selected for special duty when circumstances warrant it. In Texas, after years of disorder and violence, it was the disturbance control officers who retook Eastham prison by isolating gang leaders and locking them up (Pedersen, Shapiro, and McDaniel, 1988).

Today, the federal prison system has developed a model disturbance control squad called the Special Operations Response Team or SORT (Raymond and Raymond, 1991; Earley, 1992). Although there is some evidence that SORT had its origins in the Texas prison system in 1984 (Crouch and Marquart, 1989:144), Earley (1992:146) credits Warden Jerry O'Brien, who ran Leavenworth Penitentiary from 1982 to 1987, with creating the first federal SORT team as early as 1983. SORT officers are trained to control disorders with a minimum of injury to themselves and inmates. Wearing special protective helmets and body suits, they enter the cell of a difficult prisoner. Each officer is responsible for controlling a particular body part, a leg or arm. With the focus on specific goals in this way, the inmate can do little to resist or to injure himself or an officer. To the extent possible, SORT actions are taped for review. This is an example of the professional approach to the use of controlled violence that is becoming the model for today's prison administrator. SORT officers maintain a team spirit by engaging in athletic competitions with other SORT units in annual tournaments.

At Central, the correctional officer who gains the respect of both staff and inmates alike is fearless when faced with dangerous situations. Working closely with inmates in situations of isolation and vulnerability, he would not think twice should he observe an inmate with a deadly weapon. In one situation an officer was in a large open area at the entrance to the dining halls during the lunch hour when he observed an inmate attacking another with a knife. He lunged at the inmate, wrestled the knife away, and prevented a murder from taking place. Interestingly, he risked his life to protect an inmate! At Central, the officer's primary duty is to the "humane incapacitation" of dangerous felons. Evidently this is a responsibility many officers take seriously.

On the other hand, this violence can take on a negative aspect. The role of correctional officer is considered to be one of the most stressful occupational roles in contemporary society (Williamson, 1990:149–164). Correctional officers suffer from "higher than average" stress-related illnesses such as hypertension and alcoholism (Crouch, 1980:19; Cheek and Miller, 1983; Mobley, 1985; Kauffman, 1988:220–221; Williamson, 1990:149). According to Cheek and Miller (1983:111), correctional officers are more likely to report alcohol problems than police officers, with 27 percent of their New Jersey sample stating that at least one of their "five closest colleagues" had an alcohol problem. During the research at Central, two officers were killed in a one-car accident. According to local newspaper accounts, both the driver and passenger were legally intoxicated when the car skidded out of control while passing another vehicle.

It seems, too, that family problems among correctional officers are not unusual. According to one study (Cheek and Miller, 1983:111), the divorce rate among correctional officers is double the rate for blue and white collar workers. In one extreme situation, Earley (1992:119) describes a lieutenant at Leavenworth who, known for his no-nonsense approach at work, was suspected of violence at home. But this violence at home was covered up and ignored by those with whom he worked until one day one of his teen-age sons shot him to death. The fourteen-year-old fired both barrels of a shotgun at his father after his father had knocked out his older brother in a fit of rage, stating "you're next" to the fourteen-year-old (Earley, 1992:130). No criminal charges were filed.

At Stanford University, psychologist Philip Zimbardo (1982) constructed a prison in the basement of the Psychology Department building. He randomly assigned "mature, emotionally stable" young male volunteers to the roles of inmates and guards. The project was to last two weeks, but in only six days, he found that abuse on the part of some of the correctional officers had reached such proportions that it was necessary to stop the experiment. Some guards treated prisoners as "despicable animals, taking pleasure in cruelty," while prisoners were "dehumanized" (Zimbardo, 1982: 196). About one-third of the guards became "tyrannical in their arbitrary use of power" (Zimbardo, 1982:196). This research indicates that there is something about the nature of the power relationship between officer and inmate that lends itself to physical violence and the abuse of power.

A major criticism of Zimbardo's experiment is that he failed to give specific instructions to the volunteer correctional officers regarding the rules they were to apply in maintaining order, nor were limits clearly defined. In fact, the so-called guards were free to create their own rules. This is hardly the case in real prisons today. Officers are trained to abide by specific procedures, including those pertaining to the use of force. Increasingly, court decisions have defined the parameters of proper action by correctional officers for which administrators may be held responsible. At institutions like Central, officers are subject to dismissal should they engage in the use of excessive force. But this is not the case everywhere.

Crouch and Marquart (1989:78) describe a "tune-up" as the beating of a prisoner in order to teach him respect for the authority of the correctional officer. A tune-up "involved verbal humiliation, profanity, shoves, kicks, and head and body slaps" at Eastham prison in Texas, but it was the mildest of three types of officer violence employed prior to the institutionalization of more disciplined and legalistic force policies in the mid to late 1980s. An "ass-whipping" involved the use of nonlethal weapons such as blackjacks and batons and occurred in response to a major challenge to officer control, such as an inmate yelling "shut up yourself and stay the hell out of the dayroom" to an officer who had ordered inmates to keep quiet (Crouch and Marquart, 1989:79). Severe beatings were reserved for inmates who attacked staff members (Crouch and Marquart, 1989:80).

Whenever such behavior becomes routine, even if not legitimated by prison administrators, new correctional officers will be taught by the old guards how it is "really" done in the prison. In a recent case (*Hudson v. McMillian*, 1992), the U.S. Supreme Court ruled by a 7–2 majority that a "tune-up" is never justified under the Constitution's Eighth Amendment prohibition against cruel and unusual punishment. Following an argument with a correctional officer, a Louisiana state prison inmate had been beaten by two officers under the watchful eye of a supervisor; in other words, he had received a "tune-up." Although his damages were minor (he suffered some bruises and a cracked dental plate), the justices approved awarding him damages because his civil rights had been violated.

Both the U.S. Department of Justice, whose Bureau of Prisons is one of the most professionally managed prison systems in the world, and a watchdog group, Americans for Effective Law Enforcement, which is usually on the other side of these issues, supported inmate Hudson in amicus (friend of the court) briefs. The use of force that is not necessary to maintain order in the institution is excessive and constitutes brutality. From the point of view of some correctional officers, however, the ability to discipline an inmate may be the only way to teach him who is in charge.

The use of excessive force was clearly prohibited at Central. Although it is necessary from time to time to use force to quell a disturbance or move a disruptive inmate from one location to another, or even arrest a violator, these acts of violence by correctional officers are authorized and within the bounds of legality. Correctional officers understand that the use of excessive force may lead to disciplinary action or even dismissal.

Although *no* inmates who were interviewed or who responded to the questionnaire reported that they had been personally a victim of excessive force, some reported that beatings occurred in the segregation unit. One inmate (out of 96) reported being "hurt or injured" by an officer at some time during his stay, but there is no evidence from his description that inappropriate force was used. Ten (10 percent) of the sample described various threats to do bodily harm, including one "to be taken to segregation and beat up." Some of the others described threats such as "get my head busted," "get my ass busted," and "kick [my] ass." Clearly, some inmates believe that tune-ups occur in the "hole" where they are not visible to administrators.

There was one civil suit alleging the use of excessive force during the fourteen-month research period at Central, and this suit alleged the violation had occurred two years earlier. An inmate charged that three masked officers had entered his cell in the segregation unit, "beat him and used handcuffs to hang him by one leg" from a light fixture for five minutes. The jury did not find that the inmate's constitutional rights had been violated nor that he had been injured, but it did award him modest punitive damages for the hanging. Prison officials had argued that the inmate was "prone to self-inflicted injuries" and "had placed himself in a hanging position."

SYMBOLS OF VIOLENCE
IN A VIOLENT WORLD

The environment of the prison itself provides a variety of symbols of violence, which convey to the inmate, guard, and visitor alike the fundamental reality of prison life. First, there is the *body alarm*, similar to a beeper, worn by staff members who may find themselves in isolated, dangerous situations and need to summon the assistance of other staff. The body alarm reminds the officers that they are among dangerous individuals whom they cannot trust. Similarly, walkie-talkies are used by correctional officers to stay in contact with the control center, which monitors inmate location and movement throughout the institution.

At Central, dialing 2-2-2 on the nearest phone, called the *deuces*, alerts the control center that an officer is in trouble and needs assistance. The control center officer, in turn, alerts others that an officer needs assistance or that there is some other emergency requiring backup. Once alerted, all those who are available and not required to stay at a particular location for security reasons are expected to come to the assistance of the officer or staff member who sounded the alarm. This includes correctional officers, teachers, and any other regular employees who are in the vicinity. They are expected to run in the direction of the trouble.

The most generalized symbols of violence in the prison are associated with the coercive nature of the social controls employed, from metal bars or "grilles" and locked doors to metal detectors and body searches. Certainly the wall, with its gun towers, surrounding the prison grounds is ample evidence of the coercive nature of the institution. Each visitor or employee and all new inmates must pass through this wall and associated grilles before gaining access to the prison grounds. The loss of control experienced the first time the gate clangs behind you is overwhelming for visitors as well as those who realize that they are not to leave for many years to come.

On another level, there are more subtle symbols of violence conveyed to newcomers than just the physical plant. *War stories* designed to convey the dangerous nature of the prisoners are communicated to visitor and new employee alike to create proper respect for the violent nature of the prison world. One inmate was pointed out who had allegedly murdered a staff member at another institution and dismembered him. A few years earlier, as part of a plan to take over the institution, a group of prisoners (who had been removed from another prison after taking part in both large-scale property destruction and the killing of other inmates) had apparently planned to take female employees hostage during the lunch hour as they were proceeding to the officer's mess, which is behind the inmate cafeteria. Fortunately, the staff was able to thwart the planned takeover before it actually took place. Several years before that, a group of inmates assaulted three correctional officers, reportedly beating their heads against the wall. They all survived with various stages of disability, although one officer recovered sufficiently both physically and emotionally to be able to return to work. Staff members also described instances in which a female employee at another prison had been raped and murdered by an inmate and how a female staff member at another had been raped.

Significant in the minds of many staff members were the recent murders of two correctional officers by two members of the Aryan Brotherhood (AB) prison gang in the control unit at Marion Federal Penitentiary, nicknamed the "Alcatraz of the '80s" (the same prison that had housed Jack Abbott prior to his release). The fact that there were Aryan Brotherhood members at Central was brought out in a murder trial involving the killing of a black prisoner who allegedly raped (or attempted to rape) the homosexual lover ("kid") of an AB gang member (see Chapter 3). The visible presence of gang members at this prison was also a symbol of potential violence.

HOMICIDES AT CENTRAL

Following work stoppages and a major disturbance involving an assault on three officers in the early 1970s, the institution experienced a series of highly visible signs of disorder, including 8 homicides in a 26-month period and a well-publicized escape involving the commandeering of a garbage truck, which was then rammed through the rear gate. An investigation of the homicides concluded that most of the victims were long-term inmates who were killed "in retaliation for something they had done." Several of the homicides had been provoked by some sort of dispute, often involving "homosexual entanglements."

Another inquiry in the early 1980s investigated reports that homicides at Central were racially motivated. Black inmates complained that the previous six to nine murders had been racially motivated slayings of blacks by whites. According to the staff, there were only four to six murders during the three-year period prior to the investigation.

According to institutional records, there were five murders and one attempted murder during the period under investigation. In four of these five murders, two involved blacks killing blacks, one involved two whites killing a Hispanic prisoner, and one a white killing a black. The author was unable to discover the racial characteristics of the assailant and victim in the fifth murder, but the attempted murder involved a white assailant and a white victim. In other words, there appears no systematic racial bias in homicides here. Moreover, the homicide rate was relatively stable from the late 1970s through the middle '80s, at about one or two per year.

Only one murder during the past twenty years may have been explicitly racially motivated. In the mid-1970s, the murder of a white convict, who was himself a convicted murderer, by a group of black inmates was in apparent retaliation for the killing of a black prisoner by a white group at another prison. This was during a period of racial violence in American prisons as racially motivated prison gangs appeared to be taking hold.

There were three murders and one attempted murder from mid-1984 through mid-1985.[1] The first incident began with a dispute between two inmates. It seems that one inmate had pulled a knife on the other early that morning. When he was approached later by a few friends of the inmate he had threatened, he pulled a knife again. Later that day, three inmates approached the one who had pulled the knife during the lunch hour, when inmates are milling about, going to and from the cafeteria. At this time, case managers, correctional counselors, and supervisors are available to chat informally with inmates and keep an eye on them. Several officers jumped the assailants to prevent the knifing by separating the combatants. While the officers were restraining the first prisoner, one of the others broke loose and fatally stabbed him.

The second murder occurred in the cell block reserved for "fags and losers" (an appellation used by staff and inmates alike), inmates who have a record of mental illness or are "known" homosexuals. Inmates with prior histories of mental illness or who were currently on medication (about 50 of the 1250 total) were assigned to this unit. Just after the wake-up call one morning, two inmates entered the cell of another and stabbed him to death. After this incident, another inmate in this unit described barricading his door at night to protect himself against unexpected intruders before he was fully awake in the morning.

The attempted murder is typical of the type of situations that generates violence here and elsewhere. A prisoner who was described by officials as a sexual predator had attempted to "pressure" another inmate for sex. This inmate had requested and received a transfer to another prison for his own protection. For some inexplicable reason, this inmate was transferred back from the other prison and was housed in the segregation unit. During the recreation period, the prisoner who had been pressured reached for a "shank" (homemade knife) while his cuffs were off and slashed the throat of the assailant who had been placed in segregation at the same time. It is evident that this prisoner had learned that if he wanted to do his time without being "turned out" or becoming someone's "kid," he would have to display his willingness to use deadly force to protect himself.

Assaults involving homemade knives disproportionately involve aggressive homosexual activity. These disputes are made worse when they cross racial or ethnic lines. Most such assaults are intended not to kill but to maim and to send a message regarding the willingness of the assailant to stand up to any threats. Because of an effective emergency system, most stabbing victims at Central survive these attacks, and the inmates know this. Although a small percentage of the inmate population at Central can be described as sexual predators, a disproportionate amount of the deadly violence at Central appears to result from their activity.

The third murder, which remained unsolved at the time, occurred during the noon hour on the third tier of one of the dormitory units. An older, white bank robber who had a long prison sentence was found stabbed to death in a unit that was not his own. This inmate was a lone wolf who had no gang or group affiliation to back him up if he got into trouble.

Unlike many prisons in which all tiers on a cell block are visible from the control center (where inmate movement is monitored), at Central each tier is on a separate floor with ordinary staircases linking the tiers. The grille (bars) with access to the main corridor is on the first of three floors. All of a sudden, there was a scrambling of staff members in response to the deuces (the 2-2-2 emergency call) as they ran to provide assistance to the officer who had discovered the stabbing victim. Throughout the afternoon, inmates were paraded through the counseling office for interrogation. Frustrated, the investigators were unable to turn up any evidence of who was guilty or why the assault occurred. No one was talking.

DEFENSIVE STRATEGIES

In their book *Coping: Maladaptation in Prisons*, Hans Toch and Kenneth Adams (1989) treat inmate infractions as symptoms of dysfunction or maladaptation to the prison environment. This behavior is maladaptive, they reason, because they "invite repercussions that are aversive" (Toch and Adams, 1989:xviii) such as being placed in segregation and loss of good time. Successful coping or adaptation to prison is indicated by participation "in programs, constructive extracurricular pursuits and links to significant others" (Toch and Adams, 1989:xxv). That adjustment to prison is viewed strictly within the officially sanctioned norms suggests that the authors fail to comprehend the dual nature of the prison world, one in which the consequences for violating the convict code may be more severe than those connected to the prison's official rewards and punishments. This is especially the case in a maximum security penitentiary where inmates come to see themselves as "doing life on the installment plan." Faced with ten or twenty years in prison, the reality of survival day to day and at night, when most officials go home, is the reality prisoners must deal with.

Successful coping in prison means responding to the "significant others" around you—those who can exploit you physically and emotionally if you are not careful. The official world becomes relatively meaningless as inmates adapt to the values and norms of the prisoners with whom they must live. Virtually all prisoners must adhere, more or less, to the convict code in order to survive in the contemporary prison.

Being Tough

Toch and Adams (1989:xx) refer to "veneers of toughness" used by inmates to "bluff" the observer into thinking they are something they are not. In a world in which showing signs of weakness may lead to sexual assault and other aversive consequences, presenting a tough image is part of survival in the contemporary prison. Interestingly, this tough image is repeatedly subject to validation from the moment one enters the prison system. Failure to meet any test may lead to a variety of subordinate roles within the inmate social system, including being "turned out" and seeking protection by becoming someone's kid, or spending time in isolation in protective custody.

Central to the tough veneer is the importance of physical space. In an environment in which space itself is scarce, the possibility of inadvertently invading another person's space is a constant source of tension. One of the concerns raised by inmates during the 1986 riot at the penitentiary in Moundsville, West Virginia, was that overcrowding had created conditions in which disputes arising out of these close living conditions could lead to violence (Hoedel, 1986).

In the most extreme cases, the convict puts a symbolic, almost tangible, wall around himself. This wall defines boundaries, both psychological and physical, that protect his sense of self-worth and self-control. One inmate, a convicted armed robber who had received additional time for assaulting an officer at another prison, said, "They [officers] can make me eat shit, but they better not touch me." In other words, he was willing to obey the rules and regulations of the institution as long as they were legitimate from his point of view. Should actions by correctional officers challenge his integrity or sense of self-worth, he would feel compelled to act to maintain his self-respect. He was also prepared to "defend" himself with deadly force if necessary should another inmate invade his personal space. That he had used violence before and was willing to do so in the future gave him the sort of status that made it possible for him to live a relatively peaceful and secure life from day to day.

In other words, the key to survival in prison is gaining a reputation for toughness and maintaining a veneer consistent with that reputation. One convict, who had a reputation for killing another inmate with his bare hands, expressed his desire to be "left alone" to do his own time. In general, those inmates who had found it necessary to defend themselves violently in the past tended to be left alone. Within the prison world, being willing to fight and, if necessary to kill is essential for survival.

Doing Gang Time vs. Doing Your Own Time

Writing about the contemporary prison system in California, John Irwin (1980) claims that convicts no longer do their "own time" as they did in the past. Instead, they now do "gang time." As early as 1972, Jacobs (1977:146) reports that half the inmates at Stateville in Illinois were gang members. But this high percentage may have had more to do with the fact that these gangs had their origins on the street rather than in the prison system. Gangs emerged in the Texas prison system in the early 1980s, yet by the mid-1980s only 8–10 percent of the inmates at Eastham, the maximum security prison, were active gang members (Marquart and Crouch, 1985:578).

Citing a 1985 survey, Crouch and Marquart (1989:203) report that gang activity occurred in only 29 of the 51 state and federal prison systems. In these systems, even when gang membership is small, the gangs tend to dominate the inmate power structure. Still, there were a large number of prison systems without gang activity. And, within each prison system, the amount of gang activity may vary from prison to prison.

Although there were gang members at Central, gang activity did not appear to dominate the inmate social system. Group affiliation of some kind was very important to a majority of inmates. Nevertheless, 30 percent indicated that they did not associate with any other prisoners, preferring to stay to themselves as much as possible. Religious affiliation was important to at least one-fourth of the inmates. The largest group, 36 percent, indicated that they hung around with people who had similar interests, usually "homeboys" who shared a similar background and came from the same neighborhood.

When asked, "What do you do to survive in prison?" most inmates said, "I mind my own business." Some added comments such as "see nothing, hear nothing, say nothing"; "keep busy"; "stay away from cliques"; "watch my back"; "try to be left alone or else with the one friend that I have"; and "I'm only doing my time, mind my business and get out of here."

Walking Around Together

In a recent description of street life in New York City, the *New York Times* (Kleinfield, 1992:32) described a *prop* as a friend who will back you up in a dispute with someone else. In order to have *juice*, or power, on the street, you must rely on friends who will stick up for you when you are in trouble. Typical of props were two friends, one the "tougher of the two," who developed an increasingly serious dispute with two classmates at Thomas Jefferson High School. Hearing that he was going to "get jumped," the weaker of the two friends, described as a " 'punk' who wanted to prove himself," shot and killed his two adversaries in the hallway of the high school.

Although the term *prop* is not used at Central, it seems to be a useful one to describe a friendship pattern that has emerged in maximum security prisons in the 1980s. Convicts at Central would say that they "walked around [the yard or corridors between cell blocks] together" to describe a relationship of mutual protection. In an atmosphere where you distrust nearly everyone, survival may depend on your ability to have someone cover your back, one close buddy whom you can trust.

Even some of the most isolated prisoners would rely on one other prisoner for mutual aid and protection. Inmates and officers often assume that these pair relationships are homosexual in nature, that is, involving a convict and his "kid." But they are not. They involve genuine friendships, often originating in ties on the street that make trust possible. For example, two bikers may have known each other or had mutual acquaintances before coming to prison, and they hook up for the purpose of providing some sort of emotional bond and material support in prison.

Earley (1992:54–62) describes such a relationship at Leavenworth between a tough convict ("no one fucks with him") and a new inmate who
asserted that he had been placed at Leavenworth by "mistake." This new inmate, who had a middle-class suburban background, liked to draw and
study mathematics. The more experienced convict had a reputation as a
sexual predator. Both inmates and guards assumed the relationship was
sexual in nature. The convict explained, "Sex is easy to find [in prison], but
a friend is damn near impossible 'cause no one trusts anyone in here"
(Earley, 1992:111). He described the need to share companionship and talk
to someone who shares your experiences to survive the isolation and bore-
dom of prison life.

At Central, the author encountered several relationships that appeared to
be similar to this relationship. In one case, the author was introduced by a
small, slender individual to his prop who was large and muscular. Pointing
to his friend, he said, "No one pushes him around," implying that the relationship provided him with a measure of protection against other inmates.
There was no hint that this relationship was sexual in nature.

Similarly, it was not uncommon to see friendship pairs of inmates who
shared common backgrounds such as membership in biker gangs or organized criminal activity. On occasion, it appeared that some of the young,
white inmates affected the attire and mannerisms of bikers (bandana, long
hair, tattoos such as "born to lose") in order to gain acceptance. Walking
around together in pairs or small groups provided a sense of safety when out
in the general population.

Why has this pattern emerged in the contemporary prison? To survive
both emotionally and physically, trust in at least one other person is necessary, but to expand this trust further is to risk exposing one's weaknesses and
making one vulnerable to exploitation. In prison, however, establishing this
bond is always tricky since the assumption that strong inmates will exploit
those who are weaker is always present. This is why some sort of external
bond or common interest is essential to creating the trust that makes this relationship possible.

Never Volunteer!

This dictum associated with the military applies even more so to convicts
today. One of the major pitfalls associated with the demise of rehabilitation
as a dominant philosophy in the prison system has been the elimination of
incentives to participate in prison programs. As a result, relatively few inmates participate voluntarily in programs designed to rehabilitate, such as
education and therapy. The convict code provides a set of norms that treat

those who do so voluntarily as cooperating with "the Man." Consequently, while many inmates privately indicated a desire to participate in self-help and other programs, it was clear that they needed a public "excuse" to do so.

In the past, an inmate could always say that he was participating in order to get "points" toward early release when his parole hearing would come up. Today there are no such points, and the tendency of parole boards is to ignore recommendations of program supervisors regarding the constructive behavior of the inmate. In these more conservative times, what counts most is the severity of the crime. With mandatory sentencing and more rigid guidelines governing sentences and parole hearing, there is even less incentive to cooperate. Once this symbolic barrier has been created, it is difficult for the average inmate to cross the line.

From the perspective of prison administrators, mandatory sentencing is a disaster. It provides little incentive for inmates to cooperate with authorities while doing time, thus creating control problems for correctional officers and their supervisors.

Program Participation

Most inmates who participated in the education programs did so because they were mandated to do so. This was true for those who required adult basic education. Inmates were not required to pursue high school diplomas, technical training, or additional education as a condition of parole. However, some of the training programs provided placement opportunities upon release, and there was some incentive to participate in order to convince authorities that you were deserving when parole hearings were scheduled. Time after time, however, inmates reported their disappointment after parole hearings because the seriousness of the crimes they had committed was the most important determinant of time served.

Participation in counseling programs depended on a relationship of trust established with one of the counselors. Interestingly, hard-core convicts were more likely to participate in group counseling programs, especially when these programs met their particular needs. These convicts knew that they had sufficient respect from their fellow prisoners that no one would suspect them of crossing the line (becoming snitches) or showing weakness.

An anger management group was especially popular. From a psychological perspective, inmates were taught to handle their rage so that they would not find themselves in situations of escalating violence. But rage itself is learned social behavior, and its expression reflects the cultural values of those who experience "righteous" anger (Katz, 1988:12–51). Consequently, from a sociological perspective, anger management contributes to a redefinition of culturally acceptable ways of expressing one's sense of injustice in disputes with fellow inmates and staff.

One special bond that provided both a basis of trust among inmates and between some of the inmates and staff was the status of Vietnam veteran. For those who attributed their criminality to the desperate economic conditions and rejections they experienced upon returning from Vietnam, both officers and inmates felt a common bond. Vietnam veterans were especially receptive to constructive programming such as drug and alcohol counseling when they had the support and understanding of fellow vets.

Clear evidence of the constructive role that programs can play in the reduction of violence in prison through the creation of trust between staff and inmates occurred in the 1989 Camp Hill (Pennsylvania) prison riot. Some inmates defended their units and staff members, preventing them from being taken hostage by rioters. In one case, an inmate in the education department assisted a staff member in escaping from the prison! In another, "inmates who went through the drug treatment program . . . fought to protect a corrections officer from attack by other inmates" and prevented other inmates from setting their quarters on fire (Senate Judiciary Committee, 1989:168).

Although there is little evidence that rehabilitation programs were effective in reducing recidivism rates (Martinson, 1974), the rehabilitation era in American prisons, especially during the 1950s and early 1960s, was its most peaceful period (Irwin, 1980:60–62). Rehabilitation programs contribute to the reduction of violence in American prisons.

Acting Crazy

Toch and Adams (1989:xxi) report that a small percentage of inmates in the New York state prison system can be classified as DDIs, "disturbed–disruptive inmates," or what the inmates call "dings." This group represents the "tip of an iceberg," the most extreme cases along a continuum of psychological disturbances linked to disruptive behavior. They argue that these extreme cases are characterized by movement back and forth between conventional correctional settings and mental health facilities. According to Toch and Adams, disruptive behavior stemming from emotional problems is a frequent source of violence in prison.

This argument, like so may psychogenic arguments concerning the causes of criminality, is circular. It assumes, by definition, that disruptive behavior is rooted in a predisposition to disrupt. But the prison environment creates a variety of incentives for inmates to engage in behavior that officials define as destructive. As we have already seen, violent behavior is an effective strategy for survival in a violent world. Violence is a form of *self-help* used by disputants in social conflicts (Marquart and Crouch, 1985:577; Silberman, 1988:524; Silberman, 1992:93). In the case of so-called dings, bizarre behavior is a distinctive, adaptive strategy for dispute *avoidance.* As on the outside, bizarre behavior is perceived as dangerous because of its unpredictability (Warren, 1979). At Central, roughly 50, or less than 5 percent, of the inmates were classified as "mental cases" and were subject to special housing and, in many cases, antipsychotic medication.

In one sense, DDIs should be vulnerable to exploitation by other inmates, yet in the prison world, they are avoided. Consequently, the environment reinforces bizarre behavior by not hassling those who engage in it. Consciously or unconsciously, vulnerable inmates learn that bizarre behavior is adaptive. For example, one inmate at Central would walk up and down the prison corridors talking loudly to himself. The more of a pariah he became, the more he fixated on this behavior, the more other inmates left him alone. Being "schizophrenic" in prison is reinforced by the relative safety playing this role provides. Another inmate, who had spent time in mental health facilities both in and out of the prison system, did his level best to avoid permanent assignment to Central. Finding himself assigned to a maximum security prison, within a few days he started destroying property such as fire extinguishers, then spat on correctional officers trying to move him into the disciplinary segregation unit. This behavior quickly paid off because he was transferred to a special program for inmates with adjustment problems.

Snitching

Providing information to staff about other inmates is a two-edged sword. This behavior may provide a short-term advantage in terms of some privilege or benefit provided by a staff member, but in the long term being a "snitch" can be quite dangerous. In response to the question, if "another inmate had given false information about you to an officer, what would you do?" several inmates indicated that they would "just beat him up" if it were not too serious. But several also indicated that, if it were serious, the convict code for snitching meant death. Responses varied from, I'd "probably knock his head off if it's serious" to "burn him out or kill him depending on what the information was." Another responded, "This type of act by an inmate usually means death," and another simply wrote in big bold letters across the page, "KILL."

Nevertheless, few actual murders at Central involved snitches, and it is clear that this prison, like all others, depends on the flow of information for its smooth operation. It has been the case at other prisons, however, that when prisoners have taken control of prisons, the first thing they did was to go after snitches and execute them. Most of the 33 inmates who were brutally murdered during the riot in New Mexico's state prison in 1980 were snitches in protective custody (Useem and Kimball, 1991:202). During the riot at Moundsville in West Virginia in 1986, three inmate snitches were killed following a kangaroo court held by the inmates (Hoedel, 1986; Martin and Zimmerman, 1990:727). In his book on the "criminal mind," Samenow (1984:145) writes that " 'don't snitch' is a code among inmates. The price of squealing on another con may be a beating or even death." Earley (1992:59) quotes a prison psychologist at Leavenworth: "If you [the inmate] go to the guards, you will be known as a snitch and that can get you killed."

For a brief period of time, the policy at Central was to encourage staff members to make the names of their informants known when specific accusations regarding misconduct of another inmate were involved. This policy expressed an appropriate concern for the due process rights of those accused of a crime who have the constitutional right to confront their accusers, at least in the free world. But this is a limited right for prisoners if it is "hazardous to institutional safety" (Krantz, 1988:233).

Although recognizing the due process rights of inmates reflects current trends in professionalism and bureaucratic-legalism in corrections (see Chapter 6), it has potential side effects that must also be taken into account. To reveal the names of snitches, even if only to other staff members, puts them at risk and breaks down the limited amount of trust that exists between inmates and staff that makes the prison run smoothly. Many serious problems have been averted, including situations that could have led to riots, because of information provided by snitches. The confidentiality of informants is essential to the effective management of the modern prison (see Marquart and Roebuck, 1986).

THE CONVICT CODE

The old convict code, characterized by a set of norms governing the behavior of inmates, had its origin in the streets. The old code reflected the norms of the professional thief, "don't snitch" and "do your own time" (Irwin, 1980:12). Convicts were also expected to "be cool and tough, that is, to maintain respect and dignity; not to show weakness; to help other thieves; and to leave most other prisoners alone" (Irwin, 1980:12; Sykes and

Messinger, 1960:6–8). Convicts also indicated their loyalty and group cohesion by their adherence to the convict code (Tittle, 1969:72).

The basic elements of the code have not changed, but they have become transformed in three ways. First, there has been a change in emphasis to *toughness* as a central part of the new convict identity in the 1980s (Irwin, 1980:193). Second, there has been a change from the focus of loyalty to the prisoner population as a whole to a focus on *loyalty to one's own group*, usually defined in racial or ethnic terms (Irwin, 1980:194). At the extreme, this means a shift from "doing your own time" to doing "gang time" (Jacobs, 1977:157). Third, the sanctions associated with violations of the code, such as snitching, and correspondingly with maintaining one's dignity, that is, a "tough" image, requires a willingness to go to the *extremes of violence*, including killing the transgressor.

From the convict's point of view, the routine denial of privileges by officers is to be expected as part of the deprivations associated with incarceration. The officer is just "doing his job." But when any man, inmate or officer alike, "disrespects" him, the convict feels compelled to do something about it. This disrespect may be the result of what appears to be the arbitrary use of discretionary authority, or it may be the invasion of personal space, a threat to the individual's personal integrity that results in acts of violence.

For the contemporary convict, ethnic or racial identification has become important. Many groups that have taken hold in prison provide an ideological basis for racial doctrines that contribute to racial conflict within prisons (see Chapter 3). A white convict, who was doing time in a maximum security federal penitentiary, explained that the swastika tattoos on his body were "a symbol for the white people in prison . . . it's a symbol of our culture—white" (Raymond and Raymond, 1991; also see Earley, 1992:46).

The toughness aspect of the convict code has become central in large part because of the dominant role played today by these state-raised youth. Youth prisons are generally the most violent and degrading. The strongest and most aggressive dominate these institutions. At a critical stage in the formation of the adolescent's identity, the state becomes both mother and father to the young prisoner. The violence that is the essence of the state's system of social control becomes the major mode of identification for the young convict. Violence as the primary solution to problems becomes internalized and incorporated as a way of life.

At Central, convicts have reputations for willingness to resort to extreme violence to maintain their self-respect. Many prisoners have been transferred from other prisons because they have committed murder in these institutions. In some cases, these murders may have been motivated by defense against or retaliation for sexual predation. There is evidence that some of these murders may have stemmed from racial or ethnic hostilities related to gang activity in those prisons. With the absence of organized gang activity at Central, there was relative peace among the different ethnic groups. Consequently, even those who may have been involved in racial violence elsewhere avoided overt conflict here.

Wooden and Parker (1982:173) point out that prisoners are distinguished in today's prison by their degree of commitment to the convict code. *Convicts* are distinguished from *inmates*, who are typically older "first-termers who merely wanted to leave the prison as soon as possible." Convicts tend to act in conformity with the new convict code, which includes sexual aggression and exploitation of "weaker" inmates and members of different ethnic groups.

Roughly half the inmates at Central identify themselves as convicts. These self-described convicts were distinguished from the remaining inmates by their tendency to agree or disagree *strongly* with a series of items on a questionnaire designed to measure the convict code. Inmates were asked whether they agreed or disagreed with the following statements, "If you mind your own business in prison, people will leave you alone"; "I try to stay out of trouble, but you can't let anyone push you around and get away with it"; "It is better to tell the case managers and counselors what they want to hear rather than to tell them the truth"; "It is better to keep to yourself and do your own time at this institution"; "Suckers deserve to be taken advantage of"; "There are situations when inmates have to snitch just to get along" (a reversed item). All those who answered the questionnaire tended to agree (or disagree where appropriate) with these statements, but convicts tended to agree (or disagree) *strongly*. In other words, all prisoners give lip service to the code to some degree because the code is the operating reality of daily life in the "joint." Convicts are distinguished by their degree of commitment to the convict code.

The violent nature of the code is indicated by the fact that only the most strongly committed convicts openly expressed support for killing snitches. When convicts were asked to describe themselves, *loyalty* was the single most important trait selected. Several also indicated that being *violent* was an important part of who they were. Along with loyalty, *honesty* was also a valued trait. The emphasis on doing your own time in this institution was reflected in the frequent self-description of the individual as a *loner*. But these same individuals reported either hanging out with "homeys" or people who shared a common interest or "one other guy."

Nearly all the convicts had been in some sort of fight with another in-mate since coming to Central. Virtually all those who have *not* been in a fight define themselves as inmates. Fighting is an integral part of the convict identity, for the convict must establish his reputation at least once by fight-ing with another inmate. It becomes a rite of passage into the convict world. But an interesting pattern emerges. They have either been in fistfights (a bare majority) or have used a deadly weapon such as a knife (shank) or lead pipe, but few have done both. And virtually none have just used a nonlethal weapon such as a broomstick.

One convict explained, "I don't use my fist, you either kill your oppo-nent or don't fight because if he's not dead, he might come back on you later." Another, who described himself as "crazy," indicated that he is differ-ent in prison than on the outside because here he "plays tough." When asked, "What would you most like to change around here in order to make this institution safer?" he said, "Blow the fucker up."

THE EFFECT OF ADMINISTRATIVE
POLICY ON CONVICT NORMS
AND BEHAVIOR

It might be useful at this juncture to illustrate how administrative policies can affect the way in which the convict code can operate to shape inmate behavior. In other words, administrative policies can shape inmate behavior more effectively by taking into account their impact on the norms that regulate convict behavior. During the early to mid-1970s, inmates fre-quently carried shanks to protect themselves against assault or, at least, they would have them readily available. This was true, too, in the mid-1980s dur-ing the present research. There was a brief period, however, during the re-gime of a tough warden in the late 1970s and early 1980s, when carrying a weapon was made more difficult. One inmate expressed what happened as follows: "Back then," he said, "it was more difficult to get away with carry-ing a weapon, but on the other hand, you didn't need one as bad, because the other guy didn't have one either" [paraphrasing].

Applying this principle to the wider society, the tendency for kids in the inner city to carry weapons for "protection" as well as the tendency for middle-class suburbanites to own handguns for "protection" centers around the widespread belief that the other guy is armed. This escalation of the cycle of violence is easier to break down in a prison than it is in society as a whole, if the administration has the will to do so, through the use of metal detectors, shakedowns, and other means. It should not be surprising that many inmates favor weapons reduction programs because they, too, would like to live in a safer environment.

CONCLUSION

The contemporary prison is a violent world in which survival depends on the ability of the new prisoner to learn to adapt to the violent lifestyle of the hard-core convict. Most inmates live in fear of the more aggressive prisoners. Some adapt to prison life by becoming tough on the outside while maintaining a softer, more humane side within. Still others become hard-core convicts, willing to respond violently in response to threats to their physical well-being or self-respect. A few convicts, many of whom were state-raised youth, live a predatory lifestyle in prison, where the ability to materially and sexually exploit others is a source of power in the inmate social system.

Life in the contemporary prison centers around three relationships: props, homeys, and ethnic background. Props are close friends who will back you up no matter what happens. Homeys are usually people from the same neighborhood or community who provide a basis for trust and mutual assistance. Shared racial or ethnic background has become the central organizing principle for social life in prison. Group activities, from informal social groups to organized religion, tend to occur within homogeneous ethnic groups. Prison gangs, which originated in California as racially oriented self-defense groups, compete for control over the distribution of resources in those prisons where they have taken hold.

Today's convict code differs from the old code in three ways. It emphasizes toughness, primacy of loyalty to one's ethnic or racial group, and willingness to go to extremes, including murder, to prove oneself. Becoming an informant, or snitching, is one of the worst offenses an inmate can commit. During prison riots, in accordance with the convict code, snitches have been brutally murdered. Yet no prison could function without the smooth flow of information that informants provide.

Officers, too, must adjust to this violent world. The officer is also expected to display his toughness when relating to inmates who may resent his authority. The officer must be willing to confront aggressive inmates when necessary and to use force when inmates are unwilling to comply with regulations. Faced with prisoners who challenge their authority, officers may lose control and use excessive force. This situation is especially likely to occur in the disciplinary segregation unit where mutual hostility between inmates and officers can escalate. This is where most assaults on officers occur and where officers are most likely to abuse their authority. Recent court decisions that prohibit the use of excessive force by correctional officers in routine disciplinary situations have contributed to increased professionalism of the guard force in some institutions.

NOTE

1. The following allegations regarding these incidents are based on information available at the time and do not necessarily reflect the final outcome of court dispositions.

REFERENCES

Abbott, Jack Henry (1981). *In the Belly of the Beast*. New York: Random House.

Bowker, Lee H. (1980). *Prison Victimization*. New York: Elsevier.

Cheek, F. E. and M. D. Miller (1983). "The Experience of Stress for Correctional Officers," *Journal of Criminal Justice* 11:105–120.

Crouch, Ben M. (1980). "The Guard in a Changing Prison World." Pp. 5–45 in *The Keepers: Prison Guards and Contemporary Corrections*, edited by Ben M. Crouch. Springfield, IL: Charles C. Thomas.

Crouch, Ben M. (1986). "Prison Guards on the Line." Pp. 177–210 in *The Dilemmas of Punishment*, edited by K. Haas and G. Alpert. Prospect Heights, IL: Waveland Press.

Crouch, Ben M. and James W. Marquart (1989). *An Appeal to Justice: Litigated Reform of Texas Prisons*. Austin, TX: University of Texas Press.

Earley, Pete (1992). *The Hot House: Life Inside Leavenworth Prison*. New York: Bantam Books.

Goffman, Erving (1961). *The Presentation of Self in Everyday Life*. Woodstock, NY: Overlook Press.

Hoedel, Martha B. (1986). "Finished: Inmates Slay Three Before Yielding," *The Patriot*, January 4:A1–A2. Harrisburg, PA.

Irwin, John (1980). *Prisons in Turmoil*. Boston: Little, Brown.

Jacobs, James B. (1977). *Stateville: The Penitentiary in Mass Society*. Chicago, IL: University of Chicago Press.

Katz, Jack (1988). "Righteous Slaughter." Pp. 12–51 in *Seductions of Crime*, by Jack Katz. New York: Basic Books.

Kauffman, Kelsey (1988). *Prison Officers and Their World*. Cambridge, MA: Harvard University Press.

Keen, John Ernest (1970). *Three Faces of Being: Toward an Existential Clinical Psychology*. New York: Appleton-Century-Crofts.

Kleinfield, N. R. (1992). "The Fatal Vortex: Collision of 3 Lives in East New York," *New York Times*, March 1:1, 32.

Krantz, Sheldon (1988). *Corrections and Prisoners' Rights*. St. Paul, MN: West Publishing.

Lockwood, Daniel (1980). *Prison Sexual Violence*. New York: Elsevier.

Mailer, Norman (1981). "Introduction." Pp. ix–xvi in *In the Belly of the Beast*, by Jack Henry Abbott. New York: Random House.

Marquart, James W. and Ben M. Crouch (1985). "Judicial Reform and Prisoner Control," *Law and Society Review* 16:557–586.

Marquart, James W. and Julian B. Roebuck (1986). "Prison Guards and Snitches: Social Control in a Maximum Security Institution." Pp. 158–176 in *The Dilemmas of Punishment*, edited by K. Haas and G. Alpert. Prospect Heights, IL: Waveland Press.

Martin, Randy and Sherwood Zimmerman (1990). "A Typology of the Causes of Prison Riots and an Analytical Extension to the 1986 West Virginia Riot," *Justice Quarterly* 7:711–737.

Martinson, Robert (1974). "What Works? Questions and Answers About Prison Reform," *The Public Interest* 35:22–54.

Mobley, M. J. (1985). "Occupational Stress? Stress Has Many Implications for the Administrator," *Corrections Today* 47:18–20.

Nacci, Peter L. and Thomas R. Kane (1982). *Sexual Aggression in Prison*. Washington, DC: U.S. Federal Prison System.

Pedersen, Daniel, Daniel Shapiro, and Ann McDaniel (1988). "Inside America's Toughest Prison." Pp. 246–266 in *Order Under Law: Readings in Criminal Justice* (3rd edition), edited by R. G. Culbertson and R. Weisheit. Prospect Heights, IL: Waveland Press.

Raymond, Alan and Susan Raymond (1991). *Doing Time: Life in the Big House*. Home Box Office: February 12.

Samenow, Stanton E. (1984). *Inside the Criminal Mind*. New York: Times Books.

Schmid, Thomas J. and Richard S. Jones (1991). "Suspended Identity: Identity Transformation in a Maximum Security Prison," *Symbolic Interaction* 14:415–432.

Senate Judiciary Committee (1989). *Public Hearing on Recent Incidents at Pennsylvania State Correctional Institutions: Transcript of Proceedings*. Harrisburg, Pennsylvania, October 31.

Silberman, Matthew (1988). "Dispute Mediation in the American Prison: A New Approach to the Reduction of Violence," *Policy Studies Journal* 16:522–532.

Silberman, Matthew (1992). "Violence as Social Control in Prison." Pp. 77–97 in *Law and Conflict Management* (*Virginia Review of Sociology*, Volume 1), edited by James Tucker. Greenwich, CT: JAI Press.

Sullivan, Ronald (1990). "Author Facing Damages for Murder," *New York Times* June 6: B2.

Sykes, Gresham M. and Sheldon Messinger (1960). "The Inmate Social System." Pp. 5–19 in *Theoretical Studies in Social Organization of the Prison*. New York: Social Science Research Council.

Tittle, Charles R. (1969). "Inmate Organization: Sex Differentiation and the Influence of Criminal Subcultures," *American Sociological Review* 34:492–505.

Toch, Hans and Kenneth Adams (1989). *Coping: Maladaptation in Prisons*. New Brunswick, NJ: Transaction.

Useem, Bert and Peter A. Kimball (1987). "A Theory of Prison Riots," *Theory and Society* 16:87–122.

Useem, Bert and Peter A. Kimball (1991). *States of Siege: U.S. Prison Riots 1971–1986.* New York: Oxford University Press.

Warren, Carol A. B. (1979). "The Social Construction of Dangerousness," *Urban Life* 8:359-384.

Wheeler, Stanton (1961). "Socialization in Correctional Communities," *American Sociological Review* 26:697–712.

Williamson, Harold E. (1990). *The Corrections Profession.* Newbury Park, CA: Sage.

Wooden, Wayne S. and Jay Parker (1982). *Men Behind Bars: Sexual Exploitation in Prison.* New York: Plenum.

Zimbardo, Philip G. (1982). "The Prison Game." Pp. 195–198 in *Legal Process and Corrections,* edited by N. Johnston and L. D. Savitz. New York: Wiley.

CASE CITED

Hudson v. McMillian, 60 U.S. Law Week 4151 (Feb. 25, 1992).

3

*

The Social
Organization
of Prison Life

ife in the contemporary American prison is organized along several
dimensions. For the inmate, affiliating with others who share a common outlook on life and common experiences provides a basis for
trust and friendship essential to survival in a dangerous world. Sharing a
similar background of ethnic origin or religious affiliation has become the
major focus of social groupings among prisoners. Homeboys not only share
a common background, but they also come from the same community or
neighborhood. Under certain conditions, however, these social groups have
developed into prison gangs.

PRISON GANGS

The Emergence of Prison Gangs in America

It is difficult to be certain how and when prison gangs first emerged in the
American prison system, but it appears that the California prison system
may have been the first and the source of some of the most militant and effective of these gangs. Irwin (1980:186–192) describes these gangs as

emerging in the power vacuum created during the breakdown of the old rehabilitation regime and the politicization of the prisoners' rights movement during the late 1960s. The Mexican Mafia, Black Guerilla Family, and Aryan Brotherhood were, respectively, Hispanic, black, and white racially oriented gangs who dealt in violence, drugs, and racial politics both inside and outside the prison. Later the Nuestra Familia emerged as a Hispanic gang of rural and northern California origin to resist Mexican Mafia control and domination. (Most of the Mexican Mafia members were from Los Angeles.) During the struggle for power between the two Hispanic gangs, the Aryan Brotherhood aligned itself with the Mexican Mafia and the Black Guerilla Family with the Nuestra Familia. These alliances remain today.

Once again, a power vacuum was instrumental in creating the environment for prison gangs to emerge in Texas. In 1980 (*Ruiz v. Estelle*), a federal judge ordered the Texas prison system to end its abusive "building tender" system in which prison officials delegated to trusties the responsibility for maintaining order on the cell blocks. These building tenders were not subject to administrative controls and frequently abused their power, violating the constitutional prohibition against cruel and unusual punishment. In the absence of a plan to reorganize the prisons' control system, the inmates moved in to take control themselves, creating new gangs such as the Texas Syndicate.

Jacobs (1977:172) attributes the emergence of the prison gangs in the Illinois state penitentiary system to the emergence of a professional administration dedicated to the rehabilitation ideal, undermining the morale of the traditionally oriented guard force. Jacobs (1977:105–137) also argues that the "intrusion of the legal system" weakened the traditional authority of the officer corps. After a series of decisions granting limited First Amendment rights to prisoners concerning freedom of religion and expression, the U.S. Supreme Court granted due process rights to inmates in disciplinary hearings in *Wolff v. McDonnell* (1974). This landmark decision ended what has been called the "hands-off" doctrine in corrections in which the courts had deferred to the expertise of prison administrators in running their prisons. The *Wolff* decision weakened the authority of prison administrators. Making things worse, the politicization of Chicago street gangs at that time contributed to their militancy at Illinois' Stateville penitentiary (Jacobs, 1977:138–146). As prison gangs became more powerful, both here and elsewhere, prison administrators lost control of their institutions.

Three black gangs, the Black P Stone Nation, the Devil's Disciples, and the Vice Lords, and one Hispanic gang, the Latin Kings, became powerful competitors for control of Stateville (Jacobs, 1977:138–139). Like the

California prison gangs, they maintained ties to their outside members. Unlike the California gangs, they had their origins in the streets and hence their local base may have prevented them from becoming national groups with chapters in a variety of prisons as did the California prison gangs.

Prison Gangs at Central

Central prison had few hard-core gang members. Rather, it typically housed gang members who had to be removed from the core membership for one reason or another. One gang member had been doing time in another prison when he was pressured to join. But when he was ordered to carry out a task that he found objectionable, to involve a family member as a "mule" for drugs, he refused. He learned that a contract was out on his life and he asked for protection. He was moved to Central to isolate him from the core group.

The fact that few of the gang members at Central are core gang members does not eliminate the prospect for gang-related violence. According to prosecution witnesses, two inmates were hired to kill a black inmate who was accused by an alleged member of the Aryan Brotherhood of sexually assaulting his "kid" or homosexual lover. It was also alleged that the Aryan Brotherhood contracted the hit through the Mexican Mafia at another prison. In court, the defense argued that the murder was in response to sexual "pressure" by the victim, but it was the inmate that was pressured, along with an associate, who carried out the murder. The prosecution failed to prove its case beyond a reasonable doubt. That a murder occurred is not subject to question. That gang members were involved also does not appear to be subject to dispute. What is in dispute are the specific facts regarding who was responsible for the murder.

None of these prison gangs are native to Central prison, nor for that matter is there a highly developed gang structure. This may be because at no time in the recent history of this prison did officials truly lose control. During a period of about 26 months in the mid-1970s in the post-*Wolff* era, there were eight murders, none of which had anything to do with gangs and most of which were related to attempted sexual assaults and/or jealousies. Although these events occurred in a period of instability during the transition from the old rehabilitation regime to the new order-maintenance orientation, prison gangs never took over this prison as they did elsewhere. This may have been because of the new warden whose no-nonsense policy concerning inmate misconduct violations (no one gets away with anything), coupled with a decentralized control system designed to place correctional officers and other staff in close contact with the inmates under their supervision in their units, prevented this from happening.

Ethnic Affiliation at Central

Both the media and law enforcement officials often attribute more coherence and organization to street gangs and prison gangs than really exists. Yablonsky (1962:222–233) argues that many street gangs are better described as "near-groups," that is, associations of individuals with common interests who live in the same neighborhood but whose membership, allegiances, and leadership are constantly shifting. Because of this misperception of gang organization and structure, misconceptions also occur with respect to gangs, violence, and drug dealing (Klein, Maxson, and Cunningham, 1991). The distribution of drugs requires a level of organization and sophistication for which most street gangs are unsuited.

In prison, inmates associate with those whom they can trust, someone with whom one shares a common experience, either coming from the same neighborhood (a "homeboy," or "homey") or sharing a similar background defined in terms of either religion or ethnicity. To the extent that these two characteristics overlap, ethnicity becomes the primary basis of affiliation in the contemporary prison. This was not always the case. Irwin (1980:58–59) describes prison social organization in the 1950s and '60s as based on a system of "tips" and cliques. Tips were largely, but not exclusively, intraracial and consisted of a variety of preprison cultural orientations, identities, and activities, including criminal activity, being state-raised, or coming from the same neighborhood. Cliques were smaller groups of friends who shared common interests, including prison programs and living in the same quarters. Many of these cliques included members of different ethnic groups.

It is important that the reader not equate organized gangs with the tendency for inmates to affiliate with "homeboys." Outside affiliations based on community and ethnicity appear to be an important resource for survival in the contemporary prison. But prison gangs that develop from these associations are highly disciplined, well-organized entities with rigid hierarchies, structures, and leadership cadres (Lewis, 1980). At Central, there were no organized prison gangs, but there were members of gangs in the institution.

Religious affiliation is especially important for black prisoners at Central, many of whom converted to Islam while in prison. There were 55 blacks in the study who responded to the question about their religious preference. Of these, 24 (43.6%) indicated the Muslim faith as their current preference. Only 5 (9%) indicated that they had been raised as Muslims. In other words, fully one-third of the black prisoners had converted to the Muslim faith while in prison. Lincoln (1961:111–115) reports that when the Black Muslims first began to recruit new members in prisons in the late 1950s and '60s, the Muslim faith became an important source of self-esteem for black prisoners. Emphasis on job placement in one of the Muslim enterprises and involvement in religious activities "leave [the ex-prisoner] little time for regression or for any contacts with the criminal element" (Lincoln, 1961:114). Today, there are at least four distinct Muslim groups in American prisons, the Moorish Science Temple, the Nation of Islam (originally the Black Muslim followers of Elijah Muhammad), the American Muslim Mission, and those who identify with more traditional Moslem sects such as Shiite and Sunni.

Hanging out with "homeys" is essential to survival at Central. Homeys usually come from the same big city neighborhood. But the meaning of homey appears to have broadened to include anyone who shares a common experience and a common background, such as a fellow biker or someone who is of the same ethnic or religious background. A substantial number of black prisoners were affiliated with one of the Muslim groups. White prisoners were seen to sport biker insignia, and there were a significant number of alleged mafiosi in this institution. Hispanic prisoners seemed to be the least well organized with few programs and groups available to them. But a nascent Hispanic leadership had emerged and convinced the administration to celebrate a major Hispanic holiday during the summer.

The tendency of the media and prison officials, like other law enforcement officials, to reify gang membership leads to misconceptions regarding the existence and nature of ethnic groupings in prison. Earley (1992:265) identifies the "DC Blacks" gang as a dominant force at Leavenworth federal penitentiary. At Central, officials linked the "Moors" (members of the Moorish Science Temple) to the "DC Blacks" group, because this is a dominant religious affiliation for blacks from Washington, D.C. Although there were black prisoners at Central from the District of Columbia and vicinity, there was little evidence of a single, coherent, organized prison gang.

Cuban prisoners, too, constitute a distinctive grouping at Central, but the constant moving of Cuban prisoners from prison to prison left little opportunity for a coherent leadership structure to emerge. Following the Mariel boat lift in 1980, Castro released a large number of mental patients and former prisoners who joined the disenchanted in their escape to freedom in the United States. The American government rounded up about two thousand suspected convicts in order to return them to Cuba. But

Castro said no. At first, nearly all the prisoners were kept at the federal prison in Atlanta and then gradually dispersed to other prisons. Those who are doing time at Central have been convicted of committing other crimes while in the community or while incarcerated elsewhere. But like those at Atlanta, they have little hope for release because Cuba does not want them and they are undesirables as far as U.S. Immigration is concerned. In effect, they face life in prison no matter what they do, whether they violate the law or not! Consequently, Cuban prisoners tend to have developed a reputation for ruthlessness, because they are seen by others as having nothing to lose.

Italian-American prisoners, many of whom were convicted members of organized crime groups, support one another even when they were not from the same community. This sort of behavior has led observers of organized crime to infer that there is some sort of national alliance of Italian-American organized crime gangsters. There was little evidence that these gangsters knew one another, except by reputation (often media enhanced), prior to coming to prison. Organized crime is primarily a local phenomenon dependent on the corruption of local officials and police. To the extent that extralocal ties have been forged by local gangsters, the prison system has played a major role in creating opportunities for contact between gang members. Like other prisoners, Italian-American prisoners form a loosely knit group based on shared ethnicity rather than specific organizational membership.

When asked, fully one-fourth of the prisoners indicated that religious affiliation was one of the most important bases of association and identification at this prison. Almost all of the black prisoners who considered religion important were Muslims. Black Protestants and others typically associated with crime partners or homeboys. For several white Protestants, religious affiliation was important. The black nationalism associated with the Muslim faith and ethnic pride as a basis of affiliation has created a counterreaction among some white prisoners toward white supremacist religious doctrines. Many white Protestants joined purely religious prison organizations such as Yokefellows. A few Hispanic prisoners indicate that Catholicism is an important source of identification, and they tend to associate with other Hispanic Catholics.

ATTITUDES AND BEHAVIOR OF STAFF

Ramirez (1983) points out that procedural regularity in law enforcement, especially in prison, is a function of the visibility of the decision-making process. Racial bias and other manifestations of the abuse of discretionary power are made possible when decision making occurs behind closed doors.

Central is under constant scrutiny by public officials. One possible explanation is the existence of a prisoners' rights organization in the local community that provides free legal assistance in parole hearings and in lawsuits involving allegations of civil rights violations. As a result, Central has been the subject of several governmental inquiries concerning the abuse of power, especially abuse that may be racially motivated. In each case, although problems have been identified (and no prison is without some management problems), there has been no evidence of systematic bias in the enforcement of regulations.

One of the consequences of prisoners' rights cases has been to increase the level of visibility of decision making behind prison walls. From *Wolff v. McDonnell* (1974), which created due process rights for inmates, to *Hudson v. McMillian* (1992), which treats the use of excessive force by correctional officers as a violation of the Eighth Amendment's prohibition against cruel and unusual punishment, the U.S. Supreme Court made a number of decisions that ended the "hands-off" doctrine and imposed a new legalistic, bureaucratic regime on American prisons (Jacobs, 1977:102–104; Crouch and Marquart, 1989:221–238).

At first, prison administrators, including those at Central, resented these decisions because they interfered with their autonomy in running their prisons and, in particular, resented those who represented prisoners in their lawsuits. In some cases, prison administrators who did not plan for the inevitable changes that were necessary to effectively manage their prisons lost control to prison gangs (Marquart and Crouch, 1985). But not at Central. The work of prisoners' rights advocates has created an atmosphere in which officials who are responsive to the law have become more professional in their roles as prison administrators. In recent years, a more positive, constructive relationship between prison personnel and prisoners' rights advocates has emerged.

The Effect of Race on the Enforcement of Regulations

The labeling of prisoners as troublemakers because of a previous record of disciplinary infractions can be a source of racial bias in the the enforcement of prison regulations (Poole and Regoli, 1980:942–945). Officers may come to expect trouble from those who already have been labeled as troublemakers. To the extent that there is racial bias in the initial classification of inmates as dangerous because of earlier biases in arrest and sentencing practices (Poole and Regoli, 1980:942–945), black inmates are more likely to be placed in secure living quarters and subject to closer scrutiny. Consequently, misconduct by black inmates is more likely to be detected, contributing to the accumulation of an official history of misconduct. This process is called *deviance amplification.*

Inmates at Central are assigned to their living quarters according to the Adult Internal Management System (AIMS) developed by psychologist Herbert C. Quay (1984). The most aggressive inmates are placed in secure cell blocks. The least aggressive are usually assigned to open dormitories. The objective is to separate the most aggressive prisoners from those whom they are most likely to victimize, reducing the overall incidence of violence. Thus, to the extent that black inmates are more likely than whites to be labeled as dangerous due to the deviance amplification process, they are more likely to be housed in secure living quarters. This arrangement is especially problematic for black inmates who are less aggressive and must therefore learn to survive in this environment—sometimes creating a self-fulfilling prophecy as these inmates learn to survive through more aggressive conduct. In addition, correctional officers are more likely to write *shots* (incident reports) on black inmates for minor infractions because they are labeled as more dangerous and placed in more secure facilities, increasing surveillance and the expectation that minor infractions will lead to major ones (see discussion of labeling theory, Chapter 5).

At Central, there was no evidence of racial bias in the enforcement of regulations once a formal complaint was filed. Blacks and whites were equally likely to be found guilty, that is, nearly all the time. And sentences were distributed equally in terms of both the number of days in segregation and the loss of "good time" (statutory reduction of sentence for good behavior). Although inmates widely believe that there is no chance of being found innocent in the face of charges brought by staff members, this was not the case. One of the reasons that there are so many formal findings of guilt is that when the evidence is less rigorous or consistent with minor violations, staff members are more likely to resolve cases informally at the unit level. In such cases, inmates might be required to sweep floors or clean latrines for a specified period of time. On occasion, employees have gone to bat for inmates whom they believed were not guilty. In one case, an inmate was accused of participating in a disturbance, for which the consequences in terms of additional prison time would have been great. Nevertheless, a staff member who had worked with this inmate and could provide evidence of his whereabouts during the disturbance stood up against what was evidently an erroneous identification by others.

Marquart and Crouch (1985:567) describe the use of "racial epithets, name calling, derogation, threats of force, and other scare tactics" as a form of intimidation used by correctional officers in response to challenges to their authority. But at this time the old guard was still in control at Eastham penitentiary. None of the inmates at Central mentioned the use of racial epithets or name calling in the questionnaires, although in interviews a few inmates reported that some officers expressed prejudicial attitudes in their interactions with inmates. Because institutional policy reflects a professional concern for equal and fair treatment of inmates regardless of ethnic and racial background, these attitudes on the part of a few officers appear to have little or no impact on the treatment of prisoners. This is a manifestation of the professionalism that results from public pressure and legal scrutiny of official conduct in prisons. Moreover, many of the officers, including those in positions of responsibility, are from minority groups.

At Central, housing assignments and job placement within the institution are made without reference to racial or ethnic background. Housing in more secure cell blocks depends on the inmate's history of violence and escape attempts. Job assignments depend on the inmate's training and education, as well as security risks. But officials do act affirmatively to some extent to avoid the appearance of racial bias, especially in housing assignments, by balancing racial groupings whenever it appears that one unit is likely to become too homogeneous (see Quay, 1984:3).

RELIGIOUS EXPRESSION IN PRISON

Today, prisons recognize the diversity of the prison population by acknowledging the many ways in which different ethnic and racial groups express their religious beliefs. This was not always the case. It took a series of lawsuits by the Black Muslims in the 1960s to establish their fundamental right to religious expression in prison (Krantz, 1988:160–164). At first, the courts determined that the Black Muslims did not constitute a "bona fide religious group" (Krantz, 1988:160). By the end of the 1960s, the Black Muslim faith was recognized as a religion by the courts. The religious needs of Muslims, mostly of African American heritage, have been met at Central through the recognition of their different sects and the hiring of an imam.

Native Americans have established the right to worship in traditional ways. The criminal activity of many of the Native Americans who were doing time at Central seemed to be a response to the harsh living conditions their peoples have been subject to as a result of their military defeat decades ago. These were self-respecting, dignified individuals with genuine commitments to their traditional culture. It appears, however, that some inmates make claims of Native American heritage based on the identification of one Native American ancestor. With no experience or ties to Native American culture, the special status and recognition that comes with Native American identity in prison provides an incentive to assert such claims. Ties to religious and ethnic traditions provide an important means for survival in prison, both physically and emotionally.

Prisons have also been required to recognize the religious rights of white supremacist groups who adhere to racial doctrines supported by a variety of churches related to the "British Israelite" tradition. In the United States, these churches are part of what is called the "Christian Identity" movement (Aho, 1990:18–21). Followers of the Christian Identity church "believe the White, Anglo-Saxon, Germanic and kindred people to be God's true, literal Children of Israel. Only this race fulfills every detail of Biblical Prophecy" (Melton, 1988:625). They believe that white Christian Americans represent the lost tribes of Israel and are the only true Israelites, who have come to the United States of America to fulfill biblical prophecy (Aho, 1990:83–104; Melton, 1988:626).

The most well known of the Christian Identity churches is the Aryan Nations (Church of Jesus Christ Christian), which recruits members from groups such as the Aryan Brotherhood prison gang (Aho, 1990:61). Although many white prisoners adhere to various white supremacy doctrines, and the Christian Identity movement provides some degree of coherence to their beliefs, Aho (1990:61) reports that, as a *religious* doctrine, the Christian Identity movement has not been effective in attracting a large number of prisoners. Unlike the Muslim movement among black prisoners, which has provided a degree of organization and leadership over the years, white supremacist groups appear to be more fragmented.

STAFF–INMATE RELATIONS

Positive Aspects

On the individual level, a surprising number of supportive relationships existed between inmates and staff at Central. Many staff members had friendly relationships with inmates. Unit management fosters this by promoting correctional officers with the greatest amount of rapport to *correctional counselors* whose primary function is to assist inmates in dealing with problems generated in their day-to-day lives. The correctional counselor role is ideally suited to the role of dispute mediator, whether this involves other inmates, staff members, or institutional policies as a whole. The effective counselor can explain institutional policies to the inmate, preventing problems before they occur. The counselor can also play a major role in settling disputes between inmates before they erupt in violence (Silberman, 1988).

In general, there were many helping roles in this institution: staff psychologists, teachers, correctional counselors, and case managers (formerly called caseworkers). The primary duty of all staff is to maintain order in the institution. For this reason, during emergencies all staff were expected to fulfill a security function. This central obligation creates a fundamental contradiction with the helping role both on a personal (self-identity) level and as far as behavior is concerned. Should, as it must inevitably happen, a psychologist or teacher be forced to play such a dual role, he or she must deal with this fundamental contradiction. Even when there is no emergency, because classes in the education programs were underenrolled (there is no incentive for inmates to participate and a great deal of pressure from their peers not to do so), teachers could be assigned to temporary security duty. All staff must be prepared to patrol the yard during fog to prevent escapes. And all staff must be trained in the use of firearms and maintain proficiency.

Staff members who identify primarily with the helping roles employed a variety of strategies to deal with the contradiction between these roles and the institutional emphasis on the primacy of security. One strategy was to systematically avoid participating in security training, including going to the shooting range. Another strategy was to detach oneself from one's prior commitment to the reform and rehabilitation of inmates. This adaptive strategy appears to be more common than the first. After years of seeing released inmates return to prison, many staff members become resigned to the failures of the rehabilitation ideal and come to accept the notion that hardcore offenders are unlikely to change.

Those who choose the first adaptive strategy experience great emotional strain and eventually transfer to less secure settings. Some of those who choose the second adaptive strategy mark time much the way the convicts do, counting the days until retirement. Still others see their primary task as the maintenance of security and experience little conflict. Those who began their careers as correctional officers before becoming counselors or case managers appeared to experience few conflicts.

Negative Aspects

Popular in correctional psychology today is the belief that criminal behavior is determined by the *criminal personalities* of those who engage in such behavior (Yochelson and Samenow, 1977). In his extensive review of the criminal psychology literature, Gibbons (1992:158–168) illustrates the logical and empirical flaws in most psychogenic explanations of criminal behavior. Criminal personality theory, like earlier theories concerning the "psychopathic" or "sociopathic" character of convicted criminals, is fundamentally tautological (circular) in nature. The psychologist observes the criminal conduct, infers a criminal "state of mind" from these observations, then argues that this state of mind or "criminal personality" caused the behavior. Furthermore, these theories are typically based on *post factum* observations of *convicted* criminals who are assumed to have committed their crimes because of a "propensity" to do so. Psychologists rarely have criminals available for systematic study who have not been caught. These earlier approaches were discredited because it was found that personality variables explained very little criminal behavior when compared with economic and social conditions (Gibbons, 1992:154).

But criminal personality theory has yet to be subject to systematic test. Its popularity among correctional psychologists today is rooted in the belief that criminality is so deeply anchored in fundamental character flaws that it is virtually untreatable. This belief provides a ready rationale for frustrated members of the helping professions to throw up their hands and orient themselves toward control strategies rather than attempts to rehabilitate. After a while, said one staff member who had majored in the social sciences in college, you lose your faith in the textbook theories and accept the reality of prison life; these are bad guys who need to be locked up for a long time.

Alienation or powerlessness is one of the most important contributors to violence among inmates (see Chapter 5). Alienation increases both hostility toward staff and the level of assaultiveness among inmates. From the perspective of the inmate, an order from a guard to move along may appear "arbitrary" and as a source of "frustration." This is especially true whenever there is a shift in correctional officer assignments on the cell block or a newly hired officer is assigned to a cell block. To the inmate, these officers are trying to "prove themselves." One articulate and insightful inmate reported that he often takes out his resentment toward officers on available targets, other inmates. When the officer is white and the inmate is black, resentment may be directed toward white inmates, adding to racial antipathies in the prison.

In his book on Leavenworth prison, Earley (1992:200) describes a situation in which an inmate comes to believe that the hassles he had with an officer became "personal." Locked up in the "control unit" (segregation) in the federal penitentiary at Marion, a reputed leader of the Aryan Brotherhood prison gang stabbed and killed a correctional officer because "it was like I was a little kid again walking home from school and that bully . . . was picking on me" (Earley, 1992:201). Although the officer may believe that he is "just doing his job," the inmate in segregation comes to resent the power that is exercised over him, controlling all of his activities twenty-four hours a day.

It should not be surprising, then, that the vast majority of assaults on staff members occurs in the disciplinary segregation unit, the jail within the jail, at Central. Here, in conditions that can become quite oppressive, inmates may indeed take control measures as "personal." The segregation unit in the summer was extremely hot, with little ventilation. A giant fan at one end of the corridor blows continuously with an unendingly loud roar that makes it difficult to hear or think. When inmates have been particularly unruly (a favorite is to throw a caustic mixture of feces and urine in the faces of officers as they pass by), the small openings in the solid doors (with windows) may be closed to protect the officers from this sort of assault. It is here that most inmate–staff violence erupts.

DRUGS AND SEX AS
SOURCES OF DISPUTES

Most disputes between inmates at Central centered around the distribution of drugs and homosexual activity. Staff members often added a third source of disputes, gambling, but this was less of a problem than it had been in the past. One indicator of the infrequency of disputes over gambling debts was the often repeated statement that there were "no fistfights" at Central. While this was not literally true—there were indeed many fistfights—this statement had important symbolic meaning. It meant that an inmate had better be prepared to use deadly force—with a "shank" or homemade knife—if he was going to fight at all. Some inmates may be ready to kill over drugs and sex, but fewer are willing to do so over gambling debts. Consequently, fewer inmates appeared to gamble than they did in the past when Central was a less secure, less violent prison. A very small percentage (2%) reported frequent gambling; about 25–30 percent gambled once in a while.

Marijuana use, clearly the drug of choice, was widespread at this institution. Homemade liquor, often from potato peels, was frequent but presented fewer problems for the institution since it did not involve the obvious penetration of external security. Although hard drugs would find their way into the institution through the swallowing of balloons passed to inmates when visiting family and friends in the visiting room, the method for transporting large quantities of marijuana was a mystery. On occasion, staff members have been caught transporting drugs into the prison and have been prosecuted. This is a more serious problem at some prisons where criminal prosecutions of employees are frequent (Howe, 1992). In the past, when there was more movement of prisoners to and from a minimum security facility near the prison, inmates could transfer drugs into the prison;

but such movement at this time was extremely rare unless a minimum security prisoner was subject to placement in disciplinary segregation "behind the wall."

Only 10 percent of the inmates reported "getting drunk" on occasion. Few inmates admitted being drunk frequently, because there was little opportunity to do so. Although rare, the self-defined alcoholic who admits getting drunk frequently while in prison presents disciplinary problems for the staff. In contrast, *the median estimate by inmates of the percentage of inmates who smoked marijuana was 70–75 percent!* A majority (52%) admitted that the guys they hung around with smoked a joint once in a while or "often" (about 10%). Moreover, 30 percent were willing to admit that they themselves had smoked a joint while doing time at Central. The median estimate of hard drug use (mostly heroin or cocaine) by other inmates was about 20 percent. Eighteen percent of the inmates reported that their acquaintances used hard drugs "once in a while," but only 6 percent admitted to such use themselves. No inmates appeared to be regular users of heroin or cocaine at this prison. Since these inmates were likely to overestimate the use by others and underreport their own, hard drug use appeared to be limited both in terms of its distribution and availability.

The transmission of marijuana was even reported between cells in the segregation unit! Inmates would create long strings of paper or other substances to transmit messages or goods between cells on the floor where they expected little visibility or even between windows. Thin streams of marijuana could be transmitted with little visibility. But how did the marijuana get into the maximum security lockup in the first place? It should not be surprising that the prison administration decided to crack down on marijuana use by instituting random drug testing for inmates. This created some interesting problems.

Since this was during the early period of drug testing, some staff members expressed two concerns. First, there was some concern that false positives in the testing would create management difficulties for those inmates who were then presumed guilty, affecting their good time and prospects for parole. There were several instances in which inmates who tested positive for drugs had never had a shot before, lending credibility to their claims of innocence. In addition, the *use* of marijuana was a relatively minor offense for which informal disposition might be appropriate, and the major culprits were those who were distributing the drug in the institution. Nevertheless, those presumed guilty of using marijuana were automatically detained in the segregation unit for several days until a hearing could be arranged.

A second general concern was that the disciplinary segregation unit was suddenly overwhelmed with individuals waiting for their hearings or doing time afterward. This overcrowding problem was merely symptomatic of the problems facing prisons generally, due to the drug wars. Minor offenders were clogging the system to such an extent that disciplinary hearings for more serious offenses were being delayed, and overcrowding within the jail created additional disciplinary problems. At one point, inmates who were adjudicated guilty for marijuana use were released because they had already served their time waiting for the hearing. The sense of injustice created by the first problem and the tensions caused by the second can lead to more disputes and more violence.

It is a taken-for-granted assumption among staff and inmates alike that homosexuality in prison is a major source of violence. Wooden and Parker (1982:60) report that most voluntary homosexual liaisons in prison are intraracial whereas most rapes are interracial, with black aggressors and white victims. According to Wooden and Parker (1982:60), many black and Hispanic prisoners try to "turn out" young white prisoners (convert heterosexuals into homosexuals; also see Irwin, 1980:183). Rape in prison, as on the outside, is an expression of power as much as it is sexual in purpose. As an expression of the inversion of power relations during prison riots, guard hostages have been raped by inmates (Jacobs, 1977:166; Useem and Kimball, 1987:89).

At Central, rape was an extremely rare occurrence, suggesting that the unit management system was effective in separating predators (wolves) from their victims (punks). During the 14-month research period, there was only one alleged instance, although it is conceivable that others occurred and did not come to light. A male prostitute was reported to have been lured to a deserted location for a sexual liaison where he was surprised by a group of inmates who proceeded to gang rape him. In similar situations on the outside, when female prostitutes are victimized, there is little public sympathy. In prison, we can expect no less. In fact, Wooden and Parker (1982:18) report that the sexual assault of "known" homosexuals is a common feature of prison life.

During the 1960s, draft resisters at one federal prison were raped or threatened with rape by prisoners (National Commission, 1970:584). Although it was reported that three inmates were deliberately placed in "the jungle," a unit housing "homosexual attackers," prison officials denied that such a policy existed. Moreover, the prison psychiatrist and psychologist had acted to end the practice.

It was the policy at Central that any inmate who reasonably fears sexual victimization can request to be locked up for his own protection in the administrative segregation unit. Consensual homosexual relations occurred at or above the rate in the population at large, although it is difficult to obtain a precise estimate both in prison and in society (Barringer, 1993). Self-reports and records indicated that an estimated 8 percent of the inmates participated regularly in homosexual behavior. There is some evidence of underreporting of homosexual behavior in the questionnaires, and overt behavior may not always be detected, so the actual percentage may be somewhat higher. The inmates themselves estimated, on average, 10 percent of the population "having sex with other inmates."[1] In 1948, the Kinsey studies indicated that 8 percent of males are exclusively homosexual for at least three years of their adult life (Remafedi, 1987). More recently, a Battelle Institute research group reported that only "1% of men age 20 to 39 said they'd been exclusively homosexual for the last 10 years" (Beck, Fineman, and Senna, 1993:57).

At Central, when an officer caught an inmate *in flagrante*, he was required to write his observation in precise detail because homosexual behavior was a prohibited act. In one instance, an officer discovered an inmate in bed with his lover during the evening hours. Discovering the inmate out-of-bounds in the living quarters of another inmate left the officer with little choice but to write up a shot for the infractions he had observed.

Nacci and Kane (1982:50) report that in the late 1970s, in maximum security federal penitentiaries, about 19 percent participated in homosexual acts on an ongoing basis and 30 percent reported ever doing so while in prison. Tittle (1972:67) estimated that, in the late 1960s, 23 percent of the males in a coeducational federal institution for the treatment of drug abuse were actively involved in homosexual relations, although only "11% admitted present involvement." In contrast, Wooden and Parker (1982:18) report that in a medium-security California prison, 64 percent of the prisoners engaged in homosexual behavior at some time, although only 20 percent were self-admitted homosexuals or bisexuals!

There has been an apparent decline in consensual and non-consensual homosexual behavior over time at Central, which may reflect an overall decline in its incidence in maximum security prisons. This decline and the relatively low incidence of such behavior generally requires some explanation. From the staff perspective, the separation of aggressive and non-aggressive inmates may play a role in reducing the aggressive variety. In fact, there is one cell block in which "known" homosexuals are assigned as a way of containing the violence associated with sexual exploitation in prison, since this is the group that is usually victimized (see Wooden and Parker, 1982:18).

From the inmate perspective, the convict code may provide an explanation. At one point during the research, an inmate was "pressured" by another inmate for sex. His only recourse, after repeated attempts to convey peaceably that he was not interested, was to grab a shank and stab the other man. In other words, in the contemporary violent prison, the convict code says either submit or fight. At Central, the saying goes, "there are no fistfights." At Central, if you were not prepared to submit, the code says you had better be prepared to kill in "self-defense." This evidently contributed to the lower incidence of sexual victimization.

CONCLUSION

Prison officials are increasingly under scrutiny from a variety of sources, including prisoners' rights advocates and the federal courts. This scrutiny has contributed to the professionalizing of the guard force, eliminating many of the problems that existed in the past. There may be, however, unintended side effects of otherwise objective classification systems designed to separate the most dangerous prisoners from the others. Overt racial bias in corrections has clearly diminished in recent years as more minority officers have been hired and many have since moved up the ranks to positions of responsibility.

There are many positive as well as negative aspects to relationships between staff and inmates. The role of correctional counselor at Central is especially important in reducing the alienation and hostility of inmates, thereby contributing to the reduction in assaults on both inmates and staff. As former correctional officers, these counselors have little difficulty fulfilling the central security mission of the institution. But others, such as psychologists, teachers, and social workers, may find themselves torn between their helping roles and their duty to maintain the security of the institution. On the negative side, many staff share a pessimistic view of the prospects for the rehabilitation of the inmate population. Additionally, the hostility many inmates feel toward those in authority may be redirected at safer targets, fellow inmates, especially those of different racial backgrounds.

Disputes in prison often center around the struggle for control over scarce resources such as drugs and sex. This situation can be especially problematic for the maintenance of internal security, and a clear breach of external security exists when large amounts of drugs such as marijuana can find their way inside. Sexual assault is less common at Central than in some prisons and, in general, both consensual and nonconsensual homosexual relationships appeared to be less frequent at Central. This reduced frequency appears, in part, to be due to the separation of the most aggressive prisoners from those who were more vulnerable and, in part, to the convict code, which supports the use of deadly force in "self-defense," including the defense of one's masculinity.

Prison gangs emerged in some prisons in response to a power vacuum created by administrative failures to respond to court-ordered changes in prison policies, especially when those policies involved the delegation of power to inmates. These prison gangs, which were organized along ethnic lines, competed for control over scarce resources in prison, especially the distribution of drugs. Even when there are no organized gangs as such, prison life is organized around shared ethnicity and religious background as a basis of trust and friendship.

NOTE

1. The median value of the sample estimate of homosexual activity in the general population was 10%, whereas the mean estimate was 20.6%. The former is probably more accurate since it eliminates exaggerated overestimates (and underestimates) that can affect the mean.

REFERENCES

Aho, James A. (1990). *The Politics of Righteousness: Idaho Christian Patriotism*. Seattle, WA: University of Washington Press.

Barringer, Felicity (1993). "Sex, Lies and Statistics," *New York Times,* April 18.

Beck, Melinda, Howard Fineman, and Danzy Senna (1993). "The Impact of Gay Political Power," *Newsweek.* April 26:57.

Crouch, Ben M. and James W. Marquart (1989). *An Appeal to Justice: Litigated Reform of Texas Prisons*. Austin, TX: University of Texas Press.

Earley, Pete (1992). *The Hot House: Life Inside Leavenworth Prison*. New York: Bantam Books.

Gibbons, Don C. (1992). *Society, Crime, and Criminal Behavior* (6th ed.). Englewood Cliffs, NJ: Prentice Hall.

Howe, Robert F. (1992). "11 Lorton Employees Are Charged with Drug Smuggling," *Washington Post,* October 22:B8.

Irwin, John (1980). *Prisons in Turmoil*. Boston: Little, Brown.

Jacobs, James B. (1977). *Stateville: The Penitentiary in Mass Society*. Chicago, IL: University of Chicago Press.

Klein, Malcolm W., Cheryl L. Maxson and Lea C. Cunningham (1991). " 'Crack,' Street Gangs, and Violence," *Criminology* 29:623–650.

Krantz, Sheldon (1988). *Corrections and Prisoners' Rights*. St. Paul, MN: West Publishing.

Lewis, George H. (1980). "Social Groupings in Organized Crime," *Deviant Behavior* 1:129–143.

Lincoln, C. Eric (1961). *The Black Muslims in America*. Boston: Beacon Press.

Marquart, James W. and Ben M. Crouch (1985). "Judicial Reform and Prisoner Control," *Law and Society Review* 16:557–586.

Melton, J. Gordon (1988). *The Encyclopedia of American Religions: Religious*

Creeds. Detroit, MI: Gale Research Company.

Nacci, Peter L. and Thomas R. Kane (1982). *Sexual Aggression in Prison.* Washington, DC: U.S. Federal Prison System.

National Commission on the Causes and Prevention of Violence (1970). *The Rule of Law: An Alternative to Violence.* Nashville, TN: Aurora.

Poole, Eric D. and R. M. Regoli (1980). "Race, Institutional Rule Breaking, and Disciplinary Response: A Study of Discretionary Decision Making in Prison," *Law and Society Review* 14:931–946.

Quay, Herbert C. (1984). *Managing Adult Inmates: Classification for Housing and Program Assignments.* College Park, MD: American Correctional Association.

Ramirez, John (1983). "Race and the Apprehension of Inmate Misconduct," *Journal of Criminal Justice* 11:413–427.

Remafedi, Gary (1987). "Homosexual Youth: A Challenge to Contemporary Society," *Journal of the American Medical Association* 258:222–225.

Silberman, Matthew (1988). "Dispute Mediation in the American Prison: A New Approach to the Reduction of Violence," *Policy Studies Journal* 16:522–532.

Tittle, Charles R. (1972). *Society of Subordinates.* Bloomington, IN: Indiana University Press.

Useem, Bert and Peter A. Kimball (1987). "A Theory of Prison Riots," *Theory and Society* 16:87–122.

Wooden, Wayne S. and Jay Parker (1982). *Men Behind Bars: Sexual Exploitation in Prison.* New York: Plenum.

Yablonsky, Lewis (1962). *The Violent Gang.* New York: Macmillan.

Yochelson, Samuel and Stanton E. Samenow (1977). *The Criminal Personality* (2 vols.). New York: Jason Aronson.

CASES CITED

Hudson v. McMillian, 60 U.S. Law Week 4151 (Feb. 25, 1992).

Ruiz v. Estelle, 503 F. Supp. 1265 (S.D. Tex. 1980).

Wolff v. McDonnell, 418 U.S. 539 (1974).

4

*

Violence as Social Control in Prison

here is a long history of violence in American prisons. The violence has taken the form of sporadic rioting, hostage taking, assaults on officials by inmates, the use of excessive force by correctional officers, homicides, and suicides. Each of these acts can be understood as an inevitable product of the nature of incarceration itself. But the form that this violence takes must also be understood in terms of the cultural context in which the prison system is embedded. In other words, the frequency and severity of the violence that occurs in American prisons must be understood as an expression of uniquely American values and the norms (standards of conduct) that legitimate them.

HISTORY OF VIOLENCE
IN AMERICAN PRISONS

The first half of the twentieth century, often referred to as the "Big House" era in American corrections (Irwin, 1980:1; Johnson, 1987:43), was a relatively stable period. Prisons were tightly controlled "total institutions" in which a high degree of regimentation made inmate assaults unlikely and riots relatively infrequent events (see Goffman, 1961:1–124). During the second half of the twentieth century, the post–"Big House" era, there were two major episodes of prison rioting. In 1952 and 1953, there were 25 prison riots in the United States, resulting in many injuries and property destruction (American Correctional Association, 1981:vii). These riots occurred in response to the rising expectations of the inmate population as the prison system adopted humane principles devoted to the rehabilitation of prisoners while the old guard correctional officers, entrenched in control of the daily routines of prisoners, resisted legislated reforms (McCleery, 1980). Inmates frequently rebelled in such institutions in order to bring their plight to public attention.

After a period of renewed stability, in which prisons came to be known euphemistically as "correctional institutions," pressure for additional reform came from the civil rights movement. By the late 1950s, communication between staff and inmates focused on treatment-oriented goals, the "rat" or snitch played a small role in the inmate social system, and inmate participation in education and treatment programs was up (McCleery, 1980:398). As the civil rights movement began to gain influence in the outside world, black prisoners became increasingly aware of the impact of racial injustice on their position in society as a whole and in the criminal justice system (Irwin, 1980:66–72). Black, white, and Hispanic prisoners eventually joined together in a number of protests (Irwin, 1980:86). Work stoppages were a frequent tool of the prisoners' rights movement within the prison. With growing support from prisoners' rights groups on the outside, inmates gained more rights and official authority eroded.

The more liberal, treatment-oriented approach began to lose its legitimacy as more conservative crime control strategies began to gain public favor during the late 1960s and '70s. In reaction to perceived lawlessness in the inner cities and on college campuses, the Nixon administration took the lead in calling for tougher "law and order" strategies in dealing with crime. Martinson (1974) published his famous study documenting the failures of the rehabilitation programs during the previous 20 years. Reviewing over 200 studies of prison rehabilitation programs, Martinson (1974:25) concluded, "With few and isolated exceptions, the rehabilitative efforts that have been reported so far have had no appreciable effect on recidivism." Although intended as a plea for a more rational system of treatment directed at specific types of offenders, Martinson's results were used as a pretext to change to a more punitive, control-oriented policy for all offenders. This legitimated what was already a preferred policy on the federal level and was promoted on the state level through federal government funding of local law enforcement programs (see Quinney, 1974:105–110). The American correctional system officially abandoned the rehabilitation ideal in favor of more punitive policies.

Once again, changes in public policy destabilized the prison system, and a new era of prison disturbances began. From 1968 to the present, there have been numerous prison riots, more sporadic and less concentrated than during the early 1950s (American Correctional Association, 1981:vii). These riots have been more violent than those that occurred earlier, with greater loss of life and major property destruction.

At Attica, in 1971, 39 officers and inmates were killed, primarily by New York state police as they retook the prison (Useem and Kimball, 1991:20). Four others, one officer and three inmates, were killed by inmates prior to the state police assault (Useem and Kimball, 1987:93–95). At New Mexico's Santa Fe penitentiary in 1980, the worst riot in American history in terms of sheer brutality occurred when 33 inmates were tortured and killed by fellow inmates and large parts of the institution were destroyed (Useem and Kimball, 1991:105–106).

Violence Toward Inmate Informants

Inmates who took hostages in 1986 during a riot at the Moundsville, West Virginia, penitentiary petitioned for a reduction in the size of the prison's population because it was their belief that overcrowding increased the probability of confrontations among inmates and violence was likely to result (Hoedel, 1986; Martin and Zimmerman, 1990). Three alleged "snitches" (inmate informers) were killed after mock trials conducted by inmates in control of the institution. In the New Mexico prison riot in 1980, many of the 33 inmates who were brutally murdered by other prisoners were in protective custody because of informant activity (Useem, 1985). Each of these instances of prison violence suggests that a kind of vigilante justice is operating, one that justifies taking the law into one's own hands when official systems fail to do so. This emphasis on self-help is a theme that pervades American culture.

As an expression of American values concerning self-reliance, the convict code prescribes a code of silence, which is enforced by the inmates themselves. Informing on fellow convicts or "snitching" violates the convict code and, accordingly, is punished by death. But we also see this phenomenon in other areas of social life whenever there is a code of silence designed to protect one group from the control of another. Police officers will not back up a fellow officer who squeals on another, no matter what she or he might have done, putting the officer's life at risk in dangerous situations. Similarly, organized criminal gangs require total loyalty to the group.

Violence Toward Correctional Officers

Jacobs (1977:166) reports that, in 1973, several guard hostages were raped by prisoners during a riot at Stateville in Illinois. More recently, in 1989, prison guards were brutalized by inmates who took control of the Pennsylvania state prison at Camp Hill for several days. One officer, described as a "good officer" who "never said a harsh word," was severely beaten with hammers and a baseball bat, breaking "every bone" in his face (Senate Judiciary Committee, 1989b:62). A total of 34 staff and 32 inmates were seriously injured, although there were no fatalities (Senate Judiciary Committee, 1989a:56).

Violence directed at correctional officers during riots appears to have become more lethal over the years. During a 1993 riot at the maximum security prison in Lucasville, Ohio, one of the eight guard hostages was killed in order to send a message to authorities that the inmates meant business (Smothers, 1993). Six inmates were killed in the early stages of the riot, and a seventh died later.

This pattern of sporadic outbreaks of violence suggests that the American prison system has not yet stabilized around a new policy. This situation contributes to the sense of "lawlessness" that pervades prison life, creating an atmosphere in which violent self-help flourishes. There are signs, however, of a new professionalism emerging in American prison management. The goal of these new managers is the "humane incapacitation" of the prison population through the training of officers to use force in a disciplined and restrained manner. Well-managed prisons strive to remove troublemakers from the general population and to allocate prisoners rationally to different living quarters and institutions according to their predispositions to engage in violence. Returning to the regimentation of the earlier Big House era, these new institutions are less likely to brutalize inmates than they did before, although they are, in some cases, under extremely tight controls (see Chapter 6).

The norms that govern prison life are variants of dominant cultural themes in American society. Consequently, the expression of violence in American prisons, whether routine assaults or full-blown riot, express these values. Violence in the contemporary American prison has its origins in the wider cultural context in which the prison system is embedded. The frontier culture, deeply rooted in American history and tradition, provides legitimation for violence in response to confrontations concerning both persons and property, especially among adolescent and young adult males.

AMERICA'S FRONTIER CULTURE

American society has the highest violent crime rate in the modern, industrial world. According to Elliot Currie (1985:5), "Americans have faced roughly seven to ten times the risk of death by homicide as the residents of most European countries and Japan." American women are three times more likely to be raped than German women, and Americans generally are four times more likely to be the victims of armed robbery than the British.

Americans of European and African descent have higher violent crime rates than the communities from which they or their ancestors originated. With few exceptions, most African and European countries have low homicide rates (see Archer and Gartner, 1984:106; Gibbons, 1992:260). Homicide rates among Americans of European descent averaged about 4 per 100,000 population during the 1970s and '80s (based on the FBI's *Uniform Crime Reports,* 1990:10, 48, 190; Archer and Gartner, 1984). In the 1970s, European homicide rates were less than 1 per 100,000. According to one study (Bohannon, 1960:236–237), the homicide rate among African–Americans is about six times greater than that of the average African community outside South Africa.

It is more difficult to compare violent crime rates for Hispanic Americans with Latin American crime rates, since the source of much criminal violence in both Latin America and the United States is tied to the drug trade. Many Asian countries have very low violent crime rates, but others do not. But it appears that Hispanic and Asian Americans, too, are more likely to engage in violent crime than their counterparts in Latin America and Asia.

The key to understanding the high level of violence in America is the widespread cultural legitimation of aggressive behavior and the many institutional supports for the maintenance of violence in American social life. The extent of American commitment to violent attitudes and behavior is revealed in a survey of American and Canadians commissioned in 1989 by *Maclean's,* a Canadian newsmagazine (Bilski, 1989). Despite similarities in historical experience and cultural background, Americans display in attitude and behavior a far greater level of aggression and assaultiveness than Canadians. Americans appear to value independence and aggressiveness more than Canadians do, and they often express these values as competitiveness in sports and business. Aggression has its positive aspects when it produces success in entrepreneurial endeavors, but it has its negative side, too, when it leads to physical and emotional harm.

Both the United States and Canada have frontier histories, yet only the United States has developed a frontier culture—one that has become part of the dominant value system, especially for adolescent and young adult males. Canada had its frontier, too, but it did not experience the lawlessness and outright banditry that Americans did. Nor did Canada experience a revolutionary war or a civil war that has reinforced traditions of self-reliance and rebellion against government and authority. Consequently, American frontier culture has several key elements: *autonomy, resistance to authority*, and *self-reliance*, which contribute to aggressive reactions to social conflict.

The frontier culture legitimates violence in confrontations with others over property and matters that affect personal integrity. Gun ownership is an expression of these cultural values in American society. The Canadian survey revealed that 24 percent of Americans as compared with only 3 percent of Canadians own handguns (Bilski, 1989:37). Although many Americans own rifles and shotguns for recreational purposes, most American handgun owners say that the main reason they own a handgun is for self-defense (Wright, Rossi, and Daly, 1983; Silberman, 1984). Unlike Americans, Canadians are subject to strong restrictions regarding gun ownership, including licensing for specific legitimate purposes. The success of a lobbying group such as the National Rifle Association in defeating efforts to restrict the ownership of all but a few assault rifles demonstrates how strongly these values are supported in the United States. Most Americans favor some sort of gun control, but only a minority would restrict the right of citizens to own legally licensed weapons. This commitment to frontier values, coupled with the ready availability of handguns, leads to relatively high homicide rates in the U.S. (McCaghy, 1985:120-124). The Canadian homicide rate is less than one-third that of the United States (Currie, 1985:5).

THE SUBCULTURE OF VIOLENCE THESIS

Do high levels of violence in America occur because of a number of specific *subcultures* of violence, or is there a more widespread *national culture* of violence linked to America's frontier heritage? The subculture of violence argument takes two different forms. First, there is the idea that the violent slave history of the American South has given way to a regional subculture of violence, which explains the high levels of violence in the South and among individuals of southern origin (Hackney, 1969; Gastil, 1971; Erlanger, 1975; Doerner, 1978). Second, there is the idea that lower-class culture provides a milieu that generates aggressive behavior because of its support for values such as immediate gratification and toughness (Miller, 1958).

Wolfgang and Ferracuti (1967) combine both themes in their argument that there is a distinctive black underclass subculture of violence. Similarly, Davidson (1974) argues that the machismo subculture of the young Hispanic male supports an environment in which aggression is both expected and praised, especially among poor Hispanics who have not become anglicized and middle class.

Doerner (1978) has demonstrated that there is no relationship between violent attitudes and southernness when measured in terms of current residency or residential origin. The validity of the southern regional subculture of violence thesis is further challenged by the findings of Judith and Peter Blau (1982) in their study of violent crime rates in American cities. Controlling for income inequality, the Blaus found the correlation between region and crime rates to be spurious. In other words, to the extent that southern cities have higher crime rates, it is because the income differentials between the haves and have-nots in the South are greater than elsewhere in the country.

Not only do the Blaus question the validity of the regional subculture of violence thesis, but they also raise questions regarding the existence of a subculture of violence among minority groups. They found that most of the variance in black and white *violent* crime rates could be explained by differences in levels of *racial inequality* across American cities. Violent crime rates were higher in those cities where income differentials between blacks and whites were greatest. In other words, racial injustice contributes to violent crime, especially among members of minority groups whose crime rates are significantly higher than the majority.

Further challenges to the validity of the subcultural approach to explaining violence come from studies of patterns of gun ownership among different groups in the United States (Williams and McGrath, 1978; Gallup, 1983; Wright, Rossi, and Daly, 1983; Silberman, 1984). Long guns (rifles and shotguns) are principally tied to the hunting traditions of rural white Americans and their descendants, literally and figuratively. Handguns, on the other hand, seem to be valued largely by urban Americans who see their utility as a means of self-defense and for recreational uses such as target shooting. Consistent with the general value of handgun ownership is the prediction that those who have more resources should be more likely to own handguns. Upper income Americans are more likely to own handguns than those with lower incomes. Whites are much more likely to own shotguns and rifles than blacks; although handgun ownership rates are similar for both groups, whites have a slight edge here, too. Gun ownership is a phenomenon of the privileged.

Young black men are more likely to have weapons in their possession than young white men when encountered by the police, making gun ownership among minorities more visible, but not necessarily more frequent (Reiss, 1971:93). These young men typically give the same reason for gun ownership—self-defense—as the middle-aged, middle-class white suburbanite who keeps a loaded revolver in his or her nightstand. In the last several years, gun owners in the inner cities have become younger and younger. According to recent media reports (Morganthau, 1992; Nordland, 1992), inner city high schools are required to use armed security guards and metal detectors because increasing numbers of inner city minority youth are bringing handguns to school "for protection."

THE CULTURAL LEGITIMATION
OF VIOLENCE

There is increasing evidence that American culture in general supports aggressive responses among young males as a legitimate expression of *self-help* in confrontations with others, especially other young males. Self-help refers to the idea that an individual is expected to handle disputes with others directly, without the assistance of third parties such as police or attorneys (Black, 1983:34). As a type of social control, self-help is an alternative to avoidance or informal mediation by friends, ministers, or counselors (Silberman, 1991:109–110; Black, 1993:42, n.2). If an American male has a problem with someone, his integrity depends on his ability to deal with the problem head-on. Only weaklings run away from their problems or ask someone else to help out. Because of its direct nature, those who handle disputes in this manner are often perceived as aggressive.

Research on the history of aggression in America shows a decline in violent crime rates from relatively high levels in the eighteenth and early nineteenth centuries to relatively low levels by the end of the nineteenth century (Lane, 1986; 1989). This decline reflects the civilizing effect of industrial labor for those groups who participated in both blue collar and white collar work. To the extent that minority group males have been systematically excluded from meaningful participation in the industrial labor system, their violent crime rates remained high while those of white Americans, including second-generation European immigrants, declined. Nevertheless, a residue of this early frontier culture in American society provides situationally based legitimation for violent behavior by American males in all social classes and ethnic groups. American males are expected to use violence in defense of themselves or their property, including "their" women and children. Violence in the contemporary American prison can be understood as a product of the expectation that American males should respond aggressively to threats to their integrity or property.

Dixon and Lizotte (1987) tested the regional subculture of violence thesis against its alternative frontier culture thesis and found evidence in support of the former to be wanting. Based on the National Opinion Research Center's General Social Survey, Dixon and Lizotte (1987) examined two independent clusters of attitudes toward violence. The first dimension, *violent attitudes*, reflects support for the typical macho response to immediate threats to one's "manhood" in direct confrontations in bars or other similar situations. Dixon and Lizotte found no regional variation in the expression of violent attitudes, which was supported by a minority of the population, nor did they find any connection to gun ownership.

To the extent that this response is distinctively American, it appears to be linked historically to the lawlessness of the Wild West (McGrath, 1989). Stearns and Stearns (1986) argue that, unlike the American male child, Western European children are socialized to seek third-party assistance in mediating personal disputes with others. The American male, on the other hand, would be labeled a "sissy" for such behavior.

The second cultural trait, *self-defense attitudes*, involves the legitimation of the use of violence in the defense of property ("a man's home is his castle") and the weak and defenseless (women and children). This set of attitudes, which is tied to traditional notions of male dominance, justifies the use of violence in the protection of a man's property, including "his" women and children, on a level that cannot be found in other Western societies. Although there is some regional variation in the level of support for this set of attitudes, a majority of Americans support this value in all regions of the United States. That the expression of this cultural value is statistically correlated with handgun ownership, principally for self-defense, gives credence to the use of the "self-defense" label to describe it.

One manifestation of the connection between handguns and self-defense values in American culture is found in the old movie westerns. Americans idealize the lone gunman who protects "law and order" as Gary Cooper did in *High Noon*. But these values are also manifest in the sort of vigilante justice that occurred when Bernard Goetz, the so-called subway vigilante, shot four young black men in a New York City subway (see Fletcher, 1988). Asked for five dollars by one of the four men, Goetz believed that he was in danger of being mugged. Treated as a hero by the media, Goetz was acquitted of all assault charges by a New York jury, which found him guilty only of a minor gun possession charge (Fletcher, 1988:198).

Self-Defense as a Dominant Cultural Value

Self-defense and violent attitudes reflect the *dominant* and *subterranean* values, respectively, of the frontier culture in America (Matza and Sykes, 1961; Einstadter, 1978). Dominant values are pervasive and receive widespread legitimation by the public at large. Subterranean values are often publicly disapproved by the majority but are supported in private and invoked to justify actions that might otherwise be negatively sanctioned by society.

Self-defense attitudes, linked to the defense of male prerogatives and the ownership of handguns, are widely distributed and can be seen as part of the dominant core values in America. As we have seen, most Americans support these values. Furthermore, approximately half of all American households possesses guns of some sort, and almost half of these involves handguns (Wright, Rossi, and Daly, 1983). These values are more likely to be expressed actively through gun ownership in some regions of the United States. For example, more than half (53%) of southern households have guns in the house, whereas only 21 percent of northeastern households do (Gallup, 1983). In addition, some subgroups, such as white Anglo-Saxon Protestants, are more likely than others to own guns. Nevertheless, support for these values exists, more or less, in all ethnic groups, social classes, and regions of the United States.

Violence as a Subterranean Value

Attitudes expressing machismo among young adult males receive much less explicit support. Evidently a central core value over a century ago, the civilizing process of industrialism has made the overt expression of *violent attitudes* inappropriate for a majority of Americans. These attitudes, then, are an expression of subterranean values available when necessary to justify the use of violent forms of self-help in direct confrontations with other males. Expected among adolescent males, young adults are supposed to outgrow such behavior and "channel" this aggression into more productive arenas such as business or athletics (Stearns and Stearns, 1986).

Other forms of male violence have also lost their legitimacy. During the past twenty years or so, violence against women has become increasingly criminalized, both within and outside of the family. Criminal penalties have been increased for wife beating, and marital rape has become a crime (Gelles, 1987; Pleck, 1989). Reforms in rape laws have been designed to make it easier to prosecute accused rapists (Horney and Spohn, 1991). Excessive aggression against other family members, especially children, is more likely to be socially condemned and treated as evidence of emotional disturbance (Stearns and Stearns, 1986).

Most Americans believe that physical discipline is a necessary part of child rearing (Straus, Gelles, and Steinmetz, 1980:58). In more extreme cases, beatings are seen as necessary "character builders" for preadolescent males (Straus, Gelles, and Steinmetz, 1980:69; Van Brunt, 1993). Victims of child abuse are more likely to react violently as adults, although they are not more likely to commit violent *crimes* (Zingraff and Belyea, 1986). The cycle of violence involving parents and children is part of the wider cultural support for the male prerogative in protecting his interests, including the appropriate discipline of his children. The public condemnation of child abuse has not reduced the overall incidence of family violence, but there has been a significant reduction in the incidence of more severe forms of family violence (Gelles and Straus, 1988:249). Americans still spank their children, fewer engage in child abuse.

SITUATIONAL AGGRESSION

The availability of legitimating norms for aggressive male responses to affronts by other males suggests that these values will emerge and be expressed in *situationally appropriate* cultural contexts. A high rate of violence among young adult, minority group males reflects a situational response to historically consistent and structurally based deprivations that lead to high levels of rage in minority communities (Blauner, 1969). This rage is often expressed in acts of aggression against available targets in the community, neighbors, friends, and family. Such situationally aggressive individuals often have no other criminal histories (Gibbons, 1992:262). Consequently, the so-called subculture of violence in the African American community is simply a variant of the more general frontier culture, which provides justification for acts of violence.

Situational Aggression in Prison

High rates of violence in prison, too, represent situationally appropriate cultural responses to structurally based deprivations. Irwin (1980:192–197) and Wooden and Parker (1982:172–173) have observed that the *convict* identity has become the dominant form of adaptation to long-term maximum security confinement for members of all ethnic groups. The convict code, adhered to, to some degree, by virtually all long-term prisoners, expresses distrust of staff members, prisoners who are different from oneself, and alienation from society as a whole. The code forbids all cooperation with staff members, encourages deadly violence against inmates who "snitch," and demands that the convict show no weakness in his dealings with others.

Any threat to his integrity must be met with an immediate forceful action or a credible threat of violence. Thus, the prison becomes the ideal environment to nurture and give predominance to the expression of the violent attitudes deeply ingrained in the cultural heritage of the frontier.

Like the ghetto dweller, the convict lives in a world that is structurally conducive to violence. Like the ghetto dweller, the convict (black, white, or Hispanic) has been exposed all his life to a society whose cultural values dictate that, to be a man, he must be willing to respond violently to threats to his person or property.

Not only do inmates justify violence in the name of self-defense, but correctional officers frequently lend support to such aggressive responses. Young male prisoners may be advised to defend themselves should other prisoners try to take advantage of them sexually (Bowker, 1980:13). These officers make it clear that they can do nothing to stop these attacks and the prisoner must stand up like a man or he will eventually be taken advantage of.

Correctional officers, too, have a similar code of conduct in which the respected officer is one who demonstrates that he can successfully take it and "dish it out" to inmates. He must be as "tough" as the convict. In general, violence is expected in confrontations between inmates and staff. Challenges to the authority of correctional officers are met, in some instances, with physical retaliation. Again, this is a logical extension of the cultural legitimation of the use of violence in defense of personal masculine integrity. In prison, violence is legitimated by staff and prisoners alike.

VIOLENCE AS SOCIAL CONTROL

Law, as *governmental* social control (Black, 1976:2), is distinguished from other forms of social control by its unique access to legitimate means of coercion or force. The use of force is legitimate when it is employed by authorized representatives of the community (see Weber, 1954:5; Akers, 1975:306). In modern terms, this means that agents of the state—police, prosecutors, judges, and correctional officers—have a legal monopoly on the use of violence as a means of social control.

In his book *The Behavior of Law*, Donald Black (1976) proposes a scientific theory of law based on a set of fundamental principles. For example, "*law varies directly with stratification*" (Black, 1976:13). In other words, the law is imposed as a mechanism of social control more frequently when there are status differences between disputants. Moreover, law is usually imposed on those of lower status. Similarly, Black argues that law varies directly with social integration, culture, and organization. In other words, law is a mechanism of social control that protects the wealthy, the conventional, the privileged, and the well-organized.

The principle of law in Black's theory that interests us here is "*law varies inversely with other social control*" (Black, 1976:107). This means that when state agents, such as prison officials, are unable or unwilling to exert control over a prisoner population, other forms of social control will inevitably emerge to take the place of legal controls. In some settings this may mean informal mechanisms such as ridicule or gossip, but in prison, norms are usually enforced by more violent means. Since this violence is not authorized, it is defined as illegal. This applies to both the use of excessive force by correctional officers and to assaults and homicides committed by inmates.

Observing that a good deal of social behavior is regulated by conduct that is prohibited by law, Black writes elsewhere (1983) that behavior that society labels as criminal is frequently intended to sanction behavior that violates some social norm or custom. Criminal assaults frequently occur in response to "affronts to honor" on the street or in a barroom (Black, 1983:36). Domestic violence sometimes occurs in response to the failure to perform some household duty (Black, 1983:36). Some children are beaten when they disobey their parents (Straus, Gelles, and Steinmetz, 1980:51; Gelles and Straus, 1988:33). These acts of violence reflect strong cultural traditions that authorize criminal actions, many of them violent, in support of those traditions (Black, 1993:31–36).

Although Sweden has made it illegal to spank a child under all circumstances (Currie, 1985:42), most Americans believe that it is appropriate to discipline young children by spanking them (Straus, Gelles, and Steinmetz, 1980:55). Whether or not we define these actions as criminal is a political decision that reflects the standards of conduct of the wider political community. Consequently, we see the increasing criminalization of child abuse and domestic violence in areas that were previously considered legitimate.

Violence as Social Control in Prison

It should not be surprising, then, that cultural values that legitimate the use of violence in self-defense (more broadly defined than the law allows) and the defense of one's integrity and honor should take the place of legitimate authority in prison. Violence becomes a necessary means of social control in the absence of the ability of prison authorities to provide protection to inmates whose safety and self-respect are threatened in this environment. For example, sexual pressure that remains unchallenged will leave the

an inmate is a "punk," available now and in the future as a
rtner to other inmates.

ance at Central, one inmate encountered another inmate
 the shower. To the former, this situation implied that the
latter was interested in a sexual encounter. This was taken by the first inmate
as an insult to his masculinity, which required a response in order to maintain his integrity and identity as a heterosexual male. He attacked the second inmate with a homemade knife, or "shank." His personal safety threatened, the second inmate also defended himself with a shank.

SELF-HELP IN PRISON

There are four legitimate responses to disputes that occur in prison: avoidance, informal mediation, filing a formal complaint through established
grievance procedures, or taking legal action. The first, dispute avoidance, is
not feasible in prison for most prisoners. To avoid confronting a fellow prisoner over some issue may be taken as a sign of weakness, making the individual subject to future exploitation. Nor is he able to take most complaints
to authorities for much the same reason.

In his book on California prisons, Irwin (1980:58-60) reports that, at
one time, during the correctional institution era, informal mediation of disputes among inmates was commonplace. Typically, a dispute between two
individuals would be mediated by someone who shared some common interest, for example, had been crime partners with the disputants, had come
from the same neighborhood, or had participated in the same prison rehabilitation programs. In today's violent prisons, however, factionalism among
prisoners makes accommodation difficult. Nevertheless, there are occasions
when inmates whose leadership abilities are respected by a wide array of inmates are able to mediate disputes that occur in prison. But this is more the
exception than the rule.

Formal grievance procedures are usually cumbersome and unresponsive
to inmate difficulties. Moreover, they are principally designed to handle disputes with officers and concerns about policies rather than the day-to-day
confrontation inmates experience among themselves. Legal remedies are
rarely available for most disputes that occur in prison, and when they are,
the barriers to effective legal counsel are often insurmountable. Court action is rare and only likely to occur when inmates have considerable resources and when a dispute reflects a fundamental conflict of interest between inmates and the administration of the prison.

In the outside world, a person who is verbally or physically harassed can call the police or seek legal assistance to deter the harasser. In prison, there is no one to call. Consequently, there is little choice but to engage in self-help in the settling of disputes. In prison, self-help is expressed as verbal or physical aggression, threatened or real, in order to maintain "respect."

Violence in prison should *not* be understood as an indication of the breakdown of social order. Rather, it expresses and supports the existing code of conduct governing prison life today. Threats to honor, sexual harassment, and informing on fellow inmates ("snitching") are serious violations of the convict code. The use of violence as a form of self-help is an inevitable consequence of the social organization of the contemporary prison. But this violence is situationally legitimated by the self-defense and violent attitudes derived from the wider cultural context, the frontier culture, of American society.

CONCLUSION

America's frontier culture legitimates the use of direct self-help rather than the reliance on legal institutions in a variety of situations that involve the defense of male prerogatives regarding property and persons. In addition, a substantial number of Americans in all regions justify violent responses in defense of threats to male egos. In prison and in the outside world, self-help frequently involves violence or the threat of violence in support of culturally legitimated values such as integrity, masculinity, and property.

A growing body of evidence suggests that violence in American society reflects the frontier values of the society as a whole rather than distinctive regional or ethnic subcultures. Violence is a product of the self-defense and violent attitudes of American males. The high incidence of ownership of handguns for self-defense reflects the frontier values of American society. Violent crime occurs more frequently when there is a greater disparity in incomes between the haves and have-nots, especially when that disparity is based on race.

The prison provides an ideal environment for the expression of the frontier values of American culture. Young men, raised to be independent and aggressive, have little choice but to act aggressively when faced with challenges to their personal safety or self-respect in prison. The law cannot protect them, nor can they use alternative mechanisms of social control, such as avoidance or mediation, to settle disputes. So they must rely on themselves to survive the physical and emotional deprivations of prison life.

The absence of a coherent set of policy goals in the American prison system has led to sporadic riots over the past several years, with violence directed toward correctional officers on the rise. It has also contributed to a state of anomie, made worse by overcrowding, which has created an atmosphere in which violent self-help has become the dominant pattern governing the daily lives of prisoners.

REFERENCES

Akers, Ronald L. (1975). "Toward a Comparative Definition of Law," *Journal of Criminal Law, Criminology, and Police Science* 56:301–306.

American Correctional Association (1981). *Riots and Disturbances in Correctional Institutions.* College Park, MD: Author.

Archer, Dane and Rosemary Gartner (1984). *Violence and Crime in Cross-National Perspective.* New Haven, CT: Yale University Press.

Bilski, Andrew (1989). "Portrait of Two Nations," *Maclean's,* July 3:36–37, 48–51.

Black, Donald (1976). *The Behavior of Law.* New York: Academic Press.

Black, Donald (1983). "Crime as Social Control," *American Sociological Review* 48:34–45.

Black, Donald (1993). *The Social Structure of Right and Wrong.* New York: Academic Press.

Blau, Judith R. and Peter M. Blau (1982). "The Cost of Inequality: Metropolitan Structure and Violent Crime," *American Sociological Review* 47:114–129.

Blauner, Robert (1969). "Internal Colonialism and Ghetto Revolt," *Social Problems* 16:393–408.

Bohannon, Paul (1960). *African Homicide and Suicide.* Princeton, NJ: Princeton University Press.

Bowker, Lee H. (1980). *Prison Victimization.* New York: Elsevier.

Currie, Elliott (1985). *Confronting Crime: An American Challenge.* New York: Pantheon Books.

Davidson, R. Theodore (1974). *Chicano Prisoners: The Key to San Quentin.* New York: Holt, Rinehart, & Winston.

Dixon, Jo and Alan J. Lizotte (1987). "Gun Ownership and the 'Southern Subculture of Violence,' " *American Journal of Sociology* 93:383–405.

Doerner, William G. (1978). "The Deadly World of Johnny Reb: Fact, Foible, or Fantasy?" Pp. 91–98 in *Violent Crime: Historical and Contemporary Issues,* edited by J. A. Inciardi and A. E. Pottieger. Beverly Hills, CA: Sage.

Einstadter, Werner J. (1978). "Robbery-Outlawry on the U.S. Frontier, 1863–1890: A Reexamination." Pp. 21–38 in *Violent Crime: Historical and Contemporary Issues,* edited by J. A. Inciardi and A. E. Pottieger. Beverly Hills, CA: Sage.

Erlanger, Howard S. (1975). "Is There a 'Subculture of Violence' in the South?" *Journal of Criminal Law and Criminology* 66:483–490.

Federal Bureau of Investigation (1990). *Uniform Crime Reports: Crime in the United States—1989.* Washington, DC: U.S. Department of Justice.

Fletcher, George P. (1988). *A Crime of Self-Defense: Bernard Goetz and the Law on Trial.* Chicago, IL: University of Chicago Press.

Gallup, George (1983). *The Gallup Report.* Report No. 215. Princeton, NJ: Gallup Poll.

Gastil, Raymond D. (1971). "Homicide and a Regional Subculture of Violence," *American Sociological Review* 36:412–427.

Gelles, Richard J. (1987). "Power, Sex, and Violence: The Case of Marital Rape." Pp. 135–149 in *Family Violence,* edited by R. J. Gelles. Beverly Hills, CA: Sage.

Gelles, Richard J. and Murray A. Straus (1988). *Intimate Violence.* New York: Touchstone Books.

Gibbons, Don C. (1992). *Society, Crime, and Criminal Behavior* (6th ed.). Englewood Cliffs, NJ: Prentice Hall.

Goffman, Erving (1961). *Asylums.* Garden City, NY: Anchor Books.

Hackney, Sheldon (1969). "Southern Violence," *American Historical Review* 74:906–925.

Hoedel, Martha B. (1986). "Finished: Inmates Slay Three Before Yielding," *The Patriot,* January 4:A1–A2. Harrisburg, PA.

Horney, Julie and Cassia Spohn (1991). "Rape Law Reform and Instrumental Change in Six Urban Jurisdictions," *Law and Society Review* 25:117–153.

Irwin, John (1980). *Prisons in Turmoil.* Boston: Little, Brown.

Jacobs, James B. (1977). *Stateville: The Penitentiary in Mass Society.* Chicago, IL: University of Chicago Press.

Johnson, Robert (1987). *Hard Time: Understanding and Reforming the Prison.* Monterey, CA: Brooks/Cole.

Lane, Roger (1986). *Roots of Violence in Black Philadelphia, 1860–1900.* Cambridge, MA: Harvard University Press.

Lane, Roger (1989). "On the Meaning of Homicide Trends in America." Pp. 55–79 in *Violence in America, Volume I: The History of Crime,* edited by T. R. Gurr. Newbury Park, CA: Sage.

Martin, Randy and Sherwood Zimmerman (1990). "A Typology of the Causes of Prison Riots and an Analytical Extension to the 1986 West Virginia Riot," *Justice Quarterly* 7:711–737.

Martinson, Robert (1974). "What Works? Questions and Answers About Prison Reform," *The Public Interest* 35:22–54.

Matza, David and Gresham M. Sykes (1961). "Juvenile Delinquency and Subterranean Values," *American Sociological Review* 26:712–719.

McCaghy, Charles H. (1985). *Deviant Behavior: Crime, Conflict, and Interest Groups.* New York: Macmillan.

McCleery, Richard H. (1980). "Policy Change in Prison Management." Pp. 383–400 in *A Sociological Reader on Complex Organizations,* edited by A. Etzioni and E. W. Lehman. New York: Holt, Rinehart, & Winston.

McGrath, Roger D. (1989). "Violence and Lawlessness on the Western Frontier." Pp. 122–145 in *Violence in America, Volume I: The History of Crime,* edited by T. R. Gurr. Newbury Park, CA: Sage.

Miller, Walter B. (1958). "Lower Class Culture as a Generating Milieu of Gang Delinquency," *Journal of Social Issues* 14:5–19.

Morganthau, Tom (1992). "Kids and Guns: It's Not Just New York," *Newsweek,* March 9:25–29.

Nordland, Rod (1992). "Kids and Guns: Deadly Lessons," *Newsweek,* March 9:22–24.

Pleck, Elizabeth (1989). "Criminal Approaches to Family Violence, 1600–1980." Pp. 19–58 in *Family Violence,* edited by L. Ohlin and M. Tonry. Chicago, IL: University of Chicago Press.

Quinney, Richard (1974). *Critique of Legal Order: Crime Control in Capitalist Society.* Boston, MA: Little, Brown.

Reiss, Albert J. (1971). *The Police and the Public.* New Haven, CT: Yale University Press.

Senate Judiciary Committee (1989a). *Public Hearing on Recent Incidents at Pennsylvania State Correctional Institutions: Transcript of Proceedings.* Harrisburg, Pennsylvania, October 31.

Senate Judiciary Committee (1989b). *Public Hearing on Recent Incidents at Pennsylvania State Correctional Institutions: Transcript of Proceedings.* Harrisburg, Pennsylvania, November 27.

Silberman, Matthew (1984). "Guns Don't Kill, People Kill," *Legal Studies Forum* 8:481–486.

Silberman, Matthew (1991). "Dispute Resolution in a Maximum Security Penitentiary: Alternatives to Violence." Pp. 104–120 in *Alternative Dispute Resolution in the Public Sector,* edited by M. K. Mills. Chicago: Nelson-Hall.

Smothers, Ronald (1993). "Guard Is Dead at Ohio Prison, Putting Toll at 8," *New York Times,* April 16:A12.

Stearns, Carol Z. and Peter N. Stearns (1986). *Anger: The Struggle for Emotional Control in America's History.* Chicago, IL: University of Chicago Press.

Straus, Murray A., Richard J. Gelles and Suzanne K. Steinmetz (1980). *Behind Closed Doors.* Newbury Park, CA: Sage.

Useem, Bert (1985). "Disorganization and the New Mexico Prison Riot of 1980," *American Sociological Review* 50:667–688.

Useem, Bert and Peter A. Kimball (1987). "A Theory of Prison Riots," *Theory and Society* 16:87–122.

Useem, Bert and Peter A. Kimball (1991). *States of Siege: U.S. Prison Riots 1971–1986.* New York: Oxford University Press.

Van Brunt, Lloyd (1993). "Farewell, Huck," *New York Times,* January 31:10.

Weber, Max (1954). *Max Weber on Law in Economy and Society.* Translated by E. Shils and M. Rheinstein. Cambridge, MA: Harvard University Press.

Williams, J. Sherwood and John H. McGrath (1978). "A Social Profile of Gun Owners." Pp. 51–60 in *Violent Crime: Historical and Contemporary Issues,* edited by J. A. Inciardi and A. E. Pottieger. Beverly Hills, CA: Sage.

Wolfgang, Marvin and Franco Ferracuti (1967). *The Subculture of Violence.* London: Tavistock.

Wooden, Wayne S. and Jay Parker (1982). *Men Behind Bars: Sexual Exploitation in Prison.* New York: Plenum.

Wright, James D., Peter H. Rossi, and Kathleen Daly (1983). *Under the Gun: Weapons, Crime, and Violence.* New York: Aldine.

Zingraff, Matthew T. and Michael J. Belyea (1986). "Child Abuse and Violent Crime." Pp. 49–63 in *The Dilemmas of Punishment,* edited by K. C. Haas and G. P. Alpert. Prospect Heights, IL: Waveland Press.

5

✳

The Production of Violence in Prison

There are two competing theoretical perspectives on the way in which inmates learn to survive in a hostile prison environment. The first, the *importation model*, stresses the role of experiences inmates bring to the prison from outside in shaping the way in which they adapt in prison. In an early criticism of functionalist theories of adaptation to prison life, Irwin and Cressey (1962) argued that many of the traditional "argot" roles that inmates played in prison, e.g., the "merchant," "politician," or "right guy," were *imported* from their experiences prior to coming to prison.

On the other hand, Charles Tittle (1969) found little evidence of subcultural criminal values in the attitudes and behavior of inmates he studied in a coeducational federal institution. Tittle did find, however, that men and women adapted to the "pains of imprisonment" differently, suggesting that more general cultural factors play an important role in explaining what happens in prison. Men were more likely to identify with the "convict code" and the convict group as a whole, whereas women were more likely to adapt to prison life by becoming involved in small, supportive primary groups.

The second perspective, the *deprivation model*, stresses the role that institutional conditions play in explaining the attitudes and behavior of inmates.

Central to this approach is the work of Erving Goffman in his book *Asylums* (1961). Goffman argues that prisons, as "total institutions," envelop and control the daily routines of inmates to such an extent that they have little choice but to find some adaptive strategy to survive. Total institutions "mortify" inmates to such an extent that they lose their prior sense of self shortly after entering the institution. Goffman argues that they could rebel, withdraw, identify with those in control ("convert"), or accept institutional standards as a way of life ("colonize"). No matter what the adaptive strategy, the individual is transformed into someone different from whom he or she was prior to incarceration.

In his study of a maximum security prison in New Jersey, Sykes (1958) suggested that the "pains of imprisonment" that resulted from the deprivation of fundamental needs—conventional heterosexual relationships, the love of family, and the ability to make choices—lead to the acquisition of roles in prison designed to make adaptation to limited resources possible. Hence the "merchant" negotiates deals using cigarettes as money, the "gorilla" looks for weak victims to exploit, and the "wolf" or "rapo" sexually victimizes "punks." In juvenile institutions, "bogarters" and "booty bandits" rove in gangs to take possession of the property or bodies of weaker or less organized inmates (see Bartollas, Miller, and Dinitz, 1976:55–56, 96). "Bogarters" are tough guys who regularly intimidate weaker inmates; "booty bandits" specialize in sexual exploitation. Several researchers (see Clemmer, 1940; Wheeler, 1961; Tittle, 1969, 1972; Thomas and Zingraff, 1976) have argued that new inmates undergo what has been called the *prisonization* process in which they gradually learn to adhere to the existing norms of the inmate world.

Recent research on prison life suggests that the old ways of adapting to prison, the argot roles described in earlier research (see Sykes, 1956; Sykes and Messinger, 1960:9–11; Irwin, 1980:33), have disappeared. Today, there are two primary modes of identification in prison. The first is the inmate/convict continuum, reflecting the degree of commitment to the convict code. Convicts identify with the violent world of the prison, whereas inmates still maintain their ties to the outside world. The second mode of identification is based on racial and ethnic background, which has become the primary source of group affiliation. In many prisons, organized gangs have developed around ethnic and racial identity. What this suggests is that the way in which prisoners adapt to prison life cannot be strictly defined in terms of the deprivation model. Prisons are still total institutions that deprive inmates of the fundamental necessities of life. Increasingly permeable boundaries of the prison world make prisons far less total than in the past.

Whether it is prisons that have changed or theories that were in error or incomplete, it is evident that external forces play a great role in shaping prison life today.

The previous chapter explored the external origins of prison violence rooted in the frontier culture and the attitudes and behaviors that reflect traditional American values derived from the frontier experience. We have seen how these values shape the way in which convicts justify or rationalize situational aggression. We have seen how norms or standards of conduct in prison, the "convict code," reflect the general cultural values that legitimate violence in response to threats to the convict's integrity, property, or person.

In this chapter, we examine theories of social organization and social control designed to make sense of institutional processes that affect inmate adaptation to prison life. The focus here is on the institutional conditions that explain the use or threatened use of violence as an adaptive strategy. This chapter does not make the traditional deprivation argument that the way in which inmates adjust to prison life must be understood in terms of institutional processes alone. Rather, as we shall see, inmates adapt in ways that interact in complex ways with external cultural factors.

The theories we shall examine are compliance theory (Etzioni, 1975), labeling theory (Lemert, 1951; Becker, 1963), and control theory (Hirschi, 1969). All three theories suggest that the external environment plays a critical role in understanding how internal organizational processes work. Basic to all three theories is the notion that the social control process has unanticipated side effects. Prisoners are likely to become more violent because of the fundamental nature of the institutions themselves and the way in which institutional processes are affected by outside influences.

COMPLIANCE THEORY

Compliance theory is a theory about power in organizations. Those in dominant positions in organizational structures, such as prisons, have at their disposal three kinds of *power-means*, "physical, material, and symbolic rewards and punishments," to secure "conformity with the organizational norms" (Etzioni, 1975:4). We are interested here in the physical means of social control available to prison officials and the impact this control has on the behavior of inmates.

Essential to the nature of the prison as an organization is the role that coercion, the use or threatened use of force, plays in the control of inmates. Etzioni defines *coercive power* as:

..tion, or the threat of application, of physical sanctions
..s the infliction of pain, deformity, or death; generation of
..ustration through the restriction of movement; or controlling
through force the satisfaction of needs such as those for food, sex,
comfort, and the like (Etzioni, 1975:4).

At Central, inmates are restricted to designated locations at all times.
Violators are considered out of bounds and are subject to informal or formal sanctions. If the former, they may be required to clean latrines or sweep
floors for a period of time. If the latter, they may find themselves locked up
in the segregation unit (the "hole") for a few days. Similarly, inmates may
move from one location to another for ten minutes each hour and must
have written permission to do so. The deprivation of basic needs in the total institution has been described above. There is no refrigerator to raid, but
inmates have been known to steal food in order to regain some control over
this basic need. Women are not available, but homosexual prostitutes are
readily available to those who are willing to use their services. But the loss
of safety is probably the most universally devastating experience the new inmate experiences. The coercive environment generated by the prison creates fear of assault, rape, or even death (see Schmid and Jones, 1991:417).

One Central inmate, particularly fearful of an unexpected intrusion into
his cell, described sitting and sleeping with his back to the wall at all times.
Still another was unwilling to be seen cooperating with this researcher in
order to avoid appearing "weak." And yet another was afraid that, at some
unexpected time, a member of a prison gang might attempt to kill him.

Interestingly, few inmates express overt fear of correctional officers. Reported threats by officers and rumors of the use of excessive force in "seg"
do not impinge on the daily routines of most inmates. But central to their
consciousness at all times is the reality that they live in a violent world
among violent individuals—fellow convicts—from whom violence can
strike at any time. Schmid and Jones (1991) report that, over time, many inmates lose their fear as they adapt to prison life. The very fact that these inmates take for granted the dangers of their world does not make the dangers any less real. This "hardening" of the convicts suggests that they have
become part of the problem they initially feared.

The Role of the Environment

According to compliance theory, most organizations tend to rely on one
primary type of power-means. Since the main purpose of the prison system
is to contribute to the maintenance of order in society by controlling convicted criminals who have been removed from society by the courts, pris-

ons can be expected to rely primarily on the *coercive power of the state* at their disposal. In other words, organizations are linked to their environments through the purposes they serve and the resources allocated to the organization to carry out its purpose. The fact that society expects convicted criminals to be kept under lock and key for specified periods of time makes the task of the prison system clear.

Organizations are most effective in carrying out their goals when the relationship between the power-means employed and the type of involvement of those under its control is congruent. Thus, a certain degree of *alienation,* or "negative involvement," on the part of inmates is essential to the effective functioning of prisons in *incapacitating* convicts by removing them from society. If the goal of *rehabilitation* were taken seriously, we would expect some degree of shared values as inmates willingly submitted themselves to incarceration in order to get help with their problems. But this simply does not happen. Clearly, the central purpose of prisons is the incapacitation of convicts and this generates alienative involvement in a population subject to the legitimate use of coercive power by the state.

Alienation

Alienation has several meanings (see Seeman, 1959). It is sometimes used to refer to a sense of anomie or *normlessness* when there is an absence of clear expectations guiding the individual's behavior (Durkheim, 1951:246–257; Seeman, 1959:787–788). Alienation is also experienced when life seems *meaningless* to the individual who lacks direction or purpose in life (Seeman, 1959:786–787). When individuals are subject to conflicting expectations, they may become *self-estranged* or detached from their immediate experiences (Seeman, 1959:789–790). And, finally, individuals may lose control over their daily lives. It is this final sense of alienation as *powerlessness* that is essential to our understanding of the prison experience (see Seeman, 1959:784–785; Marx, 1976).

At Central, alienation *from society* had little impact on prisoner morale or behavior. Studies measuring alienation generally rely on the sense of loss of control that people experience as citizens of society as a whole (see, especially, Neal and Rettig, 1967; Thomas and Zingraff, 1976). Sociological measures rely on indicators such as, "The world is run by people in power, and there is not much the little guy can do about it," or conversely, "In my case, getting what I want has little to do with luck."

Julian Rotter (1966), a psychologist who worked with sociologist Melvin Seeman on the conceptualization and measurement of alienation in the 1960s, developed the I/E (internal/external) Scale to measure the "locus" of control experienced by his subjects. Internal individuals experience a great deal of self-control; external individuals feel that their fate is largely determined by forces outside of their control. The alienated, or powerless, person is someone who subjectively feels that others control his or her destiny or fate. Individuals who experience a great deal of self-direction and self-control in their lives measure low on alienation.

It doesn't seem to matter one way or the other if an inmate felt alienated from society before coming to prison. Far more important to the inmate's sense of powerlessness is his experience as a prisoner. The prison experience explains the inmates' orientation toward authority and their sense of personal autonomy and self-control. To better indicate the degree of alienation among Central inmates, the author constructed an institution-specific measure of alienation in which the items of the scale were phrased in terms of the specific experiences of the inmates. These items were:

> I sometimes do things I don't like to do just to get along with other inmates.
>
> I often do things in prison I don't like to do just to get along with the staff.
>
> The staff run this institution and there is little the inmates can do about it.
>
> If they try hard, most inmates can make parole before mandatory release.

Each item was scored 1–5, from strongly agree to strongly disagree. This approach is called Likert scaling. Some items are deliberately reversed in direction to avoid yea-saying or nay-saying, i.e., situations in which respondents just say yes or no to all items regardless of their content. Actual scores ranged from 6 to 18, with 18 representing the greatest amount of alienation. Inmates were then divided into three alienation groups, low (6–9), middle (10–13), and high (14–18).

The Impact of Alienation on Prison Life

Inmates, like other subordinates in organizations, can express their alienation in a number of ways. To the extent that alienation is the consequence of the use of coercive power, it is often expressed in terms of hostility toward those who wield that power. This hostility can be expressed as sabotage in industrial firms, vandalism in public schools, or assaultive behavior in prison. In other words, coercion leads to alienation, which in turn leads to violence on the part of those subject to that coercion—that is, violence begets violence.

In prison, we can expect the greatest degree of hostility toward staff to be expressed by the most alienated inmates. These inmates experience a loss

Table 5.1 Hostility Toward Staff by Alienation (in percentages)

	DEGREE OF ALIENATION		
	Low (6–9)	Middle (10–13)	High (14–18)
Expressed Hostility Toward Officer	18.8	59.5	93.1
(Number of Inmates)	(16)	(42)	(29)

$\chi^2 = 24.99$, df = 2, $p < .001$.

of control over their own destiny attributed to the coercive power of correctional officers. One insightful inmate expressed this as follows (paraphrasing):

> When a "cop" [correctional officer] pushes me around and tells me what to do, I get real angry. Before you know it, I take it out on another convict.

This inmate is aware that his frustration leads to violent behavior that he dare not express toward the officer. Instead he attacks another inmate. He further observed that racial hostilities among inmates are sometimes the consequence of displaced aggression.

As expected, there was a significant relationship between alienation and expressed hostility toward staff at Central. Inmates were considered hostile toward staff if they had been found guilty of assaulting an officer, had threatened an officer, or expressed anger at an officer at some time during their stay at Central. Few had actually assaulted an officer, but a majority expressed anger at or threatened an officer at some time. As Table 5.1 shows, the vast majority of the highly alienated group (93.1%) expressed hostility toward the staff, whereas only about one-fifth of the low alienation group (18.8%) expressed hostility toward the staff.

The insights described by the above inmate are consistent with the statistical analysis. It seems that the more hostile the inmate is toward staff, the more likely it is that he will assault another inmate. Central inmates were asked, "Since your incarceration here at [Central]":

> Have you ever found it necessary to defend yourself in a confrontation with another inmate(s) with a knife, lead pipe, or other dangerous weapon that could cause serious injury?
>
> Have you ever found it necessary to defend yourself in a confrontation with another inmate(s) with an object that was not a weapon, such as a mop wringer, broomstick, etc.?
>
> Have you ever found it necessary to actually defend yourself in a fist fight between yourself and another inmate?

Table 5.2 Self-Reported Assaults by Hostility (in percentages)

	DEGREE OF HOSTILITY EXPRESSED TOWARD OFFICERS		
	Low (0)	*Middle (1)*	*High (2–3)*
Inmate Assaults			
Another Inmate	40.0	62.5	88.9
(Number of Inmates)	(35)	(48)	(9)

$\chi^2 = 8.42$, df = 2, $p < .01$.

Inmates who had expressed great hostility toward the staff, including threats and/or actual assaults, were more than twice as likely (88.9% vs. 40.0%) to have assaulted another inmate than those who said they had never expressed any sort of anger toward staff (see Table 5.2). In other words, alienated inmates are hostile toward staff, and this hostility, in turn, leads to assaultive conduct among inmates. Consequently, the highly alienated group can be expected to take out their hostility toward the staff by engaging in violent acts directed at fellow inmates. And this is exactly what happens. Highly alienated inmates are almost twice as likely (65.5%) as those who are in the low alienation group (37.5%) to assault another inmate at Central.

Conclusion

Violence in prison is, in part, a product of the violent nature of the institution itself. Total institutions such as prisons that rely heavily on the use of force to maintain control are, as we can see, inherently violent in nature. In a well-managed institution, attacks on officers are relatively infrequent. Consequently, the alienation, or "negative involvement" as Etzioni calls it, that results can lead to assaults on the most convenient objects—fellow inmates. Given the underlying racial tensions that exist in our prisons, it should not be surprising that many of these assaults cross racial lines.

LABELING THEORY

Labeling theory has its origins in the work of George Herbert Mead (1934), whose book *Mind, Self, and Society* focuses on the relationship between the individual and society. Mead argued that the *self* is a social product that develops through the interaction of the individual and significant others in his or her immediate environment. We all play *roles*, organized sets of activities expected of us in specific social situations. For example, we play the role of son or daughter in relationship with our parents or the role of student in relationship to our teachers. The expectations associated with these roles are derived from the rules that govern relationships in the groups we belong to. Families create obligations and duties for both parents and children. Similarly, as citizens in a political democracy, we are expected to participate in the political process in a variety of legitimate ways: voting, writing petitions, and so on.

Clearly, not everyone abides by the norms that govern the roles we are expected to perform. We may accept or reject these norms, ignore them, or violate them, depending on the amount of leeway associated with each. In the military, there is little choice but to obey orders. Families vary considerably in the ability of children to express themselves freely. And political democracies are characterized by considerable leeway in the way in which citizens participate in the political process.

When individuals choose not to obey the rules, we say that they have violated the *norms*, standards of conduct, associated with the roles they are expected to perform. Children may disobey their parents, students may do poorly on exams, and citizens may violate the laws of the community. When this happens, negative sanctions may be applied to the rule violator, and these sanctions have implications for the self implied in the role the individual performs. The student is *stigmatized* by receiving low grades on his or her official report. Poor academic performance reflects on the student's ability and his or her estimation of that ability. In other words, the student's self-esteem may be affected adversely.

Frank Tannenbaum (1938:19) first described the *labeling process* as the "dramatization of evil" applied to delinquents in a ritual ceremony called a trial in which the norm violator is identified to others and to himself/herself as a delinquent person. The symbolic transformation of the individual through the application of official sanctions and labels increases the likelihood that he or she will go on to commit further delinquencies. This is reinforced by the perception of others, and since we tend to see ourselves through the eyes of others, the adolescent who violates the rules of society becomes a delinquent in his or her own eyes.

Studies of the labeling process have also focused on the consequences of that process for those who are the recipients of deviant labels. Charles Lemert (1951:75–78) defined "secondary deviance" as the consequence of the change in an individual's personality in response to society's reaction to that individual's initial or "primary deviance." The individual takes on a new deviant role in accordance with revised expectations by significant others concerning his or her behavior. As a result, a person reorganizes his or her self-image in a manner consistent with those expectations. To the extent that the deviant label carries a strong sense of disapproval by people close to the individual, lowered self-esteem often results. Sometimes, as in the case of the delinquent gang member, status may be enhanced among his or her peers, increasing self-esteem rather than diminishing it.

Howard Becker (1963:24) wrote that becoming deviant was like a "career" in which the deviant goes through a series of transformations in "perspectives, motivations, and desires" as he or she becomes more involved in a deviant lifestyle. Segregated from conventional situations, the deviant associates with others who share similar experiences and provide support for the deviant role to which the individual has been assigned. This explains why it is so difficult to escape deviant labels once they have been acquired.

The main point of labeling theory is that the punishment of social deviance makes people more deviant than if they had not been punished. This is because the societal reaction to deviance labels the accused in such negative terms that they begin to identify themselves as deviant persons. This creates a self-fulfilling prophecy: "once a deviant, always a deviant" in the minds of the public and the person who is labeled deviant. In other words, the social control of deviance creates the deviance it is designed to eliminate.

Research Evidence

Early research (Tittle, 1975; Wellford, 1975) on criminal offenders concluded that there was little evidence to support the assumptions of labeling theory concerning secondary deviance. More recent research, however, provides some evidence in support of labeling theory as it applies to youthful offenders. These studies (Bazemore, 1985; Farrington, 1977; Harris, 1975; Horwitz and Wasserman, 1979; Klein, 1986; Klemke, 1978; Ray and Down, 1986) report that juvenile offenders who are officially labeled delinquent are more likely to pursue criminal careers than those who are treated more leniently. The difference between the earlier and later studies appears to depend on the type of population studied. Younger, first offenders are clearly the most impressionable and most likely to be transformed by the labeling process. Older offenders either have already been transformed at an earlier age or have matured to the point where their fundamental personality organization is already well formed and unlikely to change.

Research on the effect of the labeling process on prison inmates is limited for the most part to ethnographic studies of contemporary prison life. Several authors (Irwin, 1980; Wooden and Parker, 1982; Fleisher, 1989) have identified the new "convict" as a tough, aggressive individual who reacts violently at the slightest provocation. These authors argue that this new convict identity is a product of the violent world in which inmates live.

Many of the most violent convicts have been "state-raised youth" (Irwin, 1980:53–54; Johnson, 1987:85–92). They were exposed to this violent world at an early age when most vulnerable to the "massive assault" on their identities that prison creates (Berger 1963:100–101). As Goffman indicated in his book *Asylums* (1961), maximum security prisons are total institutions that *mortify*, i.e., break down, the identities of their inmates. Inmates are subject to physically degrading and psychologically terrifying experiences that make them vulnerable to identity transformations regardless of age. On the other hand, Schmid and Jones (1991) have recently shown that short-term (two years or less), first-time inmates in a maximum security prison can insulate themselves from the more radical transformations that long-term convicts undergo. They do this by playing prison roles that facilitate their survival while maintaining contact with those who support their preprison identities.

In other words, we can expect to find a range of prisoners in prison today, from the most hardened convicts who have fully embraced the convict role and prison as a way of life to inmates who are struggling to maintain their sense of who they were prior to their incarceration. One convict at Central explained that he had been institutionalized on and off since he was an adolescent. He expressed his sense of detachment from the outside world and commitment to prison as a way of life when he said, "Prison is reality . . . life beyond the wall is an illusion."

The Labeling Process at Central

The labeling process plays an important role in explaining assaultive behavior by inmates at Central. Correctional officers have a great deal of discretion when deciding whether or not to write "shots," that is, reports of inmate violations of disciplinary rules. Like police officers (see Black, 1970), correctional officers are less likely to use discretion for serious offenses than for relatively minor ones.

Three kinds of labels can affect the use of discretionary authority by correctional officers: societal, institutional, and interactional. The racial/ethnic background of the offender illustrates the role of *societal* labels on the use of discretion by correctional officers. Official classification schemes create *institutional* labels designed to identify and isolate more dangerous prisoners from the others. Finally, out of the context of daily routines and *interactions* in the contemporary prison emerges the "convict" world, in which those who have adapted to prison life and adhere to the "convict code" are labeled by others and label themselves "convicts," distinguishing themselves from others whom they refer to, with some contempt, as "inmates" (Irwin 1980:192–195; Wooden and Parker, 1982:172–173).

We are interested here in the process by which these labels are assigned as well as the effects they have on the discretionary behavior of correctional officers. We are also interested in the impact of the labeling process on the actual behavior of inmates, specifically on their self-reported assaultiveness.

Classification: The Assignment of Official Institutional Labels

At Central, correctional counselors and caseworkers apply a classification scheme, the Adult Internal Management System (AIMS), developed by psychologist Herbert C. Quay (1984). Designed to isolate the most aggressive and dangerous inmates from the others, the AIMS typology has been used in a number of correctional institutions for over 20 years (Smith and Fenton, 1978; Lauder, O'Toole, and Jones, 1981:204; Quay, 1984:ix). The purpose of the AIMS typology is to reduce the level of violence in the institution by making it difficult for the more aggressive prisoners to victimize the others. It is designed to distinguish between inmates who are aggressive and independent ("heavies") from those who are passive and dependent ("lights") or who are neither excessively aggressive nor weak ("moderates"). Lauder, O'Toole, and Jones (1981:205) report that heavies are "significantly more involved in serious incidents" than lights and moderates. Quay (1984:18–23) reports significant reductions in the level of inmate violence in those institutions that have used the AIMS typology.

Inmates are well aware of their labels and pick up on their essential features. In the inmate world, heavies are characterized by their "muscles and balls," lights are called "fags and losers," and moderates are "sane and normal." A typical heavy is a street gang member from the inner city or a member of a prison gang. Since prison gangs were not entrenched at this prison as they are elsewhere, most of the violence associated with gang activity had been committed prior to coming to this institution. Inmates with any sort of history of violence prior to entering Central were likely to be labeled as heavies. In some cases, these were individuals who were convicted of killing inmates in other institutions. Some lights may have engaged in homosexual activity before coming to prison and continue to do so while incarcerated. And some of the weaker inmates, whether gay or not, may be coerced into homosexual prostitution (see Bowker, 1980:14). The majority of lights are individuals who have not been major players in the criminal world. Many have psychiatric problems and receive medication on a regular basis. Still others committed impulsive crimes as lone bandits who were easily caught. Professional criminals and members of organized crime are usually considered "sane and normal."

During their first two weeks in the Admissions unit, inmates are classified by correctional counselors and caseworkers employing an inventory of behavioral traits and background characteristics. According to Quay (1984:7), heavies are "hostile to authority" and engage in aggressive, victimizing behavior; lights are "easily victimized by [heavies] since they often are friendless and are seen as weak, indecisive, and submissive"; moderates are "neither excessively aggressive nor dependent." Inmates are assigned according to their classification to separate living quarters or "units." Heavies are usually assigned to the cell block area of the institution, whereas moderates and lights are usually assigned to the less secure dormitory section. Each unit is supervised by special unit teams of caseworkers and correctional counselors who hear complaints, recommend job assignments, and discipline minor infractions that occur in their units.

Two additional classification schemes are employed at this institution, *security level* and *custody level*. Neither of these plays as central a role here as does the AIMS typology. Security level is used systemwide to determine the appropriate institutional placement for the inmate: minimum, medium, or maximum security. Although Central was designated as a maximum security penitentiary, only 39 percent of the population was officially classified as maximum security (5 or 6 on a 6-point scale). Most of the inmates (60%) were medium security (mostly 4s and a few 3s). Despite the variation in security designations, this system was uncorrelated with the AIMS classification and played little role in affecting the treatment of inmates once they were assigned to the institution.

Custody level, however, was strongly correlated with the AIMS classification system. The purpose of custody level is to determine the level of surveillance warranted for each inmate. *Close* custody inmates, who had a history of violence in prison or were considered an escape risk, were subject to greater surveillance. Some were subject to additional surveillance because of their perceived threat to the security of the institution. Roughly one out of seven (14%) of the inmates in the institution were classified as close custody. Almost all (98%) of the lights and moderates in the sample were classified *standard* custody, meaning that they were not monitored in any special manner. Most of the heavies (59%), however, were considered close custody. Conversely, over 90% of the close custody inmates were classified as heavies. Once an inmate has been classified as a heavy, he is usually assigned to a cell block rather than an open dormitory, making it possible to monitor his behavior more closely than other inmates.

**Table 5.3 Self-Reported Assaultiveness and Assault Record
by Institutional Classification and Self-Identity (in percentages)**

	INSTITUTIONAL CLASSIFICATION		SELF-IDENTITY	
	Heavy	Light/ Moderate	Convict	Inmate
Self-Reported Assaultiveness				
Staff Victim[a]	20.0	6.8	22.2	2.2
Inmate Victim[b]	36.0	18.6	38.9	19.6
Assault Record[c]	47.6	20.4	32.3	29.3
(Number of Inmates)	(25)	(59)	(36)	(46)

[a]$\chi^2 = 3.21$, df = 1, $p < .05$ (classification effect); $\chi^2 = 8.31$, df = 1, $p < .01$ (self-identity effect).

[b]$\chi^2 = 2.92$, df = 1, $p < .05$ (classification effect); $\chi^2 = 3.74$, df = 1, $p < .05$ (self-identity effect).

[c]$\chi^2 = 5.57$, df = 1, $p < .01$ ($N = 75$; classification effect); self-identity difference is not statistically significant.

Note: Self-reported assaultiveness is based on the two subscales. Inmates were considered assaultive if they committed at least two types of offenses. Staff victims were either threatened or actually assaulted. Inmate victims were assaulted with some sort of weapon.[3]

Given the above discussion, it should not be surprising that heavies are more than twice as likely to have acquired an assault record while at this institution than lights or moderates (47.6% vs. 20.4%; see Table 5.3).[1] Of course, committing an assault is one of the main reasons that inmates are so charged, but self-reported assault statistics reveal that there is *little actual difference in the incidence of minor assaults* among the different groups. Roughly two-thirds of all inmates expressed hostility toward or threatened a staff member at some time. And more than half of all inmates reported engaging in some sort of violence, including fistfights, with fellow inmates.

When considering more serious incidents, heavies reported that they are three times more likely (20.0% vs. 6.8%) to threaten a staff member (or worse) than lights or moderates and twice as likely (36.0% vs. 18.6%) to have used a weapon in a confrontation with another inmate (see Table 5.3). Threats to officers and assaults with weapons were always taken seriously by correctional officers. Consequently, some of the difference in the acquisition of assault records between heavies and the others can be explained by the relative frequency of more aggressive behavior in the former group.

Among those who admit assaulting other inmates, heavies were still more likely to be charged than the others. Roughly twice as many heavies who admitted assaulting another inmate had an assault record when compared with lights and moderates who did so. In the sample, there were no inmates who were falsely accused of committing an assault or threatening an officer. So it appears that the difference in acquiring an assault record depends on the likelihood of detection rather than on false accusations. Since heavies have a hard time avoiding detection because they are subject to greater surveillance, they are more likely to acquire an assault record, confirming to the classification team that their initial judgment was correct. Among those inmates who admitted assaulting another inmate, 62% of the heavies had an assault record compared with only 30% of the lights and moderates.[2]

In conclusion, we can see that the official classification system is designed to distinguish the most aggressive prisoners from the remainder in order to reduce the level of violence in the institution. By separating these groups, the overall level of violence in the institution is apparently reduced. Although heavies are likely to engage in more serious forms of aggression, there is no appreciable difference among the groups in the *overall* incidence of aggression. Those who are designated heavies are subject to greater surveillance and hence are more likely to be caught. This justifies the initial judgment of the classification team and further stigmatizes these inmates in the eyes of their controllers.

Race: The Effect of Stereotypes on the Labeling Process

Individuals who are poor, uneducated, or members of minority groups are more vulnerable to the labeling process than those who are wealthier, more educated, or members of the majority. Higher social status appears to insulate individuals from both the likelihood of detection and punishment and from the adverse effects of being labeled as deviant (Ridlon, 1988:17–19). Writing about young black males as "endangered, embittered, and embattled," Jewelle Gibbs (1992:268) argues that they are stereotyped as "deviant, dangerous, and dysfunctional" in American society. These stereotypes concerning their aggressiveness make black males especially vulnerable to negative labeling in the criminal justice system.

In their study of a large urban court, Swigert and Farrell (1977) found that stereotypes concerning violent behavior among lower-class black males led to more severe sentences for those charged with homicide. Blacks were likely to be given long prison sentences because they were less able to make bail and had less effective counsel. But they also received long prison sentences because they were perceived by court personnel who did presentence investigations as more dangerous to society than white defendants who had committed the same crime. These court officials applied what Swigert and

Farrell (1977:24) describe as the "normal primitive" stereotype to black offenders, which reflects the "popular image of individuals who are thought
to be prone to the spontaneous expression of violence." Blacks were perceived to be individuals "whose violent behavior is said to be normal within
their own social setting" (Swigert and Farrell, 1977:24).

Racial Bias in the Enforcement of Disciplinary Rules. Several studies have confirmed that there is racial bias in the enforcement of disciplinary rules in prison (Poole and Regoli, 1980; Ramirez, 1983; Adams,
1992). This occurs for two reasons: (1) pervasive cultural stereotypes concerning the aggressive nature of black males in America affect the perceptions of correctional officers and their expectations concerning the potential dangerousness of black prisoners, and (2) racial biases built into the
official classification system reinforce the perceptions of correctional officers, leading to additional biases in the way in which rules are enforced.

Summarizing the research on the relationship between race and inmate
misconduct, Adams (1992:301) concluded that studies show that blacks are
more likely to be charged with institutional violations, but results are mixed
when it comes to actual infraction rates. Earlier research reported higher infraction rates for whites (Johnson, 1966) or no racial differences (Wolfgang,
1961; Ellis, Grasmick, and Gilman, 1974). In his study of Eastern Correctional Institution, Carroll (1974:118–119) found that blacks were more
likely than whites to be reported for serious infractions. Nearly all major infractions were referred to the disciplinary board, regardless of race, but
white inmates were more likely to be disciplined for minor infractions than
blacks, whose minor infractions were treated more leniently.

More recent research on aggressive behavior reports consistent racial differences, with black inmates described as aggressors and whites as victims
(Adams, 1992). But these studies do not generally distinguish between self-
reports and official statistics or are anecdotal in nature. Studies that control
for prior criminal history and urban background report similar infraction
rates for black and white inmates (Goodstein and MacKenzie, 1984; Wright,
1989). Wright (1989) found no racial differences in self-reported aggression
(fights and arguments) or in official assault statistics, but did find that blacks
were more likely to be charged with "disruptive behavior."

Poole and Regoli (1980:942–945) suggest that blacks are more likely
than whites to be labeled as troublemakers if they already have a prior history of disciplinary infractions. They argue further that the labeling process
helps to explain the differential treatment of black inmates by correctional
officers. Blacks are caught in a vicious cycle in which past biases in the la-

beling process increase the probability that their misconduct will be detected and punished, *even in the absence of current bias.* Wright's (1989) research suggests that these biases only affect minor ("disruptive") offenses committed by black inmates and that serious assaults are prosecuted regardless of the background of the assailants.

The research reported below is designed to identify the labeling mechanism that produces the cycle of differential treatment in one particular prison. The specific mechanism is likely to vary from prison to prison since classification systems vary from system to system. At Central, the evidence suggests that blacks are more likely to be labeled as heavies and placed in more secure cell blocks. This increases the ability of officers to detect their misconduct, creating higher official assault statistics. This, in turn, reinforces the expectation that black inmates are more aggressive than whites, further contributing to their detection for minor offenses. There is no evidence that serious offenses are treated differently by officers when committed by black or white inmates. Furthermore, an examination of official disciplinary hearings revealed no racial biases in findings of guilt or in sentencing.[4]

Racial Bias in the Labeling of Prisoners. The AIMS typology reproduces many of the characteristics associated with that of the "normal primitive" stereotype found in Swigert and Farrell's (1977) study of a criminal court. By taking into account background characteristics such as employment histories and family status linked to the experiences of black inmates, the AIMS classification system can be expected to label blacks as heavies more often than whites, independent of their actual aggressiveness. Family relations, for example, are defined in conventional middle-class terms. Poor work histories reproduce racial biases in the lack of educational and job opportunities in ghetto communities.

The fact that the vast majority (over 90%) of close (maximum) custody inmates are labeled as heavies indicates that a prior history of violence plays a major role in the labeling process, although it is only one of many factors taken into account. Thus, any prior bias in the treatment of black prisoners *at any stage in the criminal justice process from arrest to prosecution* will be reproduced by the AIMS classification system. In other words, the differential treatment of black prisoners at Central is primarily a consequence of racial bias in society as a whole, rather than policies generated at this institution.

Blacks are more likely to be labeled "heavies" than whites—34 percent of the black prisoners compared with only 20 percent of the whites. Many of the white prisoners in this prison are hard-core convicts who have done time in some of the most secure facilities in the country. Consequently,

**Table 5.4 Institutional Classification by
Type of Prisoner and Race (in percentages)**

	INSTITUTIONAL CLASSIFICATION		
	Heavy	*Light/Moderate*	*(N)*
Hard-Core Convicts			
Black	57.1	42.9	(14)
White	57.1	42.9	(7)
Inmates[a]			
Black	26.5	73.5	(34)
White	0.0	100.0	(10)

[a] $\chi^2 = 3.33$, df = 1, $p < .05$.

Note: Hard-core convicts score ≥ 28 on the prisonization scale and 1–3 on the convict self-rating scale; inmates are defined as those who are not hard-core.

there is a disproportionate number of highly prisonized white inmates in this penitentiary. This fact may tend to "mask," or hide, the full impact of the racial biases in the labeling process.

To control for the effect of adaptation to prison as a way of life on the labeling process, hard-core convicts were distinguished from the remaining inmates. *Hard-core convicts* are distinguished by a high degree of prisonization and by identifying themselves as "convicts" (see p. 98). Here we find that there is no difference between white and black hard-core convicts in the likelihood that they will be defined as heavies (see Table 5.4). The principal difference is in the way in which ordinary inmates are labeled by prison officials. No white inmates were defined as heavies whereas one-fourth of the black inmates were so labeled.

The expression of aggressive attitudes and hostility toward authority (characteristics of the convict) is taken into account in the classification of prisoners as heavies. But these "tough" and "defiant" attitudes are not linked to race in the classification system, despite the subjective nature of the judgments that must be made by staff members who do the evaluations. As we can see from Table 5.4, hard-core convicts are equally likely to be labeled as heavies regardless of their racial background.

Racial Bias in Reporting Assaults. Although self-reported assault statistics were nearly identical for blacks and whites, blacks in the sample were more than three times as likely to be charged with assault at some time during their stay at this institution (36.7% vs. 10.5%; see Table 5.5). This difference can be explained by the role that the heavy label plays in

**Table 5.5 Self-Reported Assaults and
Assault Record by Race (in percentages)**

	RACE	
	Black	White
Self-Reported Assaultiveness		
Highly Assaultive (3–5)	25.0	22.7
Somewhat Assaultive (1–2)	53.6	54.6
Not Assaultive (0)	21.4	22.7
Assault Record[a]		
Assault Record	36.7	10.5
No Record	63.3	89.5
(Number of Inmates)	(56)	(22)

[a]$\chi^2 = 4.53$, df = 1, $p < .05$ (N = 68; missing data = 10).

Note: Self-reported assaultiveness is based on a scale that counts the different types of assaults reported by inmates. In general, those who commit the most serious assaults report more types of assaults.

the detection of assaults committed by black prisoners. An official label indicating a prisoner's dangerousness increases surveillance of that prisoner and hence the likelihood of detection increases. Since officers use little discretion when writing shots for serious violations, such as threats to officers and the use of weapons, we can assume that these differences in detection are limited to relatively minor offenses.[5] Heavies are placed in maximum security cell blocks where they can be watched more closely. Since blacks are overrepresented in these cell blocks, their aggressiveness is more likely to be detected.[6]

Adaptation to Prison as a Way of Life: Prisonization, the Convict Code, and the Convict's Self-Image

As a matter of survival, all inmates adhere more or less to the "convict code," but the more *prisonized* inmates demonstrate greater loyalty to the code than the others (also see Wooden and Parker 1982:172–173). A *prisonization* scale measures the inmate's adaptation to prison as a way of life and indicates the extent to which the inmate is committed to the convict code. The prisonization scale used in the study of Central was based on eight Likert-scale items (see p. 84) designed to differentiate those who adhere to the convict code from those who do not (adapted from Thomas and Zingraff, 1976, and Tittle, 1969). The maximum possible score was 40, the minimum was

8, and the average (median) was 28. Committed to the convict code, prisonized convicts see little value in being straightforward with caseworkers or counselors, prefer to mind their own business and avoid trouble, and will not be pushed around. They manifest high levels of distrust in their relationships with staff members and inmates alike.

Using a 10-point self-rating scale (see Quarantelli and Cooper, 1966) where 1 represents *convict* and 10 represents *inmate*, prisoners were asked, "Do you think of yourself as a 'convict' or as an 'inmate,' or something in between? Please circle the number that describes you best." Prisoners who scored 1–3 on the self-rating scale were considered convicts; the rest were considered inmates.

Highly prisonized inmates—those who scored at or above the median on the prisonization scale—were three times more likely to define themselves as convicts than those who were less prisonized. Three-fourths (74.3%) of those who were highly prisonized defined themselves as convicts. Conversely, almost three-fourths (70.3%) of the convicts were highly prisonized, whereas only one-fourth (23.4%) of the inmates scored at or above the median on the prisonization scale.[7] *Convicts, then, are highly prisonized individuals who have adapted to prison as a way of life.*

Labeling theory predicts that institutional labels will affect both the self-image and the subsequent behavior of the prison inmate (Becker, 1963:20–21). The self-image of the actor is altered in response to the expectations of others reflected in the official labels assigned. Those who are labeled *heavies* according to the AIMS typology are placed in separate, more secure settings and, as a result, are visibly treated differently from other prisoners. Consequently, their view of themselves is affected by being treated and defined as aggressive and dangerous persons. At Central, heavies were two to three times more likely to call themselves convicts than either lights or moderates.[8] Thus, the convict self-image, which is a result of adapting to prison as a way of life, is further reinforced by the official labeling process.

As we have seen, convicts are extremely aggressive individuals who are predisposed to respond violently to threats to themselves or their belongings. As one convict said, "[The officers] can make me eat shit, but [they] don't touch me." This convict had a history of violence in the prison system, including assaults on correctional officers. His veneer of self-protection was so strong that you could almost see an invisible shield around him. His personal space was inviolable, although he knew he was in an environment that required disciplined obedience to the rules. Paradoxically, the true convict is not likely to violate the day-to-day rules of the institution; he is often respected by the older officers and is respectful in turn.

But he will not be treated unfairly nor will he be pushed around without retaliating.

Clearly, there are several sources of the convict identity. The prisonization scale and convict self-identity both reflect adaptation to prison as a way of life. It is reasonable to ask, then, whether it is the official labeling process that affects the self-image of the convict or whether it is the convict's behavior that leads the institution to label the prisoner as aggressive? From the interviews, it appears that many inmates come to the institution with well-formed self-conceptions as convicts. These are frequently long-term prisoners who are isolated from family and friends and who have spent much of their sentence in maximum security institutions or in segregation (the "hole"). In these cases, the heavy label is assigned by the institution, in part in response to the "tough guy" self-image of the highly prisonized convict. The convict's self-image is both a product of his past experience in prison and the heavy label he is assigned at the institution.

The Effect of Self-Image on Behavior. Although those who call themselves convicts are a bit more likely than others to commit at least one assault, it is only when one considers multiple assaults that we begin to see a significant difference. Convicts are twice as likely to report committing more than one type of assault than other inmates (see Table 5.3). Most inmates find themselves in at least one situation in which they are tested and find it necessary to resort to violence in order to defend themselves and establish their integrity—"respect"—in this environment. After this, they are usually able to successfully avoid confrontations of a violent nature. Convicts, on the other hand, more frequently resort to force to settle disputes with other inmates. And when they do so, they are more likely to use weapons such as a broomstick or a shank.

Convicts are also more likely to threaten or assault staff. About two-thirds of the prisoners expressed anger toward staff at least once. But *inmates* rarely express their hostility in other ways. In fact, only one inmate (2.2%) in the sample reported threatening a staff member (see Table 5.3). Almost one-fourth (22.2%) of the *convicts*, however, do more than just express their frustration in angry remarks toward staff. These convicts threaten and, on occasion, assault staff as well as other inmates.

Despite the fact that convicts are highly likely to be labeled as heavies, and heavies are more than twice as likely to be charged with an assault than lights and moderates, convicts are no more likely than inmates to be charged with committing an assault (see Table 5.3). It seems that the convict's self-identity has no effect on the likelihood of being sanctioned for assaultive behavior. In other words, *charging* an inmate with an assault is largely dependent on his official label as an aggressive, assaultive *heavy*. On the other hand, his actual *behavior* is more closely tied to his self-perception as a tough and aggressive *convict*.

CONTROL THEORY

Contemporary control theory is most clearly stated in Travis Hirschi's book, *Causes of Delinquency* (1969). It is based on the assumption that, in the absence of a variety of social constraints, individuals would naturally be deviant. Human beings are inherently amoral at best, and at worst, immoral beings driven by their animalistic instincts to violate the social constraints of society. This theory has much in common with Freudian notions concerning the role of the superego (see Hall, 1979). For Freud, deviant impulses are driven by the basic urges of the human organism, especially the libido. Individuals internalize the standards of society through intimate contact with parents and other role models early in life. Through this contact, the superego develops to regulate the individual's behavior from within and control the impulse to satisfy one's basic needs at the expense of others. Thus, control theory as a sociological theory of human motivation is a logical extension of Freudian theories of personality.

In his book, Hirschi (1969:3–15) compares three types of theories of delinquency: strain theories, cultural deviance theories, and control theories. *Strain* theories assume that the origins of social deviance are in the frustrations and anger generated by the deprivations inherent in organized social life. Conformity is normal; deviance is not. As a type of strain theory, compliance theory explains violence in terms of the alienation experienced by individuals subject to a coercive environment.

Cultural deviance theories do not assume that either conformity or deviance are inherent in human conduct. Cultural deviance theories are relativistic in nature, that is, right and wrong can only be understood in terms of the social group's cultural values, not in general universalistic terms. From the perspective of the actors, what is right or wrong, normal or deviant, depends on the situational context in which the behavior occurs. Individuals become deviant to the extent that there are incentives in their environment to do so. Labeling theory is a type of cultural deviance theory.

Control theories assume that there is a natural human urge to do evil, and civilized human behavior depends on society's ability to contain these urges by strengthening the bonds between conventional society and the individual or by threatening the individual with punishment should he or she act in an uncivilized manner. Control theories are consistent with more politically conservative attitudes concerning the role of punishment and prisons today. The public pressures the prison system to treat prisoners like animals, lock them in cages for the rest of their lives, and throw away the key. Inmates are "herded" toward the dining halls during the noon hour for their "feeding." Crushed up against the closed grilles (bars) leading to the dining area, hundreds of inmates wait to be fed in one large eating area during a short span of time. In other words, the very nature of the prison system, by locking large numbers of individuals up in a confined space, creates the behavior that control theorists attribute to "human nature."

The psychiatric view of Yochelson and Samenow (1977), two psychiatrists at St. Elizabeth's hospital in Washington, D.C. (where Goffman did his original work on *Asylums* and where John Hinkley, the would-be assassin of President Reagan, is held), is a version of control theory that legitimates the "throw away the key" philosophy. These psychiatrists argue that it is the "criminal personality" that explains the origins of criminality for most prisoners. This criminal personality, formed early in childhood, is difficult if not impossible to treat. This suggests that rehabilitation is nearly impossible and that all one can hope to do is to incapacitate dangerous offenders for as long as possible through incarceration.

Hirschi argues that, in the absence of bonds to conventional society, the fundamental self-gratifying nature of human beings will lead them to commit crimes. These bonds are: (1) *attachment* to conventional others such as family, teachers, and ministers; (2) *commitment* to conventional lines of activity such as school, church, and the military; (3) *involvement* in conventional activities, creating less opportunity for getting into trouble; and (4) *beliefs* in conventional values so that it is necessary to rationalize or "neutralize" these values before committing crimes. Hirschi supports this theory with evidence from the study of delinquents. Kids who are poorly supervised by parents, have weak ties to church and school, are uninvolved in extracurricular activities, and rationalize their behavior by arguing that the victim somehow deserves to be victimized are likely to become delinquent.

As in research on labeling theory, there is little evidence in support of control theory for adult offenders. Yet we may expect the absence of bonds to conventional society in prison to play an important role for adult offenders because of the defining nature of the prison experience. And this is precisely what we find. *Convicts* are unlikely (only 5.6%) to receive regular, monthly visits from friends and family (see Table 5.6). More than half (58.3%) received no visits during the past six months. In comparison, almost two-thirds (65.2%) of the *inmates* received occasional or frequent monthly visits from family and friends.

Table 5.6 Number of Visits from Family and Friends by Self-Identity and Institutional Classification (in percentages)

	NUMBER OF VISITS FROM FAMILY AND FRIENDS			
	Frequent	Occasional	Rare	(N)
Self-Identity[a]				
Convict	5.6	36.1	58.3	(36)
Inmate	23.9	41.3	34.8	(46)
Institutional Classification[b]				
Heavy	13.0	30.4	56.5	(23)
Moderate	24.3	29.7	45.9	(37)
Light	13.0	65.2	21.7	(23)

[a]$\chi^2 = 6.91$, df = 2, $p < .05$.
[b]$\chi^2 = 10.16$, df = 4, $p < .05$.
Note: Frequent = averaged at least one visit per month during the past six months; occasional = fewer than six visits over the past six months; rare = no visits during the past six months.

Heavies are more than twice as likely as lights to be without visits from family and friends during the previous six months (see Table 5.6). Many moderates (about one-fourth) experience frequent, monthly visits. And about half the moderates who have had no visits during the past six months have had a family visit at least once during the past year (not shown in table). This is not so for heavies. Moreover, heavies who have had frequent visits over a six-month period are unlikely to sustain this pattern for a full year. In other words, critical to the normalizing experience of inmates is contact with family and friends at least once a year.

Convicts, most of whom are labeled as heavies, are unlikely to have frequent visits from family and friends despite the fact that there are few differences among prisoners in the number of visitors on their approved visitors lists. In other words, convicts are as likely as anyone else to have entered prison with strong support from family and friends. But over time, family and friends lose interest in visiting. This is reinforced by the removal of these convicts to geographically distant locations. In other words, attachment to conventional others insulates some prisoners from the institutional processes that transforms inmates into hard-core convicts.

Removal from conventional society for long periods of time contributes directly to changing commitments on the part of inmates as they become more prisonized and committed to the prison as a way of life. There is no evidence that this contributes directly to violent behavior. The amount of contact with friends and family is unrelated to self-reported assaultiveness or to having an assault record. Consequently, control theory would appear to have limited merit when applied to the prison context. It appears not to be the release of animal instincts that leads to more violence in prison, but links to the convict code that facilitates adaptation to prison as a way of life that explains the violence of those who are cut off from society. In other words, less *attachment* to conventional others strengthens one's attachment to unconventional lifestyles, a point consistent with cultural deviance theory rather than control theory.

Those who have jobs in the prison's industrial production facilities (about 40% of the inmates) are slightly less violent than those who have a variety of support jobs such as kitchen service and maintenance. Paid less than minimum wage, but more than other inmates, those who work in prison industries are selected because of their perceived compliance with institutional rules. Involvement in conventional activities such as educational programs, religious programs, and institutionally supported self-help groups are unrelated to self-reported assaultiveness or acquiring an assault record. Inmates become involved in conventional activities because of self-selection and recruitment by those who run the programs. There appears to be little effect of involvement in these activities on the behavior of prison inmates.

CONCLUSION

Importation and *deprivation* models distinguish between the effects of external factors and institutional conditions, respectively, on the dynamics of prison life. In the previous chapter, we have seen how external factors such as frontier values play a role in explaining the violence that occurs in American prisons. In this chapter, we have examined three theories of deviance which argue that it is the pains of imprisonment—its fundamental deprivations—that produce the violence we see in prisons today.

The first, *compliance* theory, states that the use of force to control crime, although legitimate, alienates those subject to this form of state coercion. The powerlessness that results leads to hostility toward those in authority and violence against fellow inmates.

The second, *labeling* theory, argues that the official classification of prisoners as dangerous increases the visibility of their misconduct and increases the likelihood of their detection. To the extent that racial bias in society as a whole affects both the living conditions of African Americans and their accumulation of criminal records, prison classification systems tend to reflect and reproduce this racial bias. This then increases the visibility of offenses committed by black offenders. The convict identity is both a product of

adaptation to prison as a way of life and the labeling of prisoners as dangerous. Convicts, who are tough and aggressive, are more likely than other
prisoners to threaten or assault an officer and to attack fellow prisoners with
some sort of weapon.

The third deprivation theory, *control* theory, argues that bonds to conventional society prevent individuals from seeking to gratify their basest instincts. In prison, this means that attachment to family and friends insulates
the individual from adaptation to prison as a way of life. Inmates with sus-
tained family ties are less likely to identify themselves as convicts or to be labeled by officials as heavies. There is little evidence, however, that participation in institutional programs affects the values or behavior of the prisoners.

NOTES

1. An assault is defined as an "attempt
   or threat to inflict injury upon the
   person of another" (Black,
   1979:105). A battery is defined as
   the actual use of force "which always
   includes an assault" (Black,
   1979:139). Assault as it is used here
   includes both assault and battery.
   Inmates acquire assault records for a
   variety of offenses, including assault
   with a weapon, fistfights, threatening
   an officer and "insolence." (There
   was no one in the sample who was
   charged with murder while at Central.) Insolence corresponds roughly
   to inmate self-reports of expressed
   hostility toward officers. Although
   those who merely express hostility
   toward officers are rarely charged
   with an offense, one inmate who
   referred to correctional officers as
   "fucking assholes" was charged with
   insolence. Insolence, unchecked, is
   considered by correctional officers to
   be threatening because it represents a
   challenge to their authority and
   ultimately their safety (see
   Lombardo, 1981:92–96).

2. $\chi^2 = 3.72$, df = 1, $N = 40$, $p < .05$
   (direction predicted).

3. The reader may be puzzled by the
   fact that "inmates" (last column in
   Table 5.3) report committing fewer
   assaults than official assault records
   would indicate. This can be explained by the fact that inmates tend
   to commit less serious offenses, such
   as fistfights and insolence, and the
   comparison of self-reports in this
   table is based on more serious
   violations.

4. Crouch (1985) reports similar results
   in a study of a Texas prison. He
   found that minority status did not
   play a significant role in the severity
   of punishment in official disciplinary
   hearings, although the number of
   previous visits to the disciplinary
   committee and "anti-authority
   attitudes" did play a role in determining the severity of punishment.

5. In fact, in this sample, roughly 10%
   of both blacks and whites were
   charged with the most serious offenses, assault (with or without a
   weapon) and possessing a weapon.
   Most of the remaining charges were
   for fistfights, threatening an officer,
   and insolence.

6. Since many of the officers at Central are themselves from minority groups, including those in positions of responsibility, it seems unlikely that differences in the treatment of black and white prisoners can be explained by overt racial bias in the attitudes of correctional officers.

7. The relationship between the prisonization and self-rating scales is statistically significant ($\chi^2 = 16.35$, df = 1, $p < .001$; $N = 75$).

8. 70.8% of the heavies ($N = 24$), 25.8% of the moderates ($N = 31$), and 38.1% of the lights ($N = 21$) defined themselves as convicts ($\chi^2 = 11.50$, df = 2, $p < .01$).

REFERENCES

Adams, Kenneth (1992). "Adjusting to Prison Life," *Crime and Justice: A Review of Research* 16:275–359.

Bartollas, Clemens, Stuart J. Miller, and Simon Dinitz (1976). *Juvenile Victimization: The Institutional Paradox.* Beverly Hills, CA: Sage.

Bazemore, Gordon (1985). "Delinquent Reform and the Labeling Perspective," *Criminal Justice and Behavior* 12:131–169.

Becker, Howard S. (1963). *Outsiders.* Glencoe, IL: Free Press.

Berger, Peter L. (1963). *Invitation to Sociology: A Humanistic Perspective.* Garden City, NY: Anchor Books.

Black, Donald J. (1970). "Production of Crime Rates," *American Sociological Review* 35:735–748.

Black, Henry Campbell (1979). *Black's Law Dictionary.* St. Paul, MN: West Publishing.

Bowker, Lee H. (1980). *Prison Victimization.* New York: Elsevier.

Carroll, Leo (1974). *Hacks, Blacks, and Cons: Race Relations in a Maximum Security Prison.* Prospect Heights, IL: Waveland Press.

Clemmer, Donald (1940). *The Prison Community.* Boston, MA: Christopher Publishing.

Crouch, Ben M. (1985). "The Significance of Minority Status to Discipline Severity in Prison," *Sociological Focus* 18:221–223.

Durkheim, Émile (1951). *Suicide: A Study in Sociology.* Glencoe, IL: Free Press.

Ellis, Desmond, Harold G. Grasmick and Bernard Gilman (1974). "Violence in Prison: A Sociological Analysis," *American Journal of Sociology* 80:16–43.

Etzioni, Amitai (1975). *A Comparative Analysis of Complex Organizations.* New York: Free Press.

Farrington, David P. (1977). "The Effects of Public Labeling," *British Journal of Criminology* 17:112–125.

Fleisher, Mark S. (1989). *Warehousing Violence.* Beverly Hills, CA: Sage.

Gibbs, Jewelle T. (1992). "Young Black Males in America: Endangered, Embittered, and Embattled." Pp. 267–277 in *Race, Class, and Gender,* edited by M. L. Andersen and P. H. Collins. Belmont, CA: Wadsworth.

Goffman, Erving (1961). *Asylums.* Garden City, NY: Anchor Books.

Goodstein, Lynne and Doris L. MacKenzie (1984). "Racial Differences in Adjustment Patterns of Prison Inmates: Prisonization,

Conflict, Stress, and Control." Pp. 271–306 in *The Criminal Justice System and Blacks*, edited by D. Georges-Abeyie. New York: Clark Boardman.

Hall, Calvin S. (1979). *A Primer of Freudian Psychology*. New York: Penguin.

Harris, Anthony R. (1975). "Imprisonment and the Expected Value of Criminal Choice: A Specification and Test of Aspects of the Labeling Perspective," *American Sociological Review* 40:71–87.

Hirschi, Travis (1969). *Causes of Delinquency*. Berkeley, CA: University of California Press.

Horwitz, Allan and M. Wasserman (1979). "The Effect of Social Control on Delinquent Behavior," *Sociological Focus* 12:53–70.

Irwin, John (1980). *Prisons in Turmoil*. Boston: Little, Brown.

Irwin, John and Donald R. Cressey (1962). "Thieves, Convicts and the Inmate Culture," *Social Problems* 10:142–155.

Johnson, Elmer H. (1966). "Pilot Study: Age, Race and Recidivism as Factors in Prisoner Infractions," *Canadian Journal of Corrections* 8:268–283.

Johnson, Robert (1987). *Hard Time: Understanding and Reforming the Prison*. Monterey, CA: Brooks/Cole.

Klein, Malcolm W. (1986). "Labeling Theory and Delinquency Policy," *Criminal Justice and Behavior* 13:47–79.

Klemke, Lloyd W. (1978). "Does Apprehension for Shoplifting Amplify or Terminate Shoplifting Activity?" *Law and Society Review* 12:391–403.

Lauder, Scott P., Richard O'Toole, and Paul K. Jones (1981). "Prison Class, Time, Space, and Rule Violation," *Free Inquiry in Creative Sociology* 9:204–205.

Lemert, Edwin M. (1951). *Social Pathology*. New York: McGraw-Hill.

Lombardo, Lucien X. (1981). *Guards Imprisoned: Correctional Officers at Work*. New York: Elsevier.

Marx, Karl (1976). "The Notion of Alienation (Marx)." Pp. 397–401 in *Sociological Theory: A Book of Readings*, edited by L. A. Coser and B. Rosenberg. New York: Macmillan.

Mead, George Herbert (1934). *Mind, Self, and Society*. Chicago, IL: University of Chicago Press.

Neal, Arthur G. and Salomon Rettig (1967). "On the Multidimensionality of Alienation," *American Sociological Review* 32:54–64.

Poole, Eric D. and R. M. Regoli (1980). "Race, Institutional Rule Breaking, and Disciplinary Response: A Study of Discretionary Decision Making in Prison," *Law and Society Review* 14:931–946.

Quarantelli, E. L. and Joseph Cooper (1966). "Self-Conceptions and Others: A Further Test of Meadian Hypotheses," *Sociological Quarterly* 7:281–297.

Quay, Herbert C. (1984). *Managing Adult Inmates*. College Park, MD: American Correctional Association.

Ramirez, John (1983). "Race and the Apprehension of Inmate Misconduct," *Journal of Criminal Justice* 11:413–427.

Ray, Melvin C. and Wm. R. Down (1986). "An Empirical Test of Labeling Theory Using Longitudinal Data," *Journal of Research in Crime and Delinquency* 23:169–194.

Ridlon, Florence V. (1988). *A Fallen Angel: The Status Insularity of the Female Alcoholic*. Lewisburg, PA: Bucknell University Press.

Rotter, Julian (1966). "Generalized Expectations for Internal Versus External Control of Reinforcement," *Psychological Monographs: General and Applied* 60:1–28.

Schmid, Thomas J. and Richard S. Jones (1991). "Suspended Identity: Identity Transformation in a Maximum Security Prison," *Symbolic Interaction* 14:415–432.

Seeman, Melvin (1959). "On the Meaning of Alienation," *American Sociological Review* 24:783–791.

Smith, W. Alan and Charles E. Fenton (1978). "Unit Management in a Penitentiary: A Practical Experience," *Federal Probation* 42 (September):40–46.

Swigert, Victoria L. and Ronald A. Farrell (1977). "Normal Homicides and the Law," *American Sociological Review* 42:16–32.

Sykes, Gresham M. (1956). "Men, Merchants, and Toughs: A Study of Reactions to Imprisonment," *Social Problems* 4:130–138.

Sykes, Gresham M. (1958). *The Society of Captives*. Princeton, NJ: Princeton University Press.

Sykes, Gresham M. and Sheldon L. Messinger (1960). "The Inmate Social System." Pp. 5–19 in *Theoretical Studies in Social Organization of the Prison*. New York: Social Science Research Council.

Tannenbaum, Frank (1938). *Crime and the Community*. New York: Columbia University Press.

Thomas, Charles W. and Matthew T. Zingraff (1976). "Organizational Structure as a Determination of Prisonization: An Analysis of the Consequences of Alienation," *Pacific Sociological Review* 19:98–116.

Tittle, Charles R. (1969). "Inmate Organization: Sex Differentiation and the Influence of Criminal Subcultures," *American Sociological Review* 34:492–505.

Tittle, Charles R. (1972). *Society of Subordinates*. Bloomington, IN: Indiana University Press.

Tittle, Charles R. (1975). "Labelling and Crime: An Empirical Evaluation." Pp. 157–179 in *The Labelling of Deviance*, edited by W. R. Gove. Beverly Hills, CA: Sage.

Wellford, Charles (1975). "Labeling Theory and Criminology: An Assessment," *Social Problems* 22:332–345.

Wheeler, Stanton (1961). "Socialization in Correctional Communities," *American Sociological Review* 26:697–712.

Wolfgang, Marvin E. (1961). "Quantitative Analysis of Adjustment to the Prison Community," *Journal of Criminal Law, Criminology, and Police Science* 51:607–618.

Wooden, Wayne S. and J. Parker (1982). *Men Behind Bars: Sexual Exploitation in Prison*. New York: Plenum.

Wright, Kevin N. (1989). "Race and Economic Marginality in Explaining Prison Adjustment," *Journal of Research in Crime and Delinquency* 26:67–89.

Yochelson, Samuel and Stanton E. Samenow (1977). *The Criminal Personality*, 2 vols. New York: Jason Aronson.

6

*

Crisis in Prison Administration

To the reformer of the 1960s, empowering prisoners through legal action was based on the assumption that, given the basic humanity of prisoners, treating them with more dignity would naturally result in prisoners who respected themselves and others. This would produce a more humane environment in which violence and the need for security lessened. In this environment, prisoners would naturally choose the straight path over the criminal. Inmates would be rehabilitated, and recidivism rates among those released from prison would be reduced.

A more humane prison system was to be accomplished in two ways: (1) through legal action designed to "restore" to convicted felons that which they had never had in American law—basic civil rights—and (2) through internal administrative changes, such as inmate councils designed to give prisoners a voice in the decision-making process that affected their lives. American democratic ideals foster individual responsibility because our constitutional principles assume that adults should be treated with dignity and allowed to choose their own destiny with a minimum of government intervention in their daily lives. Basic democratic freedoms, such as religion, assembly, right to counsel, due process, equality, and freedom from excessive punishment, were to be achieved through legal action, if necessary.

What these reformers failed to take into account, as did the therapeutic interveners a decade or two earlier, is the fundamentally coercive, violent nature of the prison world itself. Democratic principles are premised upon the voluntaristic nature of a free society. In prison, these freedoms become distorted as prisoners use the opportunity to enhance their control over one another to increase their access to the scarce goods of this limited society— food, drugs, sex, and power.

These reforms had the unintended effect of making prisons into more violent places than they had been before. By destroying the system of accommodation that had existed between prison administration and inmate leadership, new control structures emerged. These structures were anchored in the racial and ethnic divisions of American society and were supported by a new convict code that legitimated violent responses to threats to the new order rather than the "mind your own business" ethos of the past. Prisoners began to do "gang time" instead of "doing their own time" (Jacobs, 1977:157; Irwin, 1980:194).

In the power vacuum that was created by the development, albeit limited, of prisoners' rights, prison administrators lost control of their institutions. This was more true in some cases than in others. Both the California and Texas prison systems are good examples of what can happen in the face of aggressive legal reforms without attention to their consequences on the part of both reformers and those affected by the reforms (Irwin, 1980; Marquart and Crouch, 1985; Alpert, Crouch, and Huff, 1986; Crouch and Marquart, 1989). The federal prison system avoided many of the more extreme problems faced by some of the state prisons. There were no riots or major disturbances except for those caused by the unique situation of the detainees from Cuba who had come to the United States during the Mariel boatlift in 1980.

The federal prison system has led the way as a model of professionalism in several ways. First, it introduced the SORT officer, a highly trained, physically competent disturbance control officer who can gain control over an individual or group with a minimum of harm to both himself and the inmate involved (Federal Prison System, 1992). Second, the federal system has led the way in unit management designed to put case managers and correctional officers in a closer, controlling relationship with subsets of prisoners (Lansing, Bogan, and Karacki, 1985; DiIulio, 1989:130; Toch, 1992). Third, the federal government has taken a strong stand against the abuse of authority by correctional officers.

This chapter traces the way in which the case law evolved over the past 30 years or so to create the crisis in prison administration that followed. The discussion then turns to more recent events, both legal and administrative, that produced the *new professionalism* in prison management. We must explain how prison administrators lost control over their institutions and show how some are leading the way in regaining control by instituting policies and procedures designed to promote: (1) the fair and impartial enforcement of rules and (2) the disciplined use of force by highly trained and closely monitored correctional officers.

HISTORICAL SHIFT IN THE RELATIONSHIP BETWEEN THE COURTS AND THE PRISON SYSTEM: THE DEMISE OF THE "HANDS-OFF" DOCTRINE

Until recently, prison inmates were considered "slaves of the state" (*Ruffin v. Commonwealth*, 1871). Based on the Thirteenth Amendment's prohibition of "slavery [and] involuntary servitude, except as punishment for crime," convicted felons lost virtually all of their fundamental civil rights (Alpert, 1978:2; Esposito and Wood, 1982:114). The lack of intervention by the courts in cases involving denial of civil rights, including accusations of the use of excessive force, was justified by the "hands-off" doctrine. According to this doctrine, "courts are without the power to supervise prison administrators or to interfere with the ordinary prison rules or regulations" (*Banning v. Looney*, 1954). According to George Murphy (1973:442), a federal prison administrator who supported court intervention, the hands-off doctrine prevented review of both "those deprivations that are the inevitable concomitants of prison life" and "arbitrary and capricious decisions by prison officials or . . . unduly restrictive regulations." Murphy prophetically observes that a new doctrine was emerging at the time, one that said, "A prisoner should not be stripped of any rights other than those which would be detrimental to the administration and discipline of the institution or the program established for him" (Murphy, 1973:444). But it is clear that the courts have deferred in large measure to prison authorities to determine what is detrimental and what is not (Krantz, 1983).

The hands-off doctrine was justified on two legal grounds (Krantz, 1983). First, the principle of "separation of powers" was invoked, arguing that prison administration was an executive branch problem and the courts should not interfere. Second, in cases involving state prison systems, the federal courts took the position that these were state, not federal problems, and that in the interest of "federalism," the courts should not get involved. The courts also expressed their concern that they lacked the expertise to evaluate the management of prisons and deferred to prison authorities to determine what policies were needed to maintain security and safety in a system governing dangerous and violent men. This last point is still a major consideration in cases that do not involve "fundamental" civil rights such as those concerning First (freedom of religion and expression), Fifth (due process), and Fourteenth (equal protection and due process) Amendment rights.

The Black Muslims, also known as the Nation of Islam, played a major role in eroding the hands-off doctrine. The Muslims challenged prison authorities concerning their ability to practice their own religion in prison. Prison officials had viewed with suspicion "jailhouse conversions" to the Muslim faith. But the courts recognized this fundamental First Amendment right to freedom of religion, eroding for the first time the ability of prison officials to govern prisons without public scrutiny (Krantz, 1983).

The U. S. Supreme Court has been especially reluctant to address issues concerning the methods of social control used in the administration of prisons. In legal terms, this means that Eighth Amendment protections from cruel and unusual punishment have not been considered the sort of "fundamental" rights that should concern the courts. It was primarily because lower courts, especially in northern California, were disposed to grant First Amendment rights and limited due process rights to prisoners that the U.S. Supreme Court was compelled in 1974 to address a number of constitutional issues concerning prisoners' rights. In *Procunier v. Martinez* and *Pell v. Procunier*, both California cases, the Supreme Court addressed the prison's ability to restrict communication with the outside world, finding that there must be a "compelling state interest" in denying fundamental rights to prisoners and to those with whom they wish to communicate. The court was concerned with freedom of expression, the ability to complain, to express political views, and to receive "lewd" matter. This represents a critical limitation of the totalistic nature of control over inmates that had previously been delegated to prison officials. In *Pell v. Procunier*, *Procunier v. Hillery*, and *Saxbe v. Washington Post Co.*, all 1974 cases, the Supreme Court restricted communication with the media in the interests of security. In effect, the Court adopted a standard that required the "least restrictive environment" necessary to maintain internal security and at the same time to protect fundamental civil rights.

It was the decision in *Wolff v. McDonnell* (1974) that became symbolic of the demise of the "hands-off" doctrine. Ironically, *Wolff* was a response to prior lower court decisions that had granted broad procedural rights to inmates whenever a serious deprivation of liberty was involved, such as during parole hearings, probation revocation hearings, and disciplinary hearings in prison. In *Goldberg v. Kelly* (1970), a case involving a "grievous loss" of welfare benefits due to official malfeasance, the U.S. Supreme Court had determined that "minimum due process requirements existed," including the right to counsel and the right to an impartial tribunal (Krantz, 1988:229). Relying on *Goldberg* as precedent, the California courts required that inmates be provided with the right to counsel or counsel substitute during disciplinary hearings (*Clutchette v. Procunier*, 1971, 1974). In *Wolff*, the Supreme Court rejected the right to counsel as well as the right to confront and cross-examine witnesses as threatening to the security of the institution (see Krantz, 1988:231-241). But the Court did establish that a formal disciplinary hearing was required with 24-hour notification in writing, specifying charges and the evidence upon which this was based. Prisoners were also permitted to call witnesses on their behalf.

In *Wolff v. McDonnell,* the Supreme Court was more restrictive than the lower courts, yet paradoxically, by establishing a fundamental right to due process, disciplinary procedures involving loss of good time and segregation were subject to judicial scrutiny and review for the first time. Prison officials lost their discretionary authority over inmates, a critical asset in the maintenance of authoritarian regimes. The "hands-off" doctrine was dead.

CRUEL AND UNUSUAL PUNISHMENT

Although the "hands-off" doctrine was ended, the courts were still extremely reluctant to interfere with the administration of prison discipline. The courts distinguished between the procedural right to due process as a fundamental right and the less fundamental substantive right to be protected from Eighth Amendment violations concerning cruel and unusual punishment. For the Eighth Amendment to be violated, the treatment of a prisoner had to be so extraordinary as to "shock general conscience" before the courts would intervene (*Lee v. Tahash*, 1965). Three "tests" or rules governing cases concerning cruel and unusual punishment guided the courts at that time:

1. A punishment is "cruel and unusual" if it is "greatly disproportionate to the offense" (*Weems v. U.S.*, 1910, summarized in Krantz, 1983). Weems had been sentenced to a maximum sentence of 20 years at hard labor with ankle and leg chains for the falsification of a public document.

2. A punishment is "cruel and unusual" if it "goes far beyond what is necessary to achieve a legitimate penal aim" (*Weems v. U.S.*, 1910, summarized in Krantz, 1983).

3. A punishment must be "of such a character or consequences as to shock general conscience or be intolerable to fundamental fairness" to violate the Eighth Amendment prohibition against cruel and unusual punishment (*Lee v. Tahash*, 8th Cir. 1965).

Yet a fourth standard, rooted in the notion that the Eighth Amendment was designed to preserve the "basic dignity of man," was beginning to emerge (Krantz, 1983:177). In *Trop v. Dulles* (1958), the Supreme Court had stated that "the [Eighth] Amendment must draw its meaning from the evolving standards of decency that mark the progress of a maturing society." This standard has been the primary vehicle for court intervention in prison affairs from the late 1970s to the present.

The *Weems* standards largely focused on the nature of punishment meted out by the courts themselves. The concern over disproportionality, for example, was reflected in *Furman v. Georgia* (1972), which made the use of the death penalty in rape cases unconstitutional. But a separate line of reasoning emerged when it came to the internal workings of the prisons themselves.

Prison Conditions

The first important Supreme Court decision concerning prison conditions was *Estelle v. Gamble* (1976), a Texas case in which an inmate with a back injury argued that he had been denied adequate medical care. His complaint was rejected, but the Supreme Court established the "deliberate indifference" standard. The Court argued that prison policies that produce "unnecessary and wanton infliction of pain" through "deliberate indifference to the . . . needs" of inmates violated the Eighth Amendment. This standard would become important later on in cases involving prison overcrowding. Although the Supreme Court was inclined to reject specific claims of inmates concerning violation of their Eighth Amendment rights, with each subsequent case new standards were articulated that provided additional restraint on prison authorities.

In *Bell v. Wolfish* (1979) and *Rhodes v. Chapman* (1981), the Supreme Court reversed lower court rulings that found overcrowding to be, on the face of it, a violation of the Eighth Amendment. In *Rhodes*, the Court found that prison policies did not inflict "unnecessary and wanton pain" (the deliberate indifference standard established in *Gamble*), nor was it "grossly disproportionate to the severity of the crime" (the *Weems* test). The Court stated that overcrowding per se did not violate the prohibition against cruel and unusual punishment unless the "totality of conditions," *as a matter of policy*, resulted in deplorable living conditions (Skovron, 1988). Since the basic needs of inmates were being met, conditions were not deemed to be deplorable.

Earlier, a lower court had found an entire state prison system (Arkansas) to be in violation of the Eighth Amendment because of the cruelty perpetrated on inmates by inmate trusties who were delegated the power to do so by prison officials (*Holt v. Sarver*, 1970). It was the fact that these extreme cruelties, including electric shock torture and homosexual rape, were the consequence of official policy that the entire system was held to be in violation. This decision was affirmed by the Supreme Court in 1978 (*Hutto v. Finney*). In a similar case (*Ruiz v. Estelle*, 1980), a lower court found the Texas system in violation of the Eighth Amendment because of the delegation of authority to "building tenders," prisoner trusties who were responsible for maintaining order and discipline among the other inmates.

Thus the courts were beginning to articulate a policy that involved active intervention in the administration of prisons. During the 1980s, state prison system after state prison system was found to be in violation of the Eighth Amendment due to overcrowded conditions. Court orders to reduce populations produced early release programs in some cases and a rush to build more prisons in others (Skovron, 1988).

The Emergence of Legally Imposed Professionalism

In the late 1980s, the deliberate indifference standard became the vehicle by which the courts asserted a more active role in regulating penitentiary life, imposing on prison officials a duty to take control of prison life in a responsible manner. Federal appellate courts upheld a Washington, D.C., decision (*Morgan v. District of Columbia*, 1987) granting the right of inmates to be protected from other inmates. In a similar case (*Walsh v. Mellas*, 1988), a federal circuit court held that an inmate's rights were violated when institutional policies concerning cell placements failed to take into account gang affiliation leading to gang-related violence. Only when an inmate was victimized due to the "deliberate indifference" of prison officials were his rights violated.

The use of excessive force by prison officials was an issue addressed for the first time by the Supreme Court in *Whitley v. Albers* (1986). An inmate had been shot by a correctional officer during a disturbance. Here the court rejected the notion that prison officials had acted with "deliberate indifference" in bringing about "unnecessary and wanton infliction of pain" (the *Gamble* standard). The issue here was "whether force was applied in good faith effort to restore discipline or *maliciously and sadistically for the purpose of causing harm*" (emphasis added). Since the shooting was presumed to be part of a good faith effort to restore order to the prison, the Court decided in favor of the officer. But it is also evident from this decision that the Court is distinguishing between exigent circumstances in which prison authorities would be granted great discretion, as they had in the past, and ordinary, routine maintenance of order. Here, prison officials would be held to a greater standard, one that prohibited, *as a matter of policy*, unjustified use of excessive force. Hence, shooting prisoners to intimidate them would not be permissible. Nor would policies supporting beatings that went beyond the immediate need to restrain an unruly prisoner.

Whitley became an important precedent when, in 1992, the Supreme Court addressed the situation in which two officers in a Louisiana state prison administered a routine beating (a "tune-up") to an inmate who had challenged their authority and did this with the tacit approval of a supervisor (*Hudson v. McMillian*, 1992). Supreme Court Justice Sandra Day O'Connor, writing for the majority in a 7–2 vote, noted the distinction between Hudson's and Whitley's situation. There was no riot or disturbance here. Consequently, the standard that applied was the intentional, that is, malicious and sadistic, infliction of harm. Since this was an obvious broadening of the Court's role in regulating official conduct in prisons, O'Connor added support for her opinion by citing *Trop v. Dulles* (1958), that even a relatively minor beating was unjustified due to "the evolving standards of decency that mark the progress of a maturing society" (also mentioned in *Hutto,* 1978, and *Rhodes,* 1981). Hudson had merely suffered minor bruises and a broken dental plate. Clearly, this was a break from Gamble whose claim had been rejected, in part, because his injuries were not serious and a break from Whitley who had been shot. By 1992, a civilized society could no longer tolerate even minor abuses of authority in its prisons!

Spurred on by lawsuits concerning the humane treatment of prisoners, professional administrators, represented by Americans for Effective Law Enforcement and the U.S. Department of Justice, joined prisoners' rights advocacy groups such as the ACLU Prison Project in condemning the use of excessive force in the Louisiana prison (*Hudson v. McMillian*, 1992). Why would prison administrators, especially federal officials, support Hudson in this case? First, it makes clear that, in the federal prison system, brutality is not to be tolerated. Although the officer's code of silence might make it difficult for administrators to detect abuses, when they are discovered, something is likely to be done about it (see Earley, 1992:229). It appears that federal prison officials have taken the lead in defining the parameters of professional conduct in prison administration.

The *Hudson* case has an additional positive feature from the point of view of the professional administrator. Earlier decisions had focused on prison *policies* that produced harm. The "deliberate indifference" standard in

Gamble concerned the overall quality of medical care. *Wolfish* and *Rhodes* focused on the "totality of conditions" that led to serious deprivations. In *Whitley*, there was a disturbance at the prison and the use of potentially lethal force was reasonably within policy under such conditions. The appellate court decisions were concerned with prison policies which, through the deliberate indifference of prison administrators, led to specific harms to inmates. For the first time, the individual officer is held responsible for the harm done. In this way, in future lawsuits alleging violations of Eighth Amendment rights, prison officials can separate themselves from responsibility as long as they have in place an official policy prohibiting the use of excessive force.

THE UNINTENDED CONSEQUENCES OF LEGAL REFORMS ON THE AMERICAN PRISON SYSTEM

To understand the consequences of the demise of the hands–off doctrine and the subsequent intervention of the courts in regulating prison discipline, both procedurally (requiring due process) and substantively (limiting the boundaries of legitimate punishment), we must first understand the fundamental nature of the contemporary prison as a logical extension of the bureaucratic society in which we live today and a political system based on the rule of law.

The modern prison is a rationally organized bureaucracy in every sense of the word. Like all bureaucracies, it is hierarchically organized with responsibilities and authority assigned, in principle, according to ability and experience. There are two main divisions in prison, one focused on security and the other on programs designed to enhance the quality of life of the inmates and their prospects for rehabilitation. An associate warden for security and an associate warden for programs report to the warden who is responsible for the overall management of the institution. The typical contemporary prison gives priority to the line officers whose central concern is the security and safety of society. The program division, which includes educational programs, counseling, and job training, is also responsible for the classification of inmates, determining where they will live and work in the institution, prerelease planning, and recommendations for parole.

Unlike industrial bureaucracies, in which material objects are the focus of manipulation and control, prisons govern people who may comply or resist attempts to regulate their behavior. Like many similar people-processing organizations, prisons have a two-tiered hierarchy that virtually prohibits both movement and discourse across the barrier between the "classes" (see Goffman, 1961). As in the military, where fraternization between enlisted men and officers is prohibited, correctional officers are prohibited from becoming too friendly with inmates. The main purpose is to prevent corruption and maintain even-handed discipline. As in mental hospitals, prison inmates have their daily routines regimented by a set of bureaucratic rules designed to control even the most private aspects of their lives. They are subject to routine counts, body cavity searches, and "shakedowns" of their living quarters. Stripped of the dignity usually associated with adult life in a democratic society, inmates experience the "mortification" of their sense of identity. Their uniqueness as individuals is under attack under a system of tight regulation. Yet through all this, inmates, soldiers, sailors, and students in boarding schools all seek to accommodate to the existing control system by carving out their own space, usually in collusion with other subordinates in the institution. A special subculture emerges, derived in some measure from the dominant culture, which is shared with inmates who are undergoing the same experience (see Chapter 2 for a description of the convict code).

Prior to the first major prison reform efforts of the post–World War II era, the dominance of the line officers and security mission were obvious in what Irwin (1980:1) called the "Big House" era. The inmate social system was coopted by the guard staff through special privileges granted to inmate leaders, who in turn maintained order in the prison. Violence was controlled and limited to the intimidation of new "fish." The top cons were often sophisticated gangsters, con men, and other professional thieves. The ethnic composition of the inmate population largely reflected the white ethnic and lower class populations of the wider society and its hierarchy, where racial minorities were subject to subordinate roles and discriminatory behavior by staff and inmates alike. In some prison systems, especially in the deep South, inmate controls became institutionalized as trusties were delegated specific authority normally entrusted to guards in most prisons.

The social control system in prisons can be characterized by a delicate balance of three elements: *security, programs,* and the *inmate social system.* With each major shift in policy goals within a prison system, the existing balance of these three elements becomes destabilized. A shift in emphasis from security to treatment in the early 1950s destabilized the control system in American prisons, leading to violence both by guards who resorted to force to maintain order and inmates who rebelled through individual acts of assault and riot (McCleery, 1960). Old systems of accommodation broke down, weakening the ability of inmate leadership to control young, rebellious inmates. The old system of control lost its legitimacy as inmates were to be treated with more respect and, in the early days, as fundamentally deprived individuals who, in the proper environment could be rehabilitated. The "Big House" became the "Correctional Institution" whose primary goal was the rehabilitation of the inmate (Irwin, 1980:37).

Over the next twenty years or so, rehabilitation programs came under increasing criticism (see Martinson, 1974). At the same time, the civil rights movement and the antiwar movement created an atmosphere in prisons that led prisoners to question the fundamental legitimacy of the political and economic system that had placed them in the position they were in. Black prisoners especially came to define themselves as "political prisoners," and the prisoners' rights movement began (Reasons, 1974:360; Irwin, 1980:94–98). As we have already seen, the first successful prisoners' rights cases were initiated by the Black Muslims whose "insistence upon the collective nature of oppression marked an important step in the transformation of black consciousness" (Pallas and Barber, 1973:246). Additionally, prisoners' unions arose, work stoppages occurred, and other disruptions signaled the loss of legitimacy of the rehabilitation regime.

The mood of the country was more conservative than in the past. Public attitudes favored more "law and order," the death penalty, and getting tough on crime. The American prison system officially abandoned rehabilitation as a central goal during the mid-1970s, because it was perceived as a source of increasing disorder in prisons. The new hard line was seen as necessary to respond to new threats to security introduced by the courts, as well. The demise of the hands-off doctrine had shifted the balance of power (albeit slightly) to the prisoners and the prisoners' rights advocacy groups.

The Decoupling of Formal and Informal Control Systems in Prison

Prior to the 1970s, American society, through its political system, delegated the authority to maintain control in prisons to prison officials. There was little concern for the "dirty work" of prison life (Hughes, 1962), as prison officials were assumed to be experts who would do their job in a responsible manner. Consequently, the prison system merely reproduced and reflected the political and economic system of which it was a part.

The effect of the loss of legitimacy of the old rehabilitation regime in the 1970s might have been limited to the production of riots and other signs of disorganization, just as the loss of legitimacy of the custodial regime had 20 years earlier. According to Useem (1985), this disorganization was one of the main reasons for the riot at New Mexico's state prison in 1980 in which 33 inmates were brutally murdered by other inmates.

But, in addition to the demise of the rehabilitation ideal, the courts had questioned the legitimacy of the total control exercised by prison officials. This, in effect, separated or *decoupled* the formal power structure of the institution and the informal power structure of the inmate social system. By granting increased autonomy to inmates to control their own destiny, in terms of First Amendment rights to free expression of religion and more open communication with the outside world and limited due process rights, the courts limited the ability of prison officials to control some of the daily routines of inmates. Inmates were no longer solely dependent on prison authorities for the "goods" of life. By the late 1970s and early '80s, the courts began to regulate general prison conditions, ordering whole prison systems to end overcrowding. Finally, Eighth Amendment prohibitions against cruel and unusual treatment were directly addressed in the late 1980s and early '90s as inmates became protected from arbitrary and excessive forms of punishment.

Given the politicized climate of the time (the late '60s and early '70s), externally relevant forms of communication and identification took on more importance. Inmates began to organize themselves around their ethnic and religious identities as opposed to a generally oppositional, yet coopted, integrated power structure as they had before (Engel and Rothman, 1983:97; Carroll, 1974:89). And these groups began to compete with one another for control over scarce resources. In other words, prison gangs were formed. For black inmates, gangs became especially important in overcoming the subordinate status that they had experienced before. As black gangs organized, white inmates were often victimized (Jacobs, 1977:159). One consequence was that whites organized defensively in racially motivated groups, giving rise to groups such as the Aryan Brotherhood. For similar reasons, a variety of Hispanic gangs emerged in prison, with the Mexican Mafia becoming the most prominent.

In some situations, the loss of control was more dramatic. In Texas, for example, the *Ruiz* decision (1980) declared the entire prison system to be in violation of the Eighth Amendment prohibition against cruel and unusual punishment because of the "building tender" system. It seems that Texas had never gone through the reform movement, thus the delegitimation of the existing control structure destabilized the system very rapidly. In this vacuum, prison gangs quickly arose to fill the void. At Stateville, in Illinois, the process was more gradual but no less real (see Jacobs, 1977:173). But it was the California system that epitomized the more subtle mechanisms by which prison authorities can slowly lose control and not realize it. At one point, in desperation, California prison officials assigned different gangs to different institutions to minimize the violence (Irwin, 1980:190).

Overcrowded conditions exacerbated the fragmented relationships among inmates. Opportunities for disputes to arise without mechanisms for peacefully resolving them increased the number of assaults and homicides. A strong indicator of the disintegration of the official power structure is increased violence among inmates (Jacobs, 1977; Marquart and Crouch, 1985:575) and assaults on staff (see Light, 1991). One of the major complaints of inmates who rioted at the Moundsville Penitentiary in West Virginia in 1986 (Hoedel, 1986; Martin and Zimmerman, 1990) was that overcrowding led to an increase in the risk of inmate on inmate violence.

In addition to the formation of prison gangs, the decoupling of inmate and staff control systems made the prisons more violent (Silberman, 1992). The violent inmate world became increasingly the focus of adaptation as the new convict code emerged to replace the old inmate social system. Being tough and aggressive, not showing any weakness, became essential to survival. At the same time, the code vigorously enforces noncooperation with prison officials. During the riots of the 1980s, for example, unlike riots in previous eras, snitches were assassinated (Useem, 1985; Hoedel, 1986).

As we can see, an unintended consequence of legal reform was to decouple the relationship between the official and unofficial control systems in prison. This led to increased violence among inmates, which, in many cases, was organized along racial and ethnic lines. It also produced prison gangs that competed with one another for control over scarce resources in prison and a new, more violent convict identity supported by a convict code that expressed support for extreme violence in response to threats to personal integrity, to one's group, or to the establishment of prisoner power itself (Silberman, 1992).

THE NEW PROFESSIONALISM: CAUSES AND CONSEQUENCES

We have recently seen a decline in the dominance of prison gangs and a reduction in violence in some prison systems. This is the result of increasing professionalism in the management of prisons.

The stimulus for this new professionalism began in the 1970s with the courts demanding greater accountability of the executive branch of government, which was responsible for the supervision of prison inmates. In response to court actions, the American Correctional Association established standards for the professional administration of prisons. The federal Bureau of Prisons and several state correctional systems supported and attempted to adhere to the demand for greater accountability. A code of ethics was established by the American Correctional Association in 1975 (American Correctional Association, 1979:42). In 1978, an accreditation process began which, by 1990, included 80 percent of state correctional systems and the federal system as well (American Correctional Association, 1990:vii). In 1980, the federal government was among the first to establish standards to meet the new mandate to provide "decent, humane and safe" prisons (U.S. Department of Justice, 1981:preamble). In 1981, the American Correctional Association established guidelines for the control of riots and disturbances in prisons (American Correctional Association, 1981). It was evident that something had to be done to restore order and regain control of the prison system.

In 1987, the American Correctional Association published a set of policy guidelines that clearly reflected its responsiveness to court-ordered mandates. The goal of corrections was to provide a "humane program . . . administered in a just and equitable manner within the least restrictive environment consistent with public safety" (American Correctional Association, 1987:vii–viii).

There is some evidence that professionalism in American prisons contributes to the overall reduction in the incidence of violence, including assaults committed by inmates and civil rights violations committed by correctional officers. In his study of three state prison systems in the early 1980s, DiIulio (1989:129) found that the "quality of prison management" was the most important factor in determining the "quality of prison life," which was indicated in part by the "rates of individual and collective violence and other forms of misconduct" (also see DiIulio, 1987). In Texas, inmate homicides and assaults were reduced significantly once prison administrators took seriously the need to respond to the power vacuum created by the *Ruiz* decision (Crouch and Marquart, 1989).

Several state correctional systems have taken steps to reduce the incidence of civil rights violations during the late 1980s (U.S. Department of Justice, 1991). Others, most notably in the South, have been slow to respond. From 1986 to 1990, there was a dramatic drop in the number of civil rights complaints coming from inmates in state and federal prisons (U.S. Department of Justice, 1991). The federal prison system experienced few complaints from 1986 through 1990. During this same period (1985–88), the federal Bureau of Prisons reported a significant drop in group-related violence, especially racially motivated incidents, when compared with the early 1970s (Karacki, 1989). Two state correctional systems, Arkansas and

New York, saw the greatest decline in the number of complaints during the same period. In Texas, the number of complaints declined from a peak of 86 in 1986 to only 36 in 1990. Louisiana (which gave rise to the *Hudson* decision) and Mississippi were among the worst states, although the former showed slight improvement while the latter worsened during this period.

Changes in Prison Policies

Ramirez (1983) has pointed out that prison officials are least likely to use discretion in the enforcement of regulations when their decisions are visible to public scrutiny. The effect of *Wolff v. McDonnell* (1974) and related decisions was to force prisons to establish formal disciplinary hearings whenever inmates were threatened with serious deprivations of liberty such as loss of good time or placement in segregation. The fair and impartial enforcement of rules is consistent with professional standards in all occupations, and this is no less true in corrections. It is not surprising, perhaps, that younger, more recently hired and trained officers are more likely to go by the book and be resistant to some of the pressures that used to work in the old days regarding improper use of discretionary power.

A second area of professionalism that emerged about a decade later reflects the "precedence of legal standards" in "use of force" policies (Marquart and Crouch, 1985:583). Whenever force is used by correctional officers, some sort of official report must be filed. Marquart and Crouch describe this as the new "bureaucratic-legal order" in prison administration. Discretion yields to uniformity and the rule of law in the application of force.

One illustration of the new regime is the Special Operations Response Team (SORT). Just as the SWAT concept developed in policing as a specialized unit within police departments dedicated to meet special emergency conditions, the SORT concept developed to respond in a professional manner to prison crises. Unlike SWAT police officers who are trained in highly technical weaponry and light infantry assault approaches, SORT officers are trained to use disciplined and controlled force, without weaponry whenever possible, to gain control over an individual, group, or unit. They are protected by helmets and heavy clothing such as flak jackets, similar to those used by the military, which are designed to protect against assaults by most of the weapons convicts are likely to possess, such as knives, broom handles, or excrement (Pedersen, Shapiro, and McDaniel, 1988:263; Raymond and Raymond, 1991). Each officer is expected to be in top physical condition and an experienced body builder.

It is difficult to determine exactly who created the first SORT team. Earley (1992:146) credits Warden Jerry O'Brien, who ran Leavenworth

Penitentiary from 1982 to 1987, with creating the first *federal* SORT team (also see Federal Prison System, 1992:1). According to Earley (1992:205), the Leavenworth SORT team was used to restore order at Marion prison in 1983 after Aryan Brotherhood gang members murdered two officers in the control unit. By 1986, a sufficient number of maximum security prisons in the federal correctional system had their own SORT teams to justify the establishment of the first annual athletic SORT competition.

The main purpose of the SORT team is to intervene in crisis situations such as hostage taking and rioting and to address everyday problems created by inmates who refuse to obey an officer's orders or threaten an officer with bodily harm. Team members wear black jumpsuits, flak jackets, and riot control helmets reinforced like football helmets with special face masks. As one officer said, the uniform worn by the SORT team has "nothing to induce pain, it's just [designed] to protect them [SORT] from getting hurt" (Raymond and Raymond, 1991).

In the past, "disturbance control" officers would enter a situation in an uncontrolled manner, leading to injuries on the part of both inmates and officers. Today, there are reportedly fewer injuries. When the four- or five-member SORT squad moves in on an inmate, one grabs each arm and leg to minimize injury to themselves or the inmate (Crouch and Marquart, 1989:165; Earley, 1992:116–117). Each episode is videotaped to provide an official record of exactly what went on, protecting officers against false charges of abuse and protecting inmates from the potential for abuse (Crouch and Marquart, 1989:165; Raymond and Raymond, 1991).

In Texas, the first SORT teams were established in September, 1984 by Raymond Procunier who had been appointed director of the Texas prison system in May (Crouch and Marquart, 1989:144). Procunier had been director in four other prison systems, including the New Mexico prison system where he was brought in after the New Mexico prison riot in 1980, and the California prison system before that (Martin and Eckland-Olson, 1987:239). Procunier was considered a top professional, who was brought in as a troubleshooter on many occasions. Following the *Ruiz* decision in 1980, the power vacuum that had been created in the Texas system led to a level of chaos that was unparalleled in its history. In 1984, 200 disciplinary actions had been taken against officers who had used excessive force (Martin and Eckland-Olson, 1987:xxviii). Also in 1984, there were 25 inmate homicides, double the rate that had occurred immediately following *Ruiz* (Martin and Eckland-Olson, 1987:38).

The purpose of the SORT teams was to deal with "problem inmates who assaulted officers, refused to leave a cell, or were otherwise creating a problem; SORTs also handled shakedowns and prisoner transfers" (Crouch and Marquart, 1989:164). But it was not until 1986 that the SORT units, referred to in the media as "goon squads," effectively took control over the most dangerous prisons in Texas. The SORT teams were ordered to seize gang leaders and other troublemakers and lock them in "administrative segregation." In 1986, the first signs of improvement began to appear with a sharp decline in weapons-related assaults and weapons possession charges, although the number of fistfights increased. Clearly, the SORT teams were effectively beginning to remove weapons from the prison system. By 1987, weapons possession and assault charges dropped still further to a fraction of their earlier levels, as did fighting in general (Crouch and Marquart, 1989:201).

Prisons have always had "goon squads" who have been trained, more or less, in traditional police techniques in riot control. But these techniques are not suited to the prison environment where the use of brute force to quell an adversary is likely to exacerbate the problem rather than bring it under control. SORT teams, by exerting disciplined and controlled force, demonstrate clearly to inmates who is in charge and provide little justification for retaliation and a continued cycle of violence. The development of SORT teams symbolizes the new professionalism in corrections. Each act of force used by officers that is likely to produce injury is governed by specific rules of engagement and is subject to external review and public scrutiny.

Recoupling the Relationship Between Prison and Society

The impact of recent court decisions has been to reestablish the link between the formal (administrative) and informal (inmate) control systems in prison. In other words, the prison system has begun to respond to court decisions in a responsive manner, creating administrative structures that are consistent with court orders concerning both the procedural and substantive rights of prisoners. In so doing, the worst fears of prison administrators have not been realized. In fact, the problems that followed the earlier court decisions occurred because of the failure of prison administrators to respond to the new legal climate (Ekland-Olson and Martin, 1988).

There are three basic principles of the new professional standards that are derived from the court decisions. These principles reflect the emerging Eighth Amendment doctrine that, in the words of Justice O'Connor, "draw[s] its meaning from the evolving standards of decency that mark the progress of a maturing society" (*Hudson v. McMillian*, 1992). In terms of prison policy, this is expressed in terms of the primary goal of the prison system as the *humane incapacitation* of prison inmates (see American Correctional Association, 1987:vii–viii). Not since the early 1970s has the prison system recognized rehabilitation as its major goal. Moreover, long-term incarceration is unlikely to have a deterrent effect on the convict who is likely to become hardened by the experience, although incarceration may act as a general deterrent to the potential offender. And contemporary correctional officials are unlikely to lend legitimacy to the retributive goal of an "eye for an eye." The central purpose of maximum security prisons today is to incapacitate the career offender and those who are considered dangerous to society by removing them from that society for a considerable period of time. But it serves no constructive purpose to do so in an inhumane or unjust manner. It is simply bad management to create an atmosphere that promotes violence and unrest.[1]

The three principles of the new professionalism are:

1. *Identify and eliminate practices that promote inmate-on-inmate violence.* Separate the aggressive from the less aggressive prisoners, making certain not to put potential victims adjacent to victimizers (see Quay, 1984). Decentralize case management so that a limited number of inmates are assigned to a specific unit supervised by a team of trained case managers and counselors (see Smith and Fenton, 1978).

2. *Do not tolerate the use of excessive force.* Physical force should only be used in self-defense, the protection of life and property, and to prevent escapes. It can never be used as punishment (American Correctional Association, 1990:64).

3. *Distinguish between routine order maintenance and emergency conditions.* The prison system has always had "emergency response" or "disturbance control" teams. But these units were geared to meet the needs of unusual events, such as hostage taking and major disturbances. The courts have made clear that a great deal of leeway is granted in the use of force, including deadly force, in crisis situations, but the courts will regulate conduct involving the control of inmates in day-to-day situations. Policies and practices concerning the routine maintenance of order on a day-to-day basis must be made clear to both inmates and officers alike.

Operational Standards. To maintain order in a manner consistent with constitutional rights, it is not necessary to give up control over the inmate population. In fact, as long as treatment is consistent and fair, although strict, the above principles are not necessarily violated. The operational standards of the new professionalism are:

1. *Officials must be in control at all times.* There can be no official or unofficial delegation of authority to inmate trusties or any other group. The emergence of autonomous inmate centers of power, such as gangs, must be prevented. This can be distinguished from the legitimate expression of reli-

gious values and ethnic concerns. A well-run prison should provide outlets
for individual expression and group values under the supervision of staff.
For example, the Council of Imams of the New York State Department of
Corrections screens out representatives of more militant groups, such as the
Nation of Islam, in favor of imams from the more mainstream Sunni Mos-
lem sect (Clines, 1992:B2).

2. *Discretionary authority must be abolished to the extent possible.* This is
easier to accomplish in principle than in fact. Although it is possible to
monitor formal hearings on all levels, it is not as easy to do so given the
day-to-day discretionary decisions that correctional officers and others
such as caseworkers must make. Sensitivity training regarding racial matters
should be required of all personnel. Racial injustice, even when unintended, can be a source of conflict in prison, both among inmates and between inmates and staff.

3. *Safety and security must be the primary goal in all institutional concerns.* This
means that both the safety of inmates as well as officers should guide policy
since the two are intimately related. We have seen how institutional alienation increases hostility toward staff and assaultiveness directed at both staff
and inmates. But the solution to this problem is not always obvious. It
would be a mistake to "empower" inmates through inmate councils since
the evidence from the 1970s is that this simply enhanced the power of inmate subgroups (Engel and Rothman, 1983).

Rather, the need to assert control over one's own fate, which is essential
to the reduction of alienation and its consequences, can be accomplished in
a number of constructive ways. First, staff and inmates should be trained in
mediation techniques to settle disputes and address relational problems
(Silberman, 1988). Second, counseling should center on coping with the
stresses of daily life in prison in more constructive ways. Third, opportunities for self-expression in religion, arts, and education should be enhanced.
Fourth, and perhaps the most important of all, a living environment should
be created in which the fear of assault is not an ever-present part of the consciousness of inmates, as it is today.

Judge William Wayne Justice, who ordered the end of abuses by the
Texas Department of Corrections in the *Ruiz* case, stated, "If governmental
organizations are . . . prepared to work *with* courts in vindication of constitutional rights and not *against* them, then some degree of judicial restraint
will be in order" (Pedersen, Shapiro, and McDaniel, 1988:264). He might
have added that a degree of professional management consistent with the
fundamental principles of due process is likely to lead to a new hands-off
doctrine, restoring autonomy to prison administrators as official and informal control systems are reintegrated.

CONCLUSION

There has been a shift in the relationship between the courts and prison administration during the past 30 years. The case law concerning prisoners' rights has evolved from the hands-off doctrine of the early 1960s to a period of active intervention by the courts. In the 1970s and '80s, the courts limited the discretionary authority of prison officials and expanded prisoners' rights. Granting broad powers to prison officials under extraordinary circumstances such as disturbances and riots, the Supreme Court has recently begun to limit the use of force by officials under routine circumstances.

Changes in the case law had dramatic effects on prison conditions. The initial effect of the demise of the hands-off doctrine was the decoupling of the formal and informal control systems in prison, leading many prison administrators to lose control of their institutions. This resulted in increased levels of inmate violence, the development of racially oriented prison gangs, and sporadic riots.

During the latter part of the 1980s, a new professionalism emerged in prison administration in response to the courts' demand for reform. This new professionalism is characterized by policies and procedures designed to promote (1) the fair and impartial enforcement of rules and (2) the disciplined use of force by highly trained and closely monitored correctional officers. The level of inmate violence in some prisons has begun to decline along with the number of complaints by inmates concerning violations of their civil rights.

NOTE

1. For a discussion of the "major agreed upon manifest functions of prisons . . . reformation [rehabilitation], incapacitation, retribution, and deterrence," see Reasons and Kaplan (1975:364–365).

REFERENCES

Alpert, Geoffrey P. (1978). *The Legal Rights of Prisoners.* Lexington, MA: Lexington Books.

Alpert, Geoffrey P., Ben M. Crouch and C. Ronald Huff (1986). "Prison Reform by Judicial Decree: The Unintended Consequences of *Ruiz v. Estelle.*" Pp. 258–271 in K. C. Haas and G. P. Alpert, *The Dilemmas of Punishment: Readings in Contempo-rary Corrections.* Prospect Heights, IL: Waveland Press.

American Correctional Association (1979). *Manual of Standards for the Administration of Correctional Agencies.* Rockville, MD: Commission on Accreditation for Corrections.

American Correctional Association (1981). *Riots and Disturbances in Correctional Institutions.* College Park,

MD: American Correctional Association.

American Correctional Association (1987). *Guidelines for the Development of a Security Program.* Washington, DC: U.S. Department of Justice (National Institute of Corrections).

American Correctional Association (1990). *Standards for Adult Correctional Institutions* (3d ed.). Washington, DC: St. Mary's Press.

Carroll, Leo (1974). *Hacks, Blacks, and Cons: Race Relations in a Maximum Security Prison.* Prospect Heights, IL: Waveland Press.

Clines, Francis X. (1992). "Prison Has the Body, but Allah Has the Spirit," *New York Times,* July 2: A1, B2.

Crouch, Ben M. and James W. Marquart (1989). *An Appeal to Justice: Litigated Reform of Texas Prisons.* Austin, TX: University of Texas Press.

DiIulio, John J., Jr. (1987). *Governing Prisons: A Comparative Study of Correctional Management.* New York: Free Press.

DiIulio, John J., Jr. (1989). "Recovering the Public Management Variable: Lessons from Schools, Prisons, and Armies," *Public Administration Review* 48:127–133.

Earley, Pete (1992). *The Hot House: Life Inside Leavenworth Prison.* New York: Bantam Books.

Ekland-Olson, Sheldon and Steve J. Martin (1988). "Organizational Compliance with Court-Ordered Reform." *Law and Society Review* 22:359–383.

Engel, Kathleen and Stanley Rothman (1983). "Prison Violence and the Paradox of Reform," *The Public Interest* 73:91–105.

Esposito, Barbara and Lee Wood (1982). *Prison Slavery.* Washington, DC: Committee to Abolish Prison Slavery.

Federal Prison System (1992). "A Short History of SORT's," *Monday Morning Highlights,* May 18:1–2.

Goffman, Erving (1961). *Asylums.* New York: Anchor Books.

Hoedel, Martha B. (1986). "Finished: Inmates Slay 3 Before Yielding." *The Patriot,* January 4: A1–A2. Harrisburg, PA.

Hughes, Everett C. (1962). "Good People and Dirty Work," *Social Problems* 10:1–11.

Irwin, John (1980). *Prisons in Turmoil.* Boston: Little, Brown.

Jacobs, James B. (1977). *Stateville: The Penitentiary in Mass Society.* Chicago, IL: University of Chicago Press.

Karacki, Loren (1989). "Serious Prison Infractions," *Federal Prisons Journal* 1(1):31–35.

Krantz, Sheldon (1983). *The Law of Corrections and Prisoners' Rights in a Nutshell* (2d ed.). St. Paul, MN: West Publishing.

Krantz, Sheldon (1988). *The Law of Corrections and Prisoners' Rights in a Nutshell* (3d ed.). St. Paul, MN: West Publishing.

Lansing, Douglas, Joseph B. Bogan, and Loren Karacki (1985). "Unit Management." Pp. 342–350 in *Correctional Institutions* (3d ed.), edited by R. M. Carter, D. Glaser, and L. T. Wilkins. New York: Harper & Row.

Light, Stephen L. (1991). "Assaults on Prison Officers: Interactional Themes," *Justice Quarterly* 8:243–261.

Marquart, James W. and Ben M. Crouch (1985). "Judicial Reform and Prisoner Control: The Impact of *Ruiz v.*

Estelle on a Texas Penitentiary," *Law and Society Review* 19:557–586.

Martin, Randy and Sherwood Zimmerman (1990). "A Typology of the Causes of Prison Riots and an Analytical Extension to the 1986 West Virginia Riot," *Justice Quarterly* 7:711–737.

Martin, Steve J. and Sheldon Ekland-Olson (1987). *Texas Prisons: The Walls Came Tumbling Down.* Austin, TX: Texas Monthly Press.

Martinson, Robert (1974). "What Works? Questions and Answers About Prison Reform," *The Public Interest* 35:22–54.

McCleery, Richard (1960). "Communication Patterns as Bases of Systems of Authority and Power." Pp. 49–77 in *Theoretical Studies in Social Organization of the Prison.* New York: Social Science Research Council.

Murphy, George F. (1973). "The Courts Look at Prisoners' Rights: A Review," *Criminology* 10:441–459.

Pallas, John and Robert Barber (1973). "From Riot to Revolution." Pp. 237–261 in *The Politics of Punishment,* edited by Erik Olin Wright. New York: Harper & Row.

Pedersen, Daniel, Daniel Shapiro, and Ann McDaniel (1988). "Inside America's Toughest Prison." Pp. 246–266 in *Order Under Law: Readings in Criminal Justice* (3d ed.), edited by R. G. Culbertson and R. Weisheit. Prospect Heights, IL: Waveland Press.

Quay, Herbert C. (1984). *Managing Adult Inmates.* College Park, MD: American Correctional Association.

Ramirez, John (1983). "Race and the Apprehension of Inmate Misconduct," *Journal of Criminal Justice* 11:413–427.

Raymond, Alan and Susan Raymond (1991). *Doing Time: Life in the Big House.* Home Box Office: February 12.

Reasons, Charles E. (1974). "Correcting Corrections." Pp. 357–365 in *The Criminologist: Crime and the Criminal,* edited by C. E. Reasons. Pacific Palisades, CA: Goodyear.

Reasons, Charles E. and Russell L. Kaplan (1975). "Tear Down the Walls? Some Functions of Prisons," *Crime and Delinquency* 21:360–372.

Silberman, Matthew (1988). "Dispute Mediation in the American Prison: A New Approach to the Reduction of Violence," *Policy Studies Journal* 16:522–532.

Silberman, Matthew (1992). "The Production of Violence in the American Prison: Historical, Structural, and Cultural Contexts," *Legal Studies Forum* 16:3–20.

Skovron, Sandra Evans (1988). "Prison Crowding: The Dimensions of the Problem and Strategies of Population Control." Pp. 183–198 in *Controversial Issues in Crime and Justice,* edited by J. E. Scott and T. Hirschi. Newbury Park, CA: Sage.

Smith, W. Alan and Charles E. Fenton (1978). "Unit Management in a Penitentiary: A Practical Experience," *Federal Probation* 42 (September):40–46.

Toch, Hans (1992). "Functional Unit Management," *Federal Prisons Journal* 2:15–19.

U.S. Department of Justice (1981). *Federal Standards for Prisons and Jails: December 16, 1980.* Washington, DC: U.S. Government Printing Office.

U.S. Department of Justice (1991). "Police Brutality Study: Part III. Correctional Systems." Unpublished government document, pp. 38–46.

Useem, Bert (1985). "Disorganization and the New Mexico Prison Riot," *American Sociological Review* 50:677–688.

CASES CITED

Banning v. Looney, 348 U.S. 859 (1954).

Bell v. Wolfish, 441 U.S. 520 (1979).

Clutchette v. Procunier, 328 F. Supp. 767 (N.D. Cal. 1971).

Clutchette v. Procunier, 497 F.2d 809 (9th Cir. 1974).

Estelle v. Gamble, 429 U.S. 97 (1976).

Furman v. Georgia, 408 U.S. 238 (1972).

Goldberg v. Kelly, 397 U.S. 254 (1970).

Holt v. Sarver, 309 F. Supp. 362 (E.D. Ark. 1970).

Hudson v. McMillian, 60 U.S. Law Week 4151 (Feb. 25, 1992).

Hutto v. Finney, 437 U.S. 678 (1978).

Lee v. Tahash, 352 F.2d 970 (8th Cir. 1965).

Morgan v. District of Columbia, 263 U.S. App. D.C. 69 (D.C. Dir. 1987).

Pell v. Procunier, 417 U.S. 817 (1974).

Procunier v. Hillery, 417 U.S. 843 (1974).

Procunier v. Martinez, 416 U.S. 396 (1974).

Rhodes v. Chapman, 452 U.S. 337 (1981).

Ruffin v. Commonwealth, 62 Va. 790, 796 (1871).

Ruiz v. Estelle, 503 F. Supp. 1265 (S.D. Tex. 1980).

Saxbe v. Washington Post Co., 417 U.S. 843 (1974).

Trop v. Dulles, 356 U.S. 86 (1958).

Walsh v. Mellas, 837 F.2d 789 (7th Cir. 1988).

Weems v. U.S., 217 U.S. 349 (1910).

Whitley v. Albers, 475 U.S. 312 (1986).

Wolff v. McDonnell, 418 U.S. 539 (1974).

7

*

Widening the Net of Social Control: Community Corrections in America

There is a paradox in American corrections. The failures of the rehabilitation era of the 1950s and '60s yielded two contradictory social
movements. One was conservative, calling for more prisons, longer
prison terms, and the reinstitution of the death penalty to restore "law and
order" to American society. The second was the liberal community-based
treatment model of the 1970s, funded first by the federal government, then
later by local governments and private organizations. The theory was that
rehabilitation had failed because of the harmful prison environment. The
solution was the therapeutic community, which by providing a supportive
environment without guards or fences would better rehabilitate offenders.
At least, it was argued, these programs would be less likely to debilitate offenders than the threatening atmosphere of the maximum security penitentiary. The *decarceration* movement was born.

It is especially important today to examine the community-based reform
efforts of the 1970s in light of current concerns that prison overcrowding
has led to the release of dangerous offenders while nonviolent drug offenders fill our prisons. Several federal judges have resigned or refused to hear
drug cases because minimum mandatory sentences have created a situation
in which youthful first offenders are incarcerated for years (Kerr, 1993:24;

Koppel, 1993). New admissions to state prisons for drug offenses rose from 6.8 percent in 1980 to 32.1 percent of the total in 1990, from 9,000 inmates to 103,800 per year in just ten years (Gilliard, 1993:10). This number represents roughly double the 54,590 *total increase* in the state prison population in 1990 (Gilliard, 1993:3). In other words, there would be no annual increase in the number of state prisoners were it not for the growth in new admissions for drug offenses. According to the federal Bureau of Prisons (Koppel, 1993), the percentage of federal prisoners who are incarcerated for drug-related offenses has risen from 34 percent in 1985 to 60 percent in 1992. Most of this increase has occurred since Congress enacted mandatory minimum sentences for drug offenses in 1986. It appears that the drug wars of the late 1980s are the major cause of prison overcrowding in the 1990s.

THE DECARCERATION MOVEMENT

During the late 1960s and early '70s, the decarceration movement led to the expansion of existing community-based programs such as group homes for delinquents and therapeutic communities for drug addicts (Scull, 1977; Blackmore, 1986). In the mental health field, changes in the law made it more difficult to incarcerate people in a mental institution unless they constituted a danger to themselves or others or were clearly unable to care for themselves. But there was no equivalent legislation for juveniles and adults accused of committing crimes. The Juvenile Justice and Delinquency Prevention Act of 1974 provided additional protection for juveniles by requiring that separate facilities and programs be made available. Before that time, juveniles were frequently housed with adults, producing a great deal of violence and abuse. Although many new programs were created with seed money provided by the federal Law Enforcement Assistance Administration (LEAA), detention facilities for juveniles were expanded as well as prisons for adults.

The Reforms of Jerome Miller

There was one brief exception to the overall trend to increase simultaneously the growth of community-based programs and the prison population. Jerome Miller, a professor of social work at Ohio State University, was asked by the governor of Massachusetts to head its juvenile justice bureaucracy with the aim of transforming the system into one based on a network of small community-based programs (see Miller, 1991). By denying offenders admission to the state's institutions, they were gradually emptied until the civil service employees found themselves without inmates to supervise. Early evidence showed that the recidivism rate among delinquents dropped as they were no longer incarcerated in the schools for crime and violence that were the state's institutions (Miller, 1991:220–223). Later on, the state reinstitutionalized many of its youth in smaller, more decentralized bodies.

Two successful residential programs for delinquent boys established in the late 1950s and early '60s, the Highfields and Provo experiments in New Jersey and Utah, respectively, may have influenced Miller's later efforts in Massachusetts. By examining these two programs, we can learn why Miller's reforms appeared to reduce juvenile crime in Massachusetts, at least at the beginning. These two programs boasted reductions in recidivism rates for delinquent youth who might otherwise have been incarcerated. The Highfields program reported that 63 percent of the boys admitted to their program remained trouble free as compared with only 47 percent of a similar group of boys admitted to a nearby institution (Weeks, 1958:118). The Provo experiment reported a significant drop in the number of offenses committed by program participants four years after release (Empey and Erickson, 1972:208–209). The number of offenses committed by program participants was reduced by 49 percent when compared with only a 25 percent drop by the incarcerated group.

These programs shared a common philosophy: There must be clear and definite consequences for law violators, but these consequences should be humane and of relatively short duration. Highfields residents, aged 16 and 17, stayed on a remote estate (formerly owned by Charles Lindbergh) for four and a half months, engaged in productive work during the day, and received group counseling at night. Initially assigned at random from adjudicated delinquents who were destined to go to reformatories, the Provo residents, repeat offenders aged 14–18, lived in their home communities. They went to school or work during the day, attended group meetings after school or work, then returned home at night, for a four- to seven-month period (Empey and Erickson, 1972:9).

There is little evidence that these residents were "rehabilitated" in the conventional sense. In fact, the Provo philosophy explicitly rejected rehabilitation as an explicit goal (Empey and Erickson, 1972:13–14). Through guided group interaction counseling, both programs stressed making the residents aware of the costs of the delinquent lifestyle and the benefits of more conventional alternatives. It is evident that a significant percentage made the rational choice that crime does not pay when faced with future opportunities to break the law. This is the ideal manifestation of the "special deterrence" effect of punishment. There was little evidence of violence in these programs, either by staff or inmates.[1]

Given his apparent success in Massachusetts, Miller was asked to go to Illinois where he was met with such resistance by correctional officials that he eventually left after making little impact on the Illinois system. He was then asked by Governor Milton Shapp to come to Pennsylvania to head the reform efforts there. In Pennsylvania, the Correctional Institution at Camp Hill originally housed delinquent youth as young as age 15 along with young adults in their early to middle twenties (Adams, Leader, and Irvis, 1989:4). During this time, homosexual rape was commonplace, a typical scenario involving young juveniles victimized by so-called trusties who helped run the institution for the guards. In essence, the kids were given to the trusties in exchange for maintaining order in the institution. Inmates frequently carried weapons, typically homemade knives, to defend themselves against assault. When one 16-year-old committed suicide, hanging himself in his cell after he was raped, Miller was finally able to order the kids out of Camp Hill and create small decentralized maximum security facilities for delinquents throughout the state (Miller, 1991:230). Ironically, it was the decarceration of mental patients that made unused state facilities available to detain delinquent youth. For example, one unit, housing about 30 juveniles, was created on the grounds of a state mental institution. Such environments were far more humane and less debilitating than Camp Hill.

The Therapeutic Community Movement

Around the same time that the state of New Jersey was experimenting with Highfields for delinquents, a self-help group for drug addicts was born in California. Growing out of the Alcoholics Anonymous movement, Synanon introduced two new principles to the self-help philosophy (see Yablonsky, 1965; Sugarman, 1974). First, drug addiction was so severe that it required more than weekly meetings; rather, addicts must live together in a supportive climate for months, if not years, to overcome their dependency. Second, addiction is so encompassing a problem that a major transformation of the individual's identity from that of the "dope fiend" would require an intensive sort of group therapy that had never been tried elsewhere. The "encounter group" was developed to assault the "dope fiend" mentality of the drug addict in order to rebuild a healthy personality. Unfortunately, the therapeutic community (TC) approach reinforced the notion that "once an addict, always an addict" and, like Alcoholics Anonymous, required continual involvement in the self-help community to stay drug-free. Indoctrination focused on permanent commitment to the TC ideology and way of life. As a result, drug dependency was transformed into a dependency on being a member of the "family" of the therapeutic community.

Synanon ultimately became the "seed" that sowed a whole movement across the nation. Once a therapeutic community became too large to sustain its membership, the tendency was to split off and generate another "house" or community. In 1963, Daytop Lodge, later to be called Daytop Village, in Staten Island, New York, was created with the assistance of the leadership of Synanon and ultimately staffed by former Synanon personnel (Sugarman, 1974:8–10). Out of Daytop was born Gaudenzia House in Philadelphia a few years later, and by the early 1970s, a subsidiary of Gaudenzia House was spawned in Harrisburg (see Sugarman, 1974:132). In 1971, Rainbow Village, a prerelease facility for prisoners at a nearby prison, was converted into a full-time alternative therapeutic community. Many of the staff were ex-cons and ex-addicts from Gaudenzia and Daytop, making Rainbow Village a fourth-generation therapeutic community. Unlike its predecessors, which stressed voluntary commitment, Rainbow Village was intended as a direct sentencing alternative for drug-dependent offenders aged 17–25 who had been convicted of drug-related felonies.

The therapeutic communities of the 1970s were direct descendants of the Synanon program. In fact, Phoenix House, the largest therapeutic community program in the United States today, was also originally staffed by former Synanon personnel (Sugarman, 1974:9; Kerr, 1993:58). But Phoenix House has since been coopted by the prison system, running drug treatment units in seven New York state prisons (Kerr, 1993:26).

The therapeutic community culture was transmitted through its graduates who were able to stay drug-free by becoming role models for others. In addition to Phoenix House in New York City, other well-known descendants of Synanon are Marathon House in Providence, Rhode Island, and the Seed, a program for delinquent youth in southern Florida. This last program became well known because of a U.S. Senate investigation of reported abuses of residents, although the program "apparently was quite successful in getting young people off drugs" (Packard, 1977:80–81). Today, with conglomerates absorbing, creating, and selling off drug treatment facilities, there has been a hybridization of the therapeutic model with variations on the 12-step Alcoholics Anonymous program and the medical approach influencing contemporary treatment. Treatment has been reduced for most addicts from months or years to 28 days because of the reliance on limited insurance coverage to fund the programs rather than virtually unlimited government funding that was available twenty years ago.

In his extremely thorough case study of Daytop Village, Sugarman (1974:6) reports a success rate of 35 percent among the first 89 residents at

Daytop. Defining success in terms of remaining drug free and out of jail, Sugarman compares this with a 4 percent success rate in a control group of untreated addicts on probation. Sugarman argues that Daytop was remarkably successful in reducing the recidivism rate of addicts. A better test of its effectiveness would have been a comparison with incarcerated drug offenders. Recent studies of incarcerated drug offenders who receive no treatment while in prison report that only between 27 percent and 37 percent were reincarcerated within three years after release (Kerr, 1993:58). But the Daytop study used a much more rigorous standard of success since graduates had to be drug free as well as avoid arrest. It appears that some sort of intervention is essential to reduce the incidence of drug-related crime. It is not clear that incarceration is a more effective way of doing so.

The author found a similar success rate in his research on Rainbow Village. Among its first 60 residents, all of whom had entered the program during its first 16 months of operation, 18 graduated from the program and two more were expected to graduate soon after completion of the study 14 months later—an expected graduation rate of 33 percent. All but one remained drug free an average 7.1 months after release. But, as time went on, the success rate dropped significantly. Further examination revealed that most of the success stories involved residents who had stayed in the TC world as staff members at Rainbow Village or elsewhere. Hence the founders of the TC movement were right. To succeed in staying drug free, one had to stay a part of the movement. As opportunities to do so dried up, the failure rate increased. The TC promise is like that of a chain letter or pyramid scheme. Given the attempt to treat more and more addicts, there is a limit to the number of places available in the TC world. As time goes on, the failure rate inevitably increases as graduates return to the lack of opportunities and temptations they had experienced before. It is no surprise, therefore, that reports of success are usually limited to the early stages in the history of each community.

Assessing the research on rehabilitation efforts in correctional facilities, Martinson (1974) reported that there was no evidence that any of these programs had a significant impact on recidivism rates for adult or juvenile offenders. His report was used by conservative policy advocates to reduce funding for rehabilitation programs and to emphasize the punitive role of imprisonment.

Although there is little evidence that community-based corrections did any better than rehabilitation within prison walls, it is important to note that these programs did no worse (Martinson, 1974:46). Since community-based treatment is more humane, less destructive in the long run, and cheaper than incarceration, it makes sense to use this approach whenever feasible.

The essential reality of criminal punishment is the state's ability to coerce the individual—to limit his or her mobility or liberty. Whether this is done in the name of rehabilitation, to deter, or to incapacitate the offender, the reality for the individual is the same (see Wilson, 1980:16). Whether a parent spanks a child for "its own good" or for the good of the parent doesn't ease the pain for the child.

Widening the Net of Social Control

Community-based treatment not only failed to rehabilitate more effectively than incarceration (Lerman, 1975:206), but it was also an instrument of expanded state control over the American population (Scull, 1977). Since we were beginning to incarcerate larger numbers of people in the U.S. in the early 1970s, more than doubling the number or state and federal prisoners over the ten-year period from 1972 to 1982, community-based corrections failed to become an alternative to incarceration.[2] According to Herbert Hoelter, project director of Jerome Miller's National Center on Institutions and Alternatives, community-based programs did not act as alternatives to incarceration as intended but were "an alternative to outright release" (Blackmore, 1986:427). As prison populations expanded, community corrections were frequently used as alternatives to probation and parole, "widening the net of social control over minorities" and the poor (Blackmore, 1986:414). Moreover, crime rates were relatively stable during the 1970s, so it appears that neither incarceration nor community corrections had much impact on criminal conduct.[3]

Following a slight decline in the incarceration of drug offenders during the Carter administration in the late '70s, during the Reagan and Bush years the rate of incarceration for drug offenses grew from 6.8 percent of total admissions to state prisons in 1980 to 32.1 percent by 1990 (Gilliard, 1993:10). With increasing economic dislocation, especially among the poor and minorities, resorting to drug use to escape and drug dealing to survive became a way of life. Placed at first in alternative programs, over time these offenders became further criminalized as they accumulated criminal records. Moreover, with the development of mandatory sentencing, first offenders were increasingly likely to be placed in prison. In other words, the criminal justice system became a way of regulating the surplus labor population, that is, the unemployed (Wallace, 1981). It appears that community-based corrections became a way station for minor offenders on their way to incarceration.

In the late 1980s and early '90s, a new alternative, the short-term correctional program or "boot camp," was adopted by state and federal correctional systems. Modeled after intensive training in the military, boot camps provide tight control and regimentation of inmates for a short, usually no more than six-month, period. Preliminary evidence suggests that these programs are an effective deterrent for first-time offenders who receive short sentences as alternatives to long-term maximum security prison (MacKenzie et al., 1989). Although boot camps are not true alternatives to incarceration, they have the advantage of many of the earlier short-term community-based programs in that they do not provide the debilitating atmosphere of the prison and the inmate can see the light at the end of the tunnel before adapting to incarceration as a way of life. Critics of the boot camp argue that the authoritarian discipline in these programs is inhumane and reinforces violence among inmates (Morash and Rucker, 1990). There is some evidence that these programs have already begun to compromise their original purpose, filling bed space with inmates who are already doing time, rather than using them as an alternative to incarceration for first-time offenders. In a more recent study of boot camp graduates, MacKenzie (1991) found no evidence that their recidivism rates were reduced when compared with offenders on probation or released on parole following a period of conventional incarceration. MacKenzie (1990:47) also points out that, in some cases, boot camps contribute to "widening the net" when judges sentence potential probationers to the camps rather than those who might otherwise be incarcerated.

Ball and Lilly (1988) recently argued that the use of house arrest and electronic monitoring, "widening the net" of state control, is a "Trojan Horse" that sneaks state agents behind the line of the private/public boundary in law and custom. Looking back at twenty years of attempts at providing alternatives to incarceration, we can see that community-based treatment programs were only the first step in a long-term process of erosion of the sanctity of the home and community. In the late twentieth century, we have first seen the intrusion of state agencies in the community, resisted derogatorily in terms of the NIMBY ("not in my back yard") phenomenon, and now we see intrusions into the home as well. One of the advantages of the boot camp programs is that they do not diffuse the boundary between public and private realms of social control. Offenders are removed from society when subject to the coercive controls of the state. Ball and Lilly (1988:163) express their concern that "we are headed for the totally disciplined 'carceral' society" that Michel Foucault (1979) envisioned in his book, *Discipline and Punish: The Birth of the Prison*. One could also ask: To what extent we have taken the first step toward the Orwellian world of *1984* in which the public realm has totally penetrated the private?

The Demise of the Decarceration Movement

Public enthusiasm for community corrections waned in the late 1970s for a variety of reasons. Federal policy to promote these programs disappeared as a more conservative approach to law enforcement gained favor. The earlier programs were "seeded" with federal grants that assumed that local governments would take on more and more of the costs over time. At first, the zero-cost option for local governments meant that there was little to lose by authorizing such programs locally. Over time, however, it became clear to local officials that it was "cheaper" to send an inmate to state prison where costs would be born by the state government than to pay for alternative programs for convicted felons. Work release programs remained strong in many locations for misdemeanants and reduced costs for these offenders. In other words, policies that increasingly criminalized certain behaviors, especially those that were drug-related, created an economic incentive to incarcerate. In the long run, however, imprisonment costs a great deal more overall than community-based treatment (Blackmore, 1986:413).

COERCION IN GROUP HOMES
FOR DELINQUENTS

River Valley Village (a pseudonym) was established in a beautiful mountain retreat in the heart of rural Pennsylvania about 25 years ago. Its founder was a deeply religious man with no other training but as the manager of a local supermarket who believed that with love and understanding, delinquent youth would soon turn to God and give up their evil ways. Staffed at first by Mennonite conscientious objectors who had refused military service during the Vietnam War, the program began with the highest of ideals and sincere motivations. But to everyone's surprise, these rural, small-town troublemakers defied the staff, refused to abide by the program's dictates, and continued to get into trouble. In a rapid turnabout, a new chief "counselor," an ex-Marine, was hired to replace the COs. A bare cinder-block cell, euphemistically referred to as a "time-out" room, was built in the basement for residents to have an opportunity to reflect upon their misdeeds. On his first day at River Valley Village, the new counselor slapped a resident across the face so hard that they were forced to take him to the hospital for treatment. The new regime was established.

This short anecdote illustrates that there is always the potential for violence in all correctional programs, no matter how benign their initial intentions. In this particular case, the absence of expertise in handling delinquent youth, coupled with naive good intentions, led this program to rely on a religious ideology that says that if your motivations were not essentially good, they must be evil, and that evil must be controlled until it changes—"spare the rod and spoil the child."

Two Studies of Group Homes for Delinquents

The above description of River Valley Village, based on interviews and records obtained during a single site visit in the early 1970s, was an eye-opener to this researcher concerning the inevitable consequences of removing individuals from their homes and communities and placing them against their will in even the most benign situation. The coercive nature of criminal punishment creates its own logic, driving even the most caring individuals to engage in acts of violence despite themselves.

Group homes normally house between 6 and 12 adjudicated delinquents between the ages of 13 and 17. As an alternative to placement in more secure facilities, they are designed for first offenders who commit serious crimes such as burglaries and drug dealing. Assaultists are not suited to the minimum security environment nor are multiple offenders who have done time in institutions. Nevertheless, many group homes fill their beds with youth whose criminal conduct has elements of violence and those who have been in more secure facilities.

The author conducted two in-depth studies of group homes, one in 1972 and the second in 1975 and 1976. The first study was on Fellowship House, a program run by a religious ministry to convicted criminals. The second was a comparative study of three group homes run by professional youth workers in juvenile probation departments and youth service bureaus in rural and small-town settings. The purpose of the youth service bureaus was to divert delinquent youth from the criminal justice system into alternative placements such as individual foster homes and group homes run by professionals and volunteers (often college students). Providing more structure than a single-family foster home, group homes were typically run by a married couple or single person who lived in the home and were assisted by caseworkers and/or volunteer counselors.

One of the difficulties that Fellowship House had was the importation of institutional norms and values through the placement of delinquents who had already experienced institutional life. Residents who had already been in institutions saw themselves and acted very differently from those who had not. They were "tough guys" who sought to control other residents through threats and intimidation. One such resident used acts of "rage" to intimidate other residents and staff. This resident had been orphaned at age five and placed in a so-called "children's home" that housed dependent, neglected, and delinquent youth. Because of the last group, this institution was run as if all kids were troublemakers. And, inevitably, kids quickly learned to survive by dominating others through violence and intimidation. One Central prison inmate, who had been abandoned by his parents during the Great Depression at the age of four, described his orphanage experience as the most violent in his life, more so than prison itself.

Residents in all four group homes experienced sporadic violence at the hands of staff members. In three of the homes, each event was traumatic because of its unusual character. Yet each event seemed inevitable. At Fellowship House, a graduate student in counseling who worked as an intern struck a resident after his repeated "hyperactivity" got on the intern's nerves and he exploded in anger. This action so violated the intern's sense of who he was and why he wanted to work with kids in trouble that he dropped out of the counseling program and left Fellowship House to "find himself" again.

The three professionally managed group homes in the later study were located in a coal mining town, a small industrial city, and a college town. The group home in the college town, Concern, was run by the local youth service bureau and had little structure except for the leadership provided by its director, a person with a strong religious background, and advice given by a local psychiatrist. Combining a strong belief that the causes of delinquency were rooted in inadequate childhood socialization, the staff and student volunteers provided loose supervision of a group of boys and girls who had committed relatively minor delinquencies, from shoplifting (boys and girls) and burglary (boys) to sexual promiscuity (girls). The assumption was that there was something wrong at home and that the families as well as the kids needed counseling. When one of the girls, age 15, said "fuck you" to one of the counselors, he lost his temper and hit her, knocking her down. A similar episode was reported to have occurred at Mountaintop House in the coal region. But in all three group homes, violent episodes were rare events that helped to define the boundaries of what was and was not acceptable. Clearly, staff assaults were not consistent with the goals of the programs nor the general motivations of the staff members involved. The first was pursuing a degree in counseling, the second intended a career in the ministry, and the third was a dedicated youth worker.

One cannot attribute the violent episodes in each program to variations in program structure. Fellowship House used a graded status model in which residents earned privileges associated with achieved levels of success in meeting program objectives. Concern used a loose counseling model based on a more open family-like atmosphere. Mountaintop House used a highly structured behavior modification system in which each task—from making beds to being polite to guests—earned fixed credits, which could be used to buy privileges such as free time outside the home or going to the movies. Yet despite these variations in program structure, all these programs experienced infrequent episodes of unauthorized violence. Here, we see a phenomenon not unlike the behavior of the simulated prison guards in Zimbardo's (1982) experimental prison study (see Chapter 2). Placed in a role that symbolizes the legitimate coercive authority of the state, counselors met resistance to that authority with force.

One program did not explode in acts of unauthorized violence because violence was, in fact, authorized and controlled by the staff. Success House in the industrial city housed delinquent boys who had committed crimes ranging from burglary to strong-arm robbery. Success House was run as a strict hierarchy with the toughest and strongest dominating the others. The head counselor used martial arts to control the residents during this period. Given his superior mastery of the martial arts, it was clear to the boys who was in charge. Older residents who gained privileges did so, in part, by emulating the chief counselor and learning martial arts over time. The informal social system of the kids paralleled the formal system of power and privilege created by the staff. The notion here was that the natural aggression of these boys could be channeled into an acceptable form. Paradoxically, the staff had coopted the inmate social structure in much the way staff did in the old "Big House" prisons during the first half of this century. The chief counselor relied on senior boys to help control the others.

Symbolic of the organized nature of the violence at Success House was the presence of a rifle locked in a closet that had been confiscated from one of the kids. Seeing the ownership of the gun as a natural right of any youth who was interested in hunting, the gun was kept unloaded but not removed from the house. Because the counselor was the only person with access to the key to the closet, it was clear who was in charge. When Jerome Miller, the reformer, came to town to praise this model program as a symbol of reform, he was unaware of the violent nature of this program nor of the gun in the closet next to him! It should have been no surprise that, some time later, the residents allegedly burned the place down!

What is it about the nature of group homes that makes violence, sporadic or systematic, inevitable? First, we must ask why the residents stay in the homes despite the absence of armed guards and barbed wire fences. In each group home, the alternative was made clear to all residents. Should they fail to comply with the rules and regulations of the group home, a more secure facility awaited them. At Fellowship House, residents were threatened with indeterminate commitment at a state mental hospital or confinement in a maximum security institution that was known to house older, tougher residents from the city. Residents in the other three programs were sent to more secure residential programs when they ran away or got into further trouble. For the most part, the threat of some sort of institutional confinement was held over their heads as an incentive to stay. Second, virtually all residents reported experiencing the loss of freedom associated with placement by the courts in a group home.

CONCLUSION

Punishment in the criminal justice system, because it is part of the *state* bureaucracy, must rely on *coercion* as its primary means of social control. The negative sanctions imposed on those who violate the criminal law are based on "physical sanctions such as infliction of pain, deformity, or death; generation of frustration through restriction of movement; or controlling through force the satisfaction of needs such as those for food, sex, comfort, and the like" (Etzioni, 1975:5). The common denominator of these coercive sanctions is the *loss of liberty*, the defining characteristic of the criminal law. Although penal (criminal) sanctions may include fines or restitution, what distinguishes criminal law from civil law is the ability of the state to exert control over the actions of the accused individual through arrest, prosecution, conviction, and sentencing.

Whether offenders are placed in group homes or therapeutic communities, are subject to house arrest and electronic monitoring, or incarcerated in a maximum security prison, they all share one common experience. They all objectively experience the loss of personal liberty that is the essence of penal sanctions. When so-called alternatives to incarceration supplement rather than replace more secure facilities, they widen the net of social control exerted by the state bureaucracy. From the point of view of the individual, even the first-time juvenile offender placed in a group home, the experience is one of constraint and resistance. From the community standpoint, its members are exposed in greater and greater numbers to coercive controls and the social consequences that result. Relying increasingly on state (coercive) rather than community (normative) social controls brutalizes society and legitimates the increasing use of violence in everyday life. It should be no surprise that the expansion of state controls over the past twenty years or so, from isolating increasing numbers of prisoners in maximum security prisons to increasing use of intensive probation and house arrest in the community, has contributed to increasing levels of violence on our streets.

Group homes are the least violent of residential settings because, in part, they presume the redemptive potential of the adolescent. The kids are assumed to be salvageable. For residential programs based on religious beliefs, the assumption is that with love and understanding the delinquent will turn to goodness through godliness. When this fails, we see the duality of religious beliefs in operation when it is assumed that the continuation of bad behavior is rooted in evil. At this point, with little to turn to, the controllers may resort to force. Even when the model is a therapeutic one, the frustration associated with the failure of rebellious teens to accept the good will of the "child savers" may yield the punitive impulse that results in violence.

More recent "alternatives" to incarceration such as house arrest and electronic monitoring represent more intrusive forms of state control than earlier approaches. The ability to monitor individual behavior in the home reflects a fundamental change in the state/society relationship. For the first time in human history, state agents have the ability to monitor and control behavior in private settings from remote locations. This form of punishment is the most subtle and indirect of all forms of state control. Consequently, we are less likely to see overt outbursts of violence. But if the foregoing analysis is correct, the coercive nature of such controls can be expected to transform the experiences and, in the long run, the culture of violence in society. In those communities subject to increasing intrusion of the state bureaucracy in the private sector, we can expect, in the long run, increasing violence in the home and community.

NOTES

1. The author visited Highfields in the early 1970s and found no evidence to contradict the findings reported in official and unofficial publications.

2. The number of state and federal prisoners rose from 196,183 at the end of 1972 to 413,806 by the end of 1982 (U.S. Bureau of the Census, 1978:197; Gilliard, 1993:1). By the end of 1992, the total prison population had more than doubled again to 883,593 (Gilliard, 1993:1).

3. According to victimization studies conducted by the U.S. Bureau of Justice Statistics, the violent crime rate remained almost constant between 1973 and 1980 at 33 incidents per 1,000 persons over the age of 12 (U.S. Bureau of the Census, 1990:174). Property crimes (larcenies) against individuals declined slightly, whereas property crimes against households rose slightly during the same period.

REFERENCES

Adams, Arlin M., George M. Leader, and K. Leroy Irvis (1989). *The Final Report of the Governor's Commission to Investigate Disturbances at Camp Hill Correctional Institution.* Harrisburg, PA.

Ball, Richard A. and J. Robert Lilly (1988). "Home Incarceration with Electronic Monitoring." Pp. 147–165 in *Controversial Issues in Crime and Justice*, edited by J. E. Scott and T. Hirschi. Newbury Park, CA: Sage.

Blackmore, John (1986). "Community Corrections." Pp. 412–430 in *The Dilemmas of Punishment: Readings in Contemporary Corrections*, edited by K. C. Haas and G. P. Alpert. Prospect Heights, IL: Waveland Press.

Empey, LaMar T. and Maynard L. Erickson (1972). *The Provo Experiment: Evaluating Community Control of Delinquency.* Lexington, MA: Lexington Books.

Etzioni, Amitai (1975). *A Comparative Analysis of Complex Organizations.* New York: Free Press.

Foucault, Michel (1979). *Discipline and Punish: The Birth of the Prison.* Translated by Alan Sheridan. New York: Vintage Books.

Gilliard, Darrell K. (1993). "Prisoners in 1992," *Bureau of Justice Statistics Bulletin.* Washington, DC: U.S. Department of Justice.

Kerr, Peter (1993). "The Detoxing of Prisoner 88A0802," *New York Times,* June 27:Sec. 6, 22–27, 58–59.

Koppel, Ted (1993). *Nightline,* "Judges Protest Mandatory Drug Sentences," July 14. ABC News.

Lerman, Paul (1975). *Community Treatment and Social Control: A Critical Analysis of Juvenile Correctional Policy.* Chicago, IL: University of Chicago Press.

MacKenzie, Doris Layton (1990). "Boot Camp Prisons: Components, Evaluations, and Empirical Issues," *Federal Probation* 54:44–52.

MacKenzie, Doris Layton (1991). "The Parole Performance of Offenders Released from Shock Incarceration (Boot Camp Prisons): A Survival Time Analysis," *Journal of Quantitative Criminology* 7:213–236.

MacKenzie, Doris Layton, Larry A. Gould, Lisa M. Reichers, and James W. Shaw (1989). "Shock Incarceration: Rehabilitation or Retribution?" *Journal of Offender Counseling, Services and Rehabilitation* 14:25–40.

Martinson, Robert (1974). "What Works? Questions and Answers About Prison Reform," *The Public Interest* 35:22–54.

Miller, Jerome G. (1991). *Last One Over the Wall: The Massachusetts Experiment in Closing Reform Schools.* Columbus, OH: Ohio State University Press.

Morash, Merry and Lila Rucker (1990). "A Critical Look at the Idea of Boot Camp as a Correctional Reform," *Crime and Delinquency* 36:204–221.

Packard, Vance (1977). *The People Shapers.* New York: Bantam Books.

Scull, Andrew T. (1977). *Decarceration: Community Treatment and the Deviant—A Radical View.* New Brunswick, NJ: Rutgers University Press.

Sugarman, Barry (1974). *Daytop Village: A Therapeutic Community.* New York: Holt, Rinehart & Winston.

U.S. Bureau of the Census (1978). *Statistical Abstract of the United States: 1978*

(99th ed.). Washington, DC: U.S. Government Printing Office.

U.S. Bureau of the Census (1990). *Statistical Abstract of the United States: 1990* (110th ed.). Washington, DC: U.S. Government Printing Office.

Wallace, Don (1981). "The Political Economy of Incarceration Trends in Late U.S. Capitalism: 1971–1977," *Insurgent Sociologist* 10:59–66.

Weeks, H. Ashley (1958). *Youthful Offenders at Highfields: An Evaluation of the Effects of Short-Term Treatment of Delinquent Boys.* Ann Arbor, MI: University of Michigan Press.

Wilson, James Q. (1980). " 'What Works?' Revisited: New Findings on Criminal Rehabilitation," *The Public Interest* 61:3–17.

Yablonsky, Lewis (1965). *Synanon: The Tunnel Back.* Baltimore, MD: Penguin Books.

Zimbardo, Philip G. (1982). "The Prison Game." Pp. 195–198 in *Legal Process and Corrections,* edited by N. Johnston and L. D. Savitz. New York: Wiley.

8

*

Coercion in a Therapeutic Community

T o understand what happens in the therapeutic community, we must first understand the effects of the different types of power, coercion and normative power, on the alienative involvement or moral commitment of those subject to that power. In Chapter 5 (pp. 83–86), we saw how the use of coercion, the use or threatened use of force, leads to alienation and violence in the prison world. In contrast, normative power relies on persuasion through the manipulation of *symbolic* sanctions, rewards and punishments, in the media, in rituals associated with traditional values and beliefs and in the context of interpersonal communication in everyday life (Etzioni, 1975:5). For Etzioni, under normal circumstances, normative power should yield positive responses, or *commitment*, by those subject to its control.

There is evidence, however, that the extreme use of force, as in the terrorizing of someone who is in the total control of another, may lead to commitment instead of alienation. When a hostage begins to sympathize with the hostage taker and accepts his or her message, the hostage experiences a psychological mechanism called "identification with the aggressor" (Wrong, 1988:111–112). Ever since Swedish hostages demonstrated support for their hostage takers after their release, the mass media has referred to this

147

phenomenon as the "Stockholm syndrome." Thus some Jewish concentration camp prisoners identified with the Nazis who ran the camps and, in a few cases, assisted them in managing other Jewish prisoners (see Bettelheim, 1943:447–452; Rashke, 1982:186, 187). And Patty Hearst, after being kidnapped by the Symbionese Liberation Army while she was a student at Berkeley in 1974 and raped repeatedly while being kept in a dark closet for several weeks, became a "willing" member of the gang and participated in some of its illegal activities, including bank robbery. Under certain conditions, then, coercion may lead to conversion to the perspective of the controllers when they exert total control over the person. Thus the individual is placed in a childlike status of total dependency on the adult and, like a child, begins to internalize the values of the adult.

There also is evidence that the use of normative power to excess may produce effects similar to that of coercion. Religious cults, for example, rely primarily on normative power to "brainwash" their potential membership. Seeking volunteers from the community, cult leaders become excellent manipulators of culturally meaningful symbols. By exerting total control of the physical and cultural milieu of the group, the cult is able to convert new members to its ideology (Lifton, 1987:212–216). But conversion is likely only when recruits share the fundamental values of the group. Lofland (1966:31–62; also see Lofland and Stark, 1965:868) has shown that converts to a religious cult must accept religious values as important in their lives before they can be successfully recruited. And it is these values that cult leaders manipulate. Since these organizations rely, in part, on breaking down the individual's sense of themselves, or *identity*, tied to earlier experiences, they may attempt to disorient the individual at first through techniques such as sleep deprivation and altered diet (Hassan, 1988:67). But it is the total control of the symbolic life of the potential recruit that is central to the conversion process.

During the Korean War, the Chinese Communists controlled the ability of POWs to communicate with the outside world, allowing only negative information to come through (Schein, 1956). This "demoralizes" the victim and makes him or her susceptible to new ways of thinking. Skinner and Winckler (1969) report that, in Communist China, periods of revolutionary fervor were followed by periods of alienation and demoralization. During the Cultural Revolution between 1966 and 1969, the most active core of ideologically committed loyalists, the Red Guards, were rewarded with prestige and status, whereas others were subject to degradation and humiliation (see Ling, 1972).

Michel Foucault (1979:3–31) distinguishes between forms of punishment, such as torture, directed at the body and forms of punishment, based on "psychiatric expertise," directed at the mind. Using Foucault's distinction between body and mind, coercion can be understood as social control of the body, whereas normative power is social control of the mind. Foucault argued that traditional forms of punishment, such as torture, did violence to the body in order to send a message to the public regarding who was in charge and the consequences of violating their authority. In other words, coercion serves a deterrent function. There was little concern for the alienation of the masses as long as coercion produced conformity.

Modern forms of punishment, such as the penitentiary, are designed to control the mind as well as the body (Foucault, 1979:30, 269). By subjecting the convict to ritualized obedience to rules and regulations, the importance of discipline is symbolized as necessary for modern industrial labor. Yet, even in the earliest days of the penitentiary system, the effort to control the minds of the prisoners backfired, producing even more seriously alienated, hostile, and dangerous felons (Foucault, 1979:264–272). And so it appears that assaults on the mind, the person's sense of self-worth and identity, have a similar impact on the individual as does the use of coercion. Normative power, in the extreme, does violence to the mind, especially when those in power rely on degrading the individual to accomplish their goals (for a discussion of "moral force," or psychic violence, see Wrong, 1988:27–28).[1]

Therapeutic communities are characterized by an absence of overt violence on the part of staff or inmates. Instead, they rely exclusively on persuasion and the manipulation of the self-esteem of residents through their control over meaningful prestige symbols. During the author's nearly year-long, in-depth observation of Rainbow Village, there were no incidents of physical assaults in the Village (see Chapter 7, p. 135, for a description of the history of this community). But there were numerous attacks on the integrity, or sense of worthiness, of the membership. Shaved heads, wearing baby bottles around one's neck, or wearing dunce caps are traditional forms of humiliation that were no longer used in Rainbow Village by the time the research had begun. Being called "stupid" or labeled a "dope fiend," however, was commonplace.

DEGRADATION RITUALS:
MORTIFICATION OF THE SELF[2]

Erving Goffman (1961:43–48), in his study of total institutions, such as mental institutions and prisons, described the mortification process as the stripping away of the individual's "identity kit" through the "loss of self-determination," "assaults upon the self," and "stress." Essential to this process are degradation rituals such as "searching, stripping, bathing, spraying, and the taking of personal property" found in American jails (Irwin, 1985:68). In mental institutions, prisons, and concentration camps, the official relationship of domination and subordination between staff and inmates legitimates these procedures as necessary for the maintenance of order.

The therapeutic community does not have the rigid two-tier structure of the typical total institution. Because many of the staff members are ex-addicts and former residents, there is a degree of unity between staff and residents that is not found in other total institutions. Consequently, the mortification process in the therapeutic community is more subtle than in the prison or asylum. Always done for the good of the victim, degradation rituals are justified in terms of their therapeutic objectives.

Degradation Rituals in a Therapeutic Community

The Prospect Chair. Humiliation and self-doubt are the principal tools of domination in the therapeutic community. The resident is constantly made aware of the fact that to leave this "benevolent" environment is to face the overt violence of the prison world. In Rainbow Village, the new resident spent 24 hours in the "prospect chair," strategically placed near the entrance to the large mansion in which the residents were housed. (At the time Rainbow Village consisted of two houses, one in the "inner city" and one along a scenic riverview front at the edge of the city.) Whenever a resident displayed behavior for which expulsion was a possibility (for example, threats of violence), she (or he) might be made to sit in the prospect chair and contemplate where she "really" wishes to be. The choice to stay is made within the context of the fear of going to prison.

About one-third of the residents chose to leave the Village within one month of the program. They tended to have a relatively strong self-image and in many cases had already experienced prison life. It is often the uncertainty of the dangers of prison that fosters the greatest anxiety for prisoners, and this fear was manipulated by the Rainbow staff. Those who chose to leave said that they would rather face the dangers of prison than face the prospect of someone "messing with my head." Those who chose to stay showed signs of feelings of inadequacy that made them more vulnerable to manipulation.

Typical of the sort of dilemma residents were faced with was the situation faced by Mark. Mark was a young, working-class white man who smoked marijuana on occasion. He was not an addict nor was he a dealer. Nevertheless, Mark was caught up in a large-scale sting operation by local and state police, who reported great success in the media because of the large number of arrests made. One can only assume that Mark helped to make the police statistics a success. He had "sold" a small amount of marijuana to an undercover "narc" who had befriended him in a local bar, asking him for a couple of joints. Mark complied and asked to be compensated for the exchange. This is not an uncommon pattern of behavior among recreational users and in no way signals addiction or drug dealing. Yet to gain acceptance in the Rainbow community (and avoid going to prison), Mark had to admit that he had failed as a human being because he was a "dope fiend," someone who was condemned to the potential for drug dependency for the rest of his life.

The ex-addicts who ran Rainbow Village knew that Mark was having a difficult time committing himself to the program. After three months, Mark was asked for a commitment; either he was to accept the "family" or leave. Residents referred to the sense of despair that comes with giving up your old self and relationships as the "90-day blues." Sugarman (1974:95–96) describes this as a "hump" in the moral career of the resident who gets depressed or "goes into a bag" when faced with personal crises such as the one faced by Mark. Mark spent hours contemplating whether to stay or leave, looking despondently at the nearby river. To stay meant the loss of his fiancee and his opportunity to work on the fast cars he loved. To leave meant the fear of prison. He stayed.

Entry into the Program. During the first year or so of its existence, Rainbow Village staff followed the therapeutic community tradition while interviewing prospective new members. Visiting the local jail, they would ask why the new "prospect" wanted to gain admission. Initially, most prospects would state that they did not want to be in jail. Guiding the responses, staff would wait until the prospect indicated in some manner that he wanted to get help for his drug problem. Using an operant conditioning strategy, staff would reinforce two statements: (1) "I want to get out of jail" and (2) "I want help," then reinforce these statements with approval. Then staff would challenge the credibility of the statements, taunting the prospect to show that he or she really wanted to get out and really wanted help. The prospects would be encouraged over a long period of time (hours, if necessary) to intensify their feelings. In other words, they had to show that they could "get into" the intense emotionality of the TC world. Those who would or could scream out at the end were admitted. From the beginning, we see the prospect exposed to a degrading, self-mortifying process, something that continues more or less throughout the program. Persuaded that this was not a "professional" way to proceed, Rainbow staff changed over time to a less emotive interviewing strategy, relying on their experience as former addicts to determine whether or not the prospect was sincere.

Loss of Privacy. As a result of these changes, new recruits to the Rainbow family were less prepared for the "bizarre" behavior they were about to encounter. They were about to see behavior that was radically different from what they were used to on the street or in jail—touching and hugging apparent strangers, emotional outbursts, public harangues for misconduct, and residents describing their innermost feelings and fears to others in encounter groups. But it is the *loss of privacy* that hits the new resident hardest. Always in the presence of at least one other Rainbow member, prospects are not alone at any time during the first month. Nor were they permitted to communicate with anyone from outside the Village. This is similar to the mechanism used in religious cults to begin the process of breaking down the person's old precult identity and make him or her compliant to the demands of the cult leaders.

Contracting. A resident might try to confide in another about some feeling or action in an attempt to create a special bond between them. This was called *contracting* and was strictly forbidden. All feelings and actions were required to be in the open and shared with the community as a whole. To do otherwise required the other resident to inform on the violator. As in other tightly controlled systems, informing is essential to effective control. Here we see a total assault on individuality.

The norms governing behavior in the therapeutic community contradict one of the most sacred rules in the prison world. In prison, snitching, although commonplace, is prohibited by the convict code. In the therapeutic community, informing on both the misdeeds and private feelings of fellow residents was required and enforced by residents and staff alike.

The Pull-Up. The new resident is likely to experience a *pull-up* as the first direct attack on his or her sense of self-worth. A pull-up is a deliberate attempt to publicly embarrass the individual who has been observed to violate a Village rule concerning daily conduct, such as cleaning ashtrays after using them. The person who observes the violation stands up, faces in the direction of the violator, and yells loudly that so-and-so is "stupid" and cannot follow the simplest directions. How can he or she expect to change as a person when she cannot do even the smallest things correctly? The accused is expected to stand there and listen, correct the mistake, and thank the accuser for calling this error to his or her attention.

The Haircut. When violations are serious or repeated, a staff member will "book" (charge the person for the offense) a *haircut,* which is a "a tirade of verbal abuse at high volume . . . [the resident is] called a 'stupid asshole' . . . that he is acting like a baby . . ." (Sugarman, 1974:57). The harangue is delivered by a group of residents who surround the accused in an isolated room. At Rainbow Village, haircuts were carried out in a darkened basement room. The resident was forced to wait outside and knock loudly, asking for permission to enter. Then the people in the room would take turns verbally abusing the accused. Residents viewed this as being "beaten up" in an environment that reminded them of the "hole," or lock-up unit, in prison.

Wearing Signs. When a resident engages in a pattern of conduct suggesting a character trait disapproved by the staff, he or she may be asked to *wear a sign* around his neck. If dependency is the problem, the sign may read, "I am a baby." For making unwise choices, such as contracting with another resident, the resident was asked to wear a dunce cap. Serious misconduct that threatened the fundamental unity of the group, like stealing, might lead to a shaved head (also see Sugarman, 1974:58–59).

Over time, Rainbow Village stopped using signs as a form of humiliation. They relied instead on verbal humiliation in encounter groups and haircuts to punish serious violations. This apparently civilizing effect was the result of input from staff psychologists who felt that this approach was overtly degrading. They did not disapprove of more subtle forms of degradation, however.

Several residents, including one male, had been prostitutes before becoming part of the Rainbow family. In one case, a senior resident, feeling guilty, admitted soliciting while off the grounds of the Village. In the past, this resident would have been asked to wear a sign that says, "I am a whore." Instead, the resident was forced to deal with the *guilt* in encounter groups and by being demoted to a position with less responsibility in the family hierarchy.

Shot Down. Each resident is assigned a specific set of duties associated with formally designated roles such as kitchen worker, maintenance worker, community relations department head, or "ramrod" in charge of internal discipline. When a resident has experienced major adjustment problems and/or failure to perform duties properly, he or she may be demoted to a lower status position in a tightly structured hierarchy of responsibilities; the resident is said to be *shot down*. Being shot down is one of the most important events in the life history of a resident, since it is here that the resident feels the greatest sense of loss of self-worth and purpose and the greatest doubt about who he or she is.

Because their new identities are so wrapped up in their relationships in the community, the residents experience this demotion as failure as a human being. It is an attack on their fundamental sense of self-worth. Should they choose to stay, this cycle of approval and disapproval intensifies their commitment to the therapeutic community's way of life. But often, residents chose at this point to leave Rainbow Village, seeking instead to find their "old" selves. In other words, being shot down and *accepting it* was the ultimate test of loyalty to the Rainbow family.

Encounter Groups. Sugarman (1974) describes the *encounter group* as a highly structured group process in which specific roles emerge such as "prosecutor" (accuser), "moralizer" (asserts what is ideologically correct behavior), "reflector" (helps the accused to see how he has hurt himself by hurting others), "therapist" (sympathizes with the plight of the accused), and "patch-up artist" (emotional healer). In the original Synanon, these were called "games" (Sugarman, 1974:68), suggesting less of a therapeutic role than the kind of "dissing" (to use contemporary jargon for *disrespect*) that was used in playing the "dozens" in prison and on the street (see Irwin, 1980:7).

For Synanon residents and many Daytop residents, these groups may have been "exciting and gratifying." But at Rainbow Village, encounter groups had taken on a much more serious tone. The purpose of each session was clearly therapeutic, meant to focus on some specific personal inadequacy that had been revealed on the part of a group member earlier in the day or week. These groups lacked the formal structure described by Sugarman, although the general process was much the same. Without signs to wear and degradation ceremonies at entry, Rainbow Village, more than its parent organizations, came to depend on the encounter group to resocialize its residents.

To begin the process, a resident "drops a slip" in an encounter box indicating how another resident has "hurt him" or "hurt the family" by his or her action and how this has offended and upset the complainant. Attributing this "slip" in proper conduct as a manifestation of personal inadequacies, the group then engages in the "merciless spotlighting of faults" (Sugarman, 1974:68) as it turns on one particular individual. In Rainbow Village, no single person played the role of "prosecutor" or "patch-up artist," but these roles shifted as different individuals contributed to the assault on the personal integrity of the accused.

In one case, a young white man, Harry, had continued to repeat his "self-destructive behavior" by violating house rules. Harry had experienced blackouts during periods of heavy doses of drugs before coming to Rainbow Village. Group members asked Harry why he wanted to hurt the "family." They proceeded to badger him until he began to shake and cry. Now, accused of being a "baby," Harry was further humiliated by suggestions that he was unmanly, a sissy, a crybaby. Having struck a nerve, the group continued to probe until Harry finally blurted out that he had been molested by his grandfather when he was seven years old. This was a repressed memory yet clearly something about which Harry experienced tremendous guilt. No one knew what had happened to him at age seven, not even Harry. But now the Rainbow family did. And he was now under the group's control.

Similarly, a young white woman, Beatrice, had prostituted herself on the street for drugs. Two distinct strategies were used to break Beatrice down in front of the group. Beatrice resented her mother for not having protected her against the ravages of the street. Beatrice was encouraged to act out her feelings of resentment by pounding a pillow, saying "I hate you" to her symbolic mother. Since this is not the sort of thing one normally allows oneself to express in public, Beatrice's emotions were captured by the group. She was encouraged to express these emotions more and more intensely until she was screaming her hate for her mother. Next, Beatrice was asked to look in the mirror. Now "I hate you" was turned on herself as her negative behavior was defined as a reflection of her hatred for her mother. Soon she was screaming "I hate you" to herself at the top of her lungs. When Beatrice admitted how she hated her old self, the group patched her up with hugs and verbal statements designed to reinforce the fact she had "gotten in touch with her feelings."

BECOMING A MEMBER OF
THE RAINBOW FAMILY

The above illustrations show how important the encounter group is to the social control of residents at Rainbow Village. Transforming the person into a committed member of the family occurs in three steps: (1) *preparation*, (2) *degradation*, and (3) *reconstruction*. This process is similar to that reported by Irwin (1985) in his study of the American jail. Irwin argues that the jail prepares inmates for life in the underclass through disintegrating, disorienting, and degrading experiences. The socially marginal person is transformed into a "street person" by a system that expels the person from conventional society. Therapeutic community residents do not experience the disintegration and disorientation that occurs in jail, but they do share the degradation experience. Unlike the dysfunctional street person, however, the therapeutic community member becomes a committed participant in a functioning social group.

The loss of privacy, isolation from the outside world, and the prohibition of contracting all *prepare* the resident for the assault on his or her sense of self-worth and identity. Pull-ups, haircuts, and being shot down (and wearing signs) serve to humiliate, or *degrade,* the person. *De-grading* implies the loss of status and loss of self-esteem that accompanies the loss of responsibilities associated with lower positions in the social hierarchy of the family. Finally, the encounter group is the place in which the now vulnerable person, suffering from a manufactured identity crisis, experiences the deepest assault on his or her moral identity, his fundamental sense of who he is. At the same time, he is supported for revealing his innermost feelings, guilt, and past misconduct.

Essential to the therapeutic community identity is the demonstrated ability to "get in touch with your feelings." Paradoxically, then, a true family member is someone who is able to reveal his or her greatest self-doubts in the group context. Thus, the new self is validated in the context of feelings of inadequacy, trapping the individual in a network of relationships that depend on taking the role of "dope fiend" for the rest of one's life. The convert, whose identity has been *reconstructed,* is hooked into a lifestyle on which he or she is dependent in order to stay drug-free. Future failure to perform at Rainbow, leading to degradation rituals such as being shot down, reawaken those negative self-feelings that are awakened in the encounter groups, causing residents to "act out." Consequently, they may get into further trouble by, for example, relapsing into drug use. The therapeutic community world reinforces the cycle of relapse and recovery that accompanies addiction (Ray, 1964). Rainbow residents soon learned that they must remain part of this or some other therapeutic community in order to remain drug free.

ESCAPE: AN ALTERNATIVE TO VIOLENCE

We have seen how the use of force as the primary instrument of social control in prison generates alienation, or feelings of powerlessness, in the inmate population. Assaulting others or threatening assault becomes a form of empowerment for those who otherwise do not have the means to control their own fate or destiny. There emerges in the contemporary prison a cultural system that legitimates violence as a means for settling disputes between prisoners and between inmates and officers. In the therapeutic community, however, the value system is quite different. Under no conditions is the use or threatened use of force permitted. In fact, any sign of inappropriate aggression is immediately punished. Aggression is channeled into the verbal arena where, as we have seen, it can take on an extraordinarily destructive form.

Expressing rage, or "coming off your belly," was a frequent event at Rainbow Village. In fact, in one administrative meeting, one of the senior staff members swore at the top of his lungs, "Fuck you," to the executive director. Although this sort of behavior is "understood," it is not condoned. Family members learn that there are "appropriate" times to express rage, for example, in groups, where one can direct this rage at a legitimate target on behalf of the community. Thus, the resident (and staff member) is expected to "hold his belly" until the appropriate time. Someone who only acted with his or her head, and never expressed intense emotions, would be chastised in group for not caring about his brothers and sisters in the family. But he would not be disciplined or "fired" for insubordination.

Suicide

How, then, can someone respond legitimately to the alienating experience of the mortification and degradation that goes on here? Angie, a white female who prostituted herself for her boyfriend to meet his need for drugs, made the mistake of violating the Rainbow "incest taboo." She was alleged to have attempted to seduce one of the men in her encounter group. Of course, this was contracting of the worst kind and Angie was put on a *ban*. (The Amish are known to follow a similar practice.) Someone who is a serious offender may be permitted to live within the confines of the community, but no one is allowed to speak with them. This is important symbolically for the rest of the community because it represents a constant reminder concerning what might happen to them should they violate the rule. But given the intensity of emotional commitment expected here and the dependency created in its residents, the impact on the banned person is devastating. Angie attempted to take her own life by slitting her wrists. Discovered in time, she did not die, but was removed from the house. Her suicide attempt had deeply offended the community in which she lived, and they would no longer accept her. Plainly, this sort of "escape" is not acceptable in the therapeutic community world.

Splittees or Dropouts

Just as it would be a mistake to assume that violence in prison is necessarily a response to a specific coercive act by a prison official, it would be a mistake to assume that dropping out of the therapeutic community is necessarily a response to a specific degrading experience. But there are instances of both. In one case, a black prisoner at Central described his feelings of hostility toward a white prisoner after a correctional officer had used his discretionary authority to "push him around." Not able to direct his hostility toward the officer, he was aware of his willingness to take his anger out on someone with whom he had had no trouble. In the therapeutic community, residents direct their anger at themselves when they have been degraded by being shot down or in some other way lost status. To avoid these negative self-feelings, the individual may decide to leave the program.

Just as the level of inmate violence in prison is related to the reliance on coercion as a means of social control, dropout rates in therapeutic communities are associated with the intensification of normative controls. Whereas escape is not a viable option for the overwhelming majority of prison inmates, violence is not a viable option for those who reside in therapeutic communities.

A person who drops out of the program is called a *splittee*. With proper contrition, splittees who returned to Rainbow Village were permitted to reenter the program. They were usually required to start the program from the beginning, as if they were newcomers.

Once a year or so, Rainbow Village would go through a crisis period in which the staff would recognize that they had "lost control" over the resident population. Too much contracting had been going on. The very fact that few residents were leaving the organization suggested that they were getting "soft." It was time to toughen up the program, remind people what the purpose of the program was. It was time to build a *tight house*.

Sugarman (1974:65) describes the "tight house" at Daytop as a response to "a slackening of discipline and purposefulness among residents." Unlike Rainbow Village, Daytop's director would call for a tight house every few months. From Daytop's point of view, Rainbow staff let residents "slide" for too long, creating more problems and instability in the long run. The intensification of demand for loyalty and commitment to the program that comes with the tight house produced an increase in the rate at which residents left the program. Within a month after a tight house in June one hot summer, approximately *one-third of the residents* left the program. The fact that it was summertime may have interacted with what went on the house to make the problem worse.

IMPACT OF THE PROGRAM ON COMMITMENT AND ALIENATION

Alienation in the Therapeutic Community

To measure the degree of alienation among residents of Rainbow Village, Rotter's I/E (internal/external) scale was administered to two groups of residents six months apart (see Rotter, 1966). A psychological measure of inner-directed (self-reliant) vs. other-directed (other-dependent) personality traits, the questions are remarkably similar to those in standard alienation scales (see discussion in Chapter 5, pp. 83–84). The internally oriented person uses his or her own personal values or standards to make judgments about the world and take action based on those judgments. This person experiences control over his or her own fate; the individual is not alienated. On the other hand, the externally oriented individual, subject to peer pressure, is likely to be impulsive in making decisions and to feel that others control his or her destiny; this is the alienated individual.

Residents of Rainbow Village became less alienated over time. In other words, older (long-term) residents were less likely to feel powerless and more likely to feel that they were in control of their own fate. Newer residents changed over time from externally oriented (measuring high on the I/E scale) to internally oriented individuals. These results were statistically significant in August (1973), but not six months later (see Tables 8.1 and 8.2).

August was the beginning of a period of intense commitment, which had followed a major weeding out of disaffected members through a tight house two months earlier. By the following February, after a long period of intense commitment, the sense of community had begun to deteriorate. Not surprisingly, it was the newcomers, the most alienated, who were likely to split (see Table 8.3 and Figures 8.1 and 8.2). When levels of alienation were on the increase, however, older residents left as well (Table 8.3). Commitment was so intense for those residents who were in the program more than 10 months that *no resident ever split who had been a resident more than 10 months* and less than 17 months. Failure to be released after 6 months of intense commitment to the program led to renewed alienation.

Residents entered Rainbow Village with a high level of alienation, or sense of powerlessness. The experience of arrest, the experience of incarceration, and the threat of further incarceration are coercive in nature and tend to alienate those who undergo these experiences. In addition, many of the residents were still dependent on drugs at the time of their admission. Consequently, it was not surprising that fully 40 percent of the residents dropped out of the program during their first three months in the program.

Table 8.1 Correlations Between Self-Rating Scales, Alienation Scale, and Length of Stay at Six-Month Intervals

	AUGUST 1973 (N = 37)	FEBRUARY 1974 (N = 46)
Identification Process		
Outsider—Member of the family	.58***	.57***
Self-Conception		
Younger—Older	.77***	.72***
Dope fiend—Responsible	.64***	.43**
Not in touch—In touch with feelings	.51***	.32*
Failure—Success	.47**	.41**
Don't understand—Understand what is expected	.45**	.46***
Think about others—Think about self	.31*	.34**
Feel like splitting—Feel like staying	.47**	.41**
Alienation		
Rotter I/E	−.39**	−.20

$*p < .05; **p < .01; ***p < .001.$

Note: Self-rating scales answer the question: "Where would you place yourself [on the scale] at this time?"

```
          1  2  3  4  5  6  7  8  9  10
Outsider __|__|__|__|__|__|__|__|__|__|____ Member of the family
```

Table 8.2 Degree of Alienation by Number of Months in Residence in August, 1973 and February, 1974

	AUGUST 1973		FEBRUARY 1974	
	Younger (0–5)	Older (6–11)	Younger (6–11)	Older (12–17)
Alienation Scale	12.8	7.1	11.0	8.8
(No. of Residents)	(12)	(9)	(12)	(9)

Note: Alienation is measured in terms of the 23-point Rotter I/E scale. There were 21 residents who were present during both administrations of the scale. Older (Phase III) residents were significantly less alienated than younger residents in August ($p < .01$; difference-of-means t-test). There is little change in their scores six months later. Note that the mean score for newer residents (0–5 months) in February was 10.6 (N = 25).

The continuing threat of incarceration and the constant assault on their sense of identity contributed to the maintenance of a high level of alienation, or sense of powerlessness, through most of their residency. Thus, it is a surprise that more residents did not drop out of the program.

**Table 8.3 Average Length of Stay for Splittees
for Periods of Increasing Commitment and Alienation**

	MEAN LENGTH OF STAY FOR SPLITTEES (IN MONTHS)	NUMBER OF SPLITTEES
Increasing Commitment (8/71–1/72)	1.3*	(10)
Increasing Alienation (2/72–7/72)	3.5*	(11)
Increasing Commitment (8/72–1/73)	1.4**	(10)
Increasing Alienation (2/73–7/73)	3.9***	(20)[a]
Increasing Commitment (8/73–12/73)	1.1	(14)[b]
Total Increasing Commitment	1.2***	(34)
Total Increasing Alienation	3.8	(31)

*$p < .05$; **$p < .01$; ***$p < .001$ (t-tests for adjacent means).
[a]Excludes four individuals who left the program without graduating after an average of 19.8 months.
[b]Excludes one individual who left the program without graduating after 22 months.
Note: Each t-test compares the mean with the adjacent mean below.

Commitment to the Therapeutic
Ideology of Rainbow Village

After observing life in Rainbow Village, the author developed a questionnaire to administer to all the community's residents in August 1973 ($N = 37$) and six months later in February 1974 ($N = 46$). This questionnaire included a set of self-rating scales based on the beliefs and values expressed by the senior residents and staff of the program (see Table 8.1). These self-rating scales identify the culturally meaningful symbols that comprise the socially constructed identity of the Rainbow Village resident. In other words, they tell us what it means to be a member of the Rainbow family.

Table 8.1 reports the zero-order correlation coefficients between identification as a member of the Rainbow family, self-concepts derived from participating in the symbolic life of the community, alienation, and length of stay. Self-definitions are reported for August and February only for those relationships that were statistically significant during both periods. It is

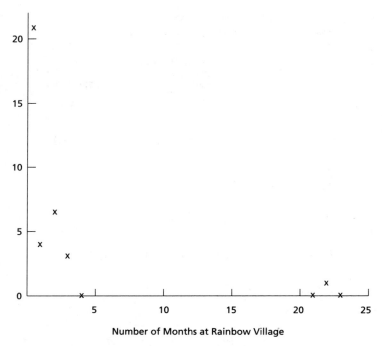

Number of Months at Rainbow Village

FIGURE 8.1 Frequency Distribution of Splittees During Periods of Increasing Commitment

assumed that these are *ways of being* inherent to the TC culture and not incident to situational factors at one point in time.

Over time, residents learn to identify with the community and begin to think of themselves as members of the Rainbow family. They think of themselves as "older," no longer a "dope fiend," and "in touch with their feelings." Experiencing more responsibility as they move up through the organizational hierarchy, they begin to see themselves as successes rather than as failures. But this success is fragile because it is tied to their experiences in the community. They also develop a clearer understanding of what is expected of them. Becoming less externally oriented, they are likely to think about their own destinies rather than simply pleasing their peers. And, finally, they are less likely to express the desire to leave the program.

Program Phases

After a one-month probationary period, residents enter Phase I of the program, a period of orientation and learning the ropes. Next, residents

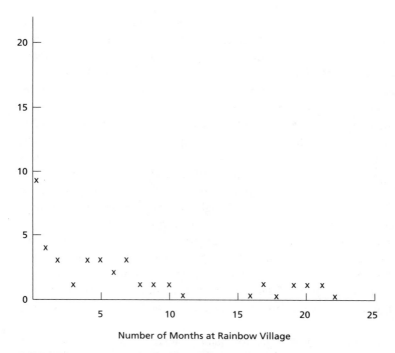

FIGURE 8.2 Frequency Distribution of Splittees During Periods of Increasing Alienation

enter Phase II, a period of intensive indoctrination where encounter groups take on a special importance. Phase III is a period of enhanced responsibility as residents assume leadership responsibilities in preparation for "graduation." During the first two years of the program, many "graduates" stayed in the program as "staff." Residents were expected to be in Phase I at least 2 months, in Phase II 3 months, and in Phase III 4 months. But this ideal was rarely achieved. Residents usually graduated within 18 months.

Phase I. Residents report feeling more like a "member of the family" over time. This is an important transition in the self-definition of the resident. Most residents report feeling like a member of the family within three months after coming into the house. This corresponds to the "three-month hump" in which the resident "begins to realize that he has become involved in something that requires a great deal of commitment" (Sugarman, 1974:97). The loss of one's old self during this period produces feelings of depression described by Rainbow residents as "the 90-day blues."

Phase II. Now that the resident is prepared for this new commitment, he or she begins to take on a new "identity kit" and comes to accept the therapeutic ideology of the community as his or her own (see Table 8.1). *Older* residents learn to accept responsibility for themselves and those around them, assuming leadership positions in the various work crews that run the house. They come to see themselves as more *responsible* over time as they give up their *dope-fiend* persona. Unlike many self-help programs such as Alcoholics Anonymous, which believe that being sober depends on accepting the belief that "once an addict always an addict," success in this program is accompanied by distancing oneself from the addict frame of reference. Critical to the therapeutic ideology at Rainbow Village is the importance of being "in touch with one's feelings." Insight concerning the source of one's emotions is viewed as critical to the resocialization process. At this stage, residents develop the reflective capacity necessary for the self-control to resist peer pressure to use drugs. Achieving *success* in terms of the program contributes to their increasing commitment to the family as they come to *understand what is expected*. Indicating this increasing commitment to the program, we find that residents feel less like *splitting* and more like *staying* over time.

It is important to note that the changes described in Table 8.1 occur within a six-month period. In other words, if the program is to work, the transformation from street junkie to reformed community member must take place rather quickly, and it does for those who choose to stay. Within six months residents report feeling like members of the family and identify fully with the ideology of the therapeutic community. This also means that there is a point beyond which residency in the community may become countertherapeutic, as alienation from the excesses of the program itself develops, usually after 16 months.

Phase III. As residents become members of the Rainbow family and begin to identify with its therapeutic ideology, they become less alienated. But the program creates such dependency that it is not until residents have been empowered with responsibilities in the program for some time that they take a more autonomous view of themselves. There isn't a significant drop in the level of alienation as measured by Rotter's I/E scale until residents have been in Phase III for some time.

As we saw above, there is a significant decrease in alienation among those in residence in August, but not six months later in February. It appears that the impact on Phase III residents was stronger during the earlier period of increasing commitment than during the later period of increasing alienation. The correlation between alienation and length of stay in August is a very strong $-.60$ ($p < .001$) for the 21 residents who remained in the program through February. But the effect was reduced in February to $-.26$ (not significant), indicating that most of the changes had occurred by August. In August, older residents (most of whom were in Phase III) were significantly less alienated than the "younger" residents (those in Phases I and II; see Table 8.2). By February, all 21 of the residents who had been tested in August were in Phase III. Yet the younger residents in August, who were now in Phase III, exhibited no less alienation than they did before. Part of the problem may have been that during a relatively stable period in the organization's history, those who had acquired responsibility at an earlier date tended to remain in control, providing little opportunity for the younger residents to experience the leadership normally experienced by Phase III residents.

To summarize, we see that there is a strong expectation for residents to become *committed* members of the Rainbow family within three months of entry into the program. This is indicated by increasing identification with the family. During the next three months, residents are expected to learn the values and beliefs associated with the therapeutic ideology of the community. Their identities are gradually reshaped as they *get in touch with their feelings* and become increasingly dependent on members of the family for self-validation. Older residents become less *alienated*; that is, they lose their sense of powerlessness once they have been in the program for some time. But this last effect is a variable function of the relative coherence in the operation of the program at different points in time.

CYCLES OF INCREASING COMMITMENT AND ALIENATION

About once a year, the staff at Rainbow Village would recognize that residents were "sliding" and the family had lost its sense of direction. Residents were "contracting" and did not demonstrate concern for their brothers and sisters. At this point there would be a call for a "tight house." A tight house usually begins with a morning meeting in which residents are expected to show their concern for their brothers and sisters by "copping out," i.e., admitting to some transgression (also see Sugarman, 1974:64–67). Since no one is without sin, everyone is expected to admit to *something*, from drug use to "stealing" food (raiding the refrigerator), to not caring enough about others. It was evident to this observer that, in some cases, residents would

manufacture minor transgressions just to get by. But as the emotions intensify and social pressure builds, residents begin copping to more and more
serious offenses, until some of the most serious problems are revealed.

The next step in tightening the house is to announce a series of negative sanctions, euphemistically called *learning experiences*, to restore order and
discipline to the family. Residents are "shot down," reduced to an earlier
phase in the program, and subject to further degradation in encounter
groups. At this point, each person must decide to accept the consequences
of his or her actions and become more committed to the program, or leave.
For those who stay, there is a significant reduction in alienation as they become more committed to the program. But this effect is significant only after a tight house has eliminated the least committed residents and rededi-
cated the Village to its mission.

The Effects of Increasing Commitment and Alienation

As we have seen above, the effect of the program on decreasing feelings of
powerlessness and increasing personal efficacy of the most senior residents is
greatest during the period following a tight house (from August through
January). Unlike the prison, where there is no escape, increasing alienation
produces more "splittees" and a higher dropout rate. Each period of increasing alienation (February through July) ends in a tight house. During this
period (of increasing alienation), the average length of stay of residents is
significantly higher than during the six-month period before and after (see
Table 8.3).

Figure 8.1 summarizes these data, showing that most residents who leave
the program during periods of increasing commitment do so within the first
month. The average length of stay for dropouts is 1.2 months (Table 8.3),
and, with one exception, no one leaves the program after three months
(Phase I). Figure 8.2 describes the dropout pattern during periods of increasing alienation. The average length of stay for dropouts is significantly
higher at 3.8 months, and almost as many residents left the program in
Phases II and III ($N = 14$) as left during the probationary period or Phase I
($N = 17$). Even here, once residents have completed 10 months in the program, they are unlikely to leave until they graduate or leave without officially graduating after 18 months.

During the first year that Rainbow Village was open, the dropout rate
was relatively stable; about 30 percent of the residents dropped out during
each six-month period (10/36 and 11/37). After a year, there were enough
residents in each phase to have a full-blown program and for the alienation
and commitment cycles to have their full effects. The average dropout rate

then began to fluctuate from a low 19.6 percent (10/51) during the first full commitment cycle to a high of 37.5 percent (25/67) during the next alienation cycle. This was again followed by a decrease to only 22.7 percent (15/66). Thus the average annual dropout rate remained the same at about 30 percent.

If we excluded those residents who dropped out in Phases II and III, the dropout rate during the year would be constant at about 20 percent. The effect of increasing alienation is to create splittees among Phase II and III residents, almost doubling the overall dropout rate to about 40 percent.

To summarize, alienation among Rainbow Village residents was quite high throughout their residency until they began to approach graduation. Were it not for the fear of imprisonment, more residents would have left. When the program was "tight," increasing commitment in Phase II and Phase III residents overwhelmed their sense of powerlessness, leading to a significant decline in the dropout rate. When commitment to the family was weakened, feelings of powerlessness became more salient, and residents split at twice the rate as before. This period of increased alienation was accompanied by a weaker impact on the sense of efficacy among the oldest residents.

COERCION IN A THERAPEUTIC COMMUNITY

The therapeutic community is an ideological organization that relies on coercion of both mind and body to control its residents. As such, alienation begins and remains high throughout residency. Therapeutic community staff control the cultural symbols residents use to facilitate adapting to institutional life. Consequently, residents become increasingly committed over time to the therapeutic culture. This is what Goffman (1961:63) calls *conversion* to the total institution as a way of life.

It appears that conversion as a form of adaptation to the total institution occurs under conditions of both physical and psychological coercion. But the potential for an alienative response is everpresent. As a result, we may see a full range of adaptive strategies to life in the total institution (see Goffman, 1961:60–66). Should controls loosen, as they inevitably do in the therapeutic community, a cycle of resistance to institutional authority develops. This is the *intransigent line* of adaptation, manifest in Rainbow Village as contracting. Residents may also *colonize* during this period as they feign commitment in order to avoid imprisonment. Those who have failed to become committed then *withdraw* from participation. Unable to withdraw

emotionally without withdrawing physically from the community, they escape or "split."

McEwen (1980) points out that prisons and therapeutic communities
share many of the characteristics of total institutions, yet vary in important
ways. They are both totalistic in character, since they control the daily routines of inmates or residents twenty-four hours a day and do so in a highly
structured manner. They differ in that membership in the therapeutic community has the appearance of voluntariness and an ideology that stresses rehabilitation and democratic participation in the governance of the institution, at least for "older" residents. Unlike staff in the therapeutic community
who rely heavily on persuasion to control residents, prison staff rely on
physical coercion as the principal means of social control. Unlike the staff in
the therapeutic community who control the cultural milieu to which residents adapt, prison officials are unable to control the cultural milieu to
which the convict adapts.

The cultural environment of the prison derives from both the dominant control resource available—force or violence—and the wider cultural
values that support violent responses in certain situations. Because prison
officials do not control the "secondary adjustments" (Goffman, 1961:54) to
institutional life of inmates, external structural, cultural, and historical
factors play a major role in determining what goes on inside prisons
(McEwen, 1980).

The cultural environment of the therapeutic community represents a
complex mix of the self-help ideology of the Synanon movement and
contemporary psychotherapeutic approaches to group treatment. Drug addicts are believed to be inadequate persons who require intensive group
therapy to change who they are and what they do. Attempts at constructing autonomous secondary adjustments by residents are periodically destroyed through writing slips, encounter groups, and the tight house. Consequently, therapeutic community staff remain in control of the normative
life of the residents and there is no equivalent of the convict code found in
prisons.

In prison and in the therapeutic community, identities are transformed
by the cultural environment in which inmates and residents reside and by
the assaults on both body and mind that occur in these otherwise different
worlds. The coercive nature of the prison world fundamentally shapes the
nature of the convict code and variations in adaptation to that code. Similarly, the coercive environment that structures the choices that residents
make in the therapeutic community shape their commitment to the
community's standards. In many ways, social control in the therapeutic
community is similar to what others have called "brainwashing" or *coercive*

persuasion (Lifton, 1961; Schein, Schneier, and Barker, 1961; also see Shinn's critique, 1987:122–143).

Throughout life in the therapeutic community, many of the apparently voluntary choices that residents must make are structured as alternatives to the threat of incarceration. For example, the prospect chair is always in evidence. And failure to accept learning experiences is frequently followed by the decision to leave, often leading to incarceration. Still other choices are structured in terms of accepting assaults on one's old identity as a precondition to acceptance by one's "brothers" and "sisters" in the "family." In fact, much of what goes on in the therapeutic community is consistent with what many claim goes on in religious cults. Yet, most of these so-called religious cults do not engage in coercive persuasion in the sense described here (Long and Hadden, 1983; Shinn, 1987:138–139). Rather, conversion is a gradual process in which individuals who are seeking solutions to life's problems receive emotional support from a group that meets their needs.

What occurred at Rainbow Village was remarkably similar to what the Chinese indoctrinators did to American POWs during the Korean War (Shein, 1956; Lifton, 1961:65–85; Shinn, 1987:128). While exposed to communist propaganda, POWs were emotionally isolated from self-validating communication from home or with fellow prisoners. They were in constant terror of what the North Korean citizenry would do to them if they were to try to escape, and they were required to make public admissions of guilt for past transgressions while appearing to publicly accept communist propaganda as a condition of improved treatment. Similarly, the therapeutic community residents were continuously exposed to the belief system of the community, isolated from family and friends, and prevented from forming special bonds with fellow residents. The public admission of past transgressions and acceptance of the will of the community was essential to the conversion process.

CONCLUSION

The therapeutic community, ideologically committed to non-violence, nevertheless relies on the threat of incarceration as an encapsulating principle. Fear of prison contributes to residents' acceptance of a therapeutic ideology that in many ways is as coercive as overt physical violence. Encounter groups attack the individual's sense of self-worth, mortifying his or her "moral identity," increasing the resident's willingness to accept the group's ideology and become the kind of person the community expects him or her to be. The therapeutic community "brainwashes" its residents through totalistic control over the symbols of communication necessary to daily life in the community. The normative controls, carried to excess, inflict emotional pain, control movement through surveillance and informing, and control the satisfaction of basic needs through threats of humiliation and degradation. Sociologists usually reserve the notion of violence to the use of physical confrontation, but there are some situations in which ideology yields excesses that do violence to the mind in addition to the body.

Rainbow Village, a coeducational, multiethnic therapeutic community of approximately 40 to 50 residents aged 17–25, was typical of the community-based approach used in the early 1970s for the treatment of drug addiction. Rainbow Village employed a number of degradation rituals designed to break down the residents' commitment to a self-destructive lifestyle. Within a few months, residents were faced with the decision to leave the program or commit themselves to an alternative way of life by becoming a member of the Rainbow family. Accepting more responsibility, they moved up the community's social hierarchy, no longer seeing themselves as "dope fiends." Dependency on drugs and life on the street was replaced, however, with dependency on the therapeutic community.

Unlike the prison world, violence is not an option in the therapeutic community. Potentially violent individuals are weeded out by ex-addicts who have "been there." Threats of violence of any kind are met with immediate sanction, if not expulsion. Faced with the constant threat of going to prison should they fail to "get in touch with their feelings," Rainbow residents were as alienated or powerless as any prison inmate, if not more so. Moreover, the assault on their old ways of thinking and reconstruction of their identities as family members represented the sort of coercive persuasion usually associated with brainwashing techniques. Consequently, the only viable option for those who rejected the program's philosophy was to leave, or "drop out," an option not usually available to the prison inmate.

NOTES

1. According to Foucault, modern forms of punishment are more intensive than older forms, including torture. The torture victim is mutilated to make a symbolic point. He is not expected to change his mind. The body is subject to violence to communicate a message to the community as a whole. But the contemporary prison controls the mind as well as the body. Intended to teach the discipline of the modern industrial era, it produces instead the hardened criminal. Hence the control over mind and body produces unintended effects.

Contemporary secret police may have perfected torture in ways that

Foucault had not conceived. No longer is the individual tortured to death in public. Rather, while imprisoned, torture is used as a way of intensifying the pains of imprisonment and the emotional harm that it does. By limiting violence to that which is necessary, the Eighth Amendment has been used to provide boundaries to state controls that

make the American prison system one of the most humane in the world. But this does not change the reality of prison nor diminish its impact on the violent nature of society itself.

2. All the names used below are pseudonyms in order to protect the identities of those involved.

REFERENCES

Bettelheim, Bruno (1943). "Individual and Mass Behavior in Extreme Situations," *Journal of Abnormal and Social Psychology* 38:417–452.

Etzioni, Amitai (1975). *A Comparative Analysis of Complex Organizations.* New York: Free Press.

Foucault, Michel (1979). *Discipline and Punish: The Birth of the Prison.* Translated by Alan Sheridan. New York: Vintage Books.

Goffman, Erving (1961). *Asylums.* Garden City, NY: Anchor Books.

Hassan, Steven (1988). *Combatting Cult Mind Control.* Rochester, VT: Park Street Press.

Irwin, John (1980). *Prisons in Turmoil.* Boston: Little, Brown.

Irwin, John (1985). *The Jail: Managing the Underclass in American Society.* Berkeley, CA: University of California Press.

Lifton, Robert J. (1961). *Thought Reform and the Psychology of Totalism: A Study of "Brainwashing" in China.* New York: Norton.

Lifton, Robert J. (1987). "Cults, Religious Totalism and Civil Liberties." Pp. 209–219 in *The Future of Immortality and Other Essays for a Nuclear*

Age, by R. J. Lifton. New York: Basic Books.

Ling, Ken (1972). *The Revenge of Heaven: Journal of a Young Chinese.* New York: Putnam.

Lofland, John (1966). *Doomsday Cult: A Study in Conversion, Proselytization, and Maintenance of Faith.* Englewood Cliffs, NJ: Prentice Hall.

Lofland, John and Rodney Stark (1965). "Conversion to a Deviant Perspective," *American Sociological Review* 30:862–875.

Long, Theodore E. and Jeffrey K. Hadden (1983). "Religious Conversion and the Concept of Socialization: Integrating the Brainwashing and Drift Models," *Journal for the Scientific Study of Religion* 22:1–14.

McEwen, C. A. (1980). "Continuities in the Study of Total and Nontotal Institutions," *Annual Review of Sociology* 6:143–185.

Rashke, Richard (1982). *Escape from Sobibor.* Boston, MA: Houghton Mifflin.

Ray, March B. (1964). "The Cycle of Abstinence and Relapse Among Heroin Addicts." Pp. 163–177 in *The Other Side: Perspectives on Deviance,* edited by Howard S. Becker. New York: Free Press.

Rotter, Julian (1966). "Generalized Expectations for Internal Versus External Control of Reinforcement," *Psychological Monographs: General and Applied* 60:1–28.

Schein, Edgar H. (1956). "The Chinese Indoctrination Program for Prisoners of War: A Study of Attempted 'Brainwashing'," *Psychiatry* 19: 149–172.

Schein, Edgar H., Inge Schneier, and Curtis H. Barker (1961). *Coercive Persuasion: A Social Psychological Analysis of "Brainwashing" of American Prisoners by the Chinese Communists.* New York: Barton.

Shinn, Larry D. (1987). *The Dark Lord: Cult Images and the Hare Krishnas in America.* Philadelphia, PA: Westminister Press.

Skinner, G. William and Edwin A. Winckler (1969). "Compliance Succession in Communist Rural China: A Cyclical Theory." Pp. 410–438 in *A Sociological Reader on Complex Organizations*, edited by A. Etzioni. New York: Holt, Rinehart & Winston.

Sugarman, Barry (1974). *Daytop Village: A Therapeutic Community.* New York: Holt, Rinehart & Winston.

Wrong, Dennis H. (1988). *Power: Its Forms, Bases, and Uses.* Chicago, IL: University of Chicago Press.

9

∗

The Social Origins of Violence in America

In Chapter 4, we explored the *cultural* origins of violence in America
and the role that the "frontier culture" has played in explaining the violent nature of young males who are incarcerated in our prison system.
We have also seen how changes in the case law concerning the regulation
of prisons has unwittingly increased the level of violence in our institutions
through the "decoupling" of the official and informal control systems that
regulate the daily lives of prison inmates. In this chapter, we turn to the
structural origins of violence in American society that contribute both directly and indirectly to violence in prison. We shall see how racial inequality contributes to the violent nature of American society, producing racial
division in society as a whole and violent confrontations between ethnic
groups in prison. The prison system reproduces the social conflicts that have
their origins in society and the violence that results.

Because the prison world is a microcosm of the larger society, and because it acts as a cauldron for the tensions that society has produced, the
prison system often releases individuals who are more dangerous than when
they entered prison. This is not only expressed in the attitudes and behavior
of the individuals who have been released after long-term incarceration, especially as juveniles or youthful offenders, but in the values and norms they

bring back to the streets. The offender who has done hard time often becomes a role model in the community to which he returns, transmitting the culture of prison life and its violent nature to the streets.

Much of what is described as the violent ghetto culture today, the expressed need to carry weapons and the easy resort to violence in response to disputes, have their origins in prison. The dependence on a group of homeboys or a single person (prop) for survival in a hostile and dangerous world in prison is replicated on the street where guns are readily available and violent confrontations over the distribution of drugs are frequent.

The purpose of this chapter is to identify the social origins of violence in society at large and to describe the mechanisms by which that violence is transmitted to the prison world. Ironically, the violent adaptations that occur in today's prisons are brought to the streets by the released convict, creating a vicious cycle of violence between society and the prison system designed to stop the violence. This chapter synthesizes new material on politics and the economy with material on prison life presented in earlier chapters in order to make sense of the interaction that occurs between prison and society.

THE STRUCTURAL ORIGINS OF VIOLENCE

Recent research on the causes of violence has identified social inequality as one of the major factors contributing to high levels of violence in the United States today. Inequality based on race, class, or gender contributes to higher rates of criminal violence, including homicide, rape, and assault (see Krohn, 1976; Braithwaite, 1979; Messner, 1980; Schwendinger and Schwendinger, 1981; Blau and Blau, 1982; Baron and Straus, 1987; Gelles and Straus, 1988:86; Caputi, 1989).[1] Cross-cultural studies link economic inequality to criminal violence in general. These studies also show that gender inequality contributes to the incidence of rape. Gender inequality in the United States has been tied to sexual violence, including rape and serial murder. Economic inequality has been linked to family violence, and racial inequality has been linked to homicide.

Economic inequality contributes to a higher incidence of violent crime in a number of ways. When poverty is made worse because of who you are rather than what you have or have not accomplished, the frustrations associated with one's relative deprivation are made worse. When economic conditions create a large underclass, the need to resort to violence in a world of scarcity increases. And when the deprivations of the underclass lead to incarceration, the racial and ethnic conflicts that result from the competition for survival in society are made worse.

Given the frontier culture that legitimates violence in response to disputes over property and persons and given the decoupling of the official and informal control systems in prison, structural inequalities on the outside exacerbate the racial and ethnic tensions inside prison. It should not be surprising, then, that much of the violence in prison has racial undertones.

Social Inequality and the Production of Violence

One of the best studies of the effect of social inequality on criminal violence was conducted by Judith and Peter Blau (1982). The Blaus examined a large number of American cities and measured the discrepancies in wealth between the haves and have nots in each city. They found that it is not poverty per se that leads to crime, but poverty in the face of wealth that does so. Property crime was especially high in those areas where the wealthy were wealthiest and the poor were the poorest. Violent crime was at its greatest in those cities where wealth was determined in part by race. In other words, violent crime is a product of racial injustice.

Violence among racial minorities is an expression of rage not unlike that expressed by colonial peoples who have been subject to foreign controls for a long period of time (see Blauner, 1969). Third World peoples in colonial settings may organize politically to overthrow their oppressors, but in America, African Americans constitute a relatively small minority. Consequently, racial tensions may erupt as they have during riots such as the one that occurred recently in Los Angeles. More often, however, the targets of criminal violence are the most available targets, members of one's own community. Consequently, African Americans are most frequently the targets of violence in African American communities.

When inequality is based on *ascribed status,* that is, status based on race, gender, age, or some other predetermined category, violence increases. The violence in Northern Ireland is a manifestation of the underclass position Catholics have experienced in a society dominated by a Protestant majority. To the extent that Palestinians are becoming a permanent underclass in Israeli society, violence in the state of Israel appears to be increasing. One of the most violent societies in the world can be found in Sri Lanka, formerly Ceylon, in which two ethnic groups, the Sinhalese and the Tamils, have been in a long-term struggle for power. Whether violence is of a criminal or political nature depends on the extent to which one group is able to dominate the political and economic system and the other has the resources to organize politically to resist domination.

Cross-cultural studies of gender inequality reveal two interesting facts. Rape is more frequent in societies characterized by a great deal of gender inequality (Schwendinger and Schwendinger, 1981), and domestic violence is widespread (see Baumgartner, 1993). Both these facts point to the importance of patriarchal relations, institutions based on the cultural and political domination of males, in explaining violence against women. Whether or not domestic violence is criminalized depends in large measure whether women are sufficiently organized politically to create legislation designed to restructure gender relations in their society (see Pleck, 1989).

Economic Instability and the Production of Violence

We have seen over the past ten to fifteen years an increase in homelessness, long-term unemployment, and most recently, a major recession. Once the leading nation in the world economy, the United States is now the greatest debtor nation in the world (*New York Times*, 1992). This rapid economic decline has been accompanied by enormous trade deficits and the export of both capital and labor to other countries (Sheinkman, 1992; Hershey, 1993). What this has meant to many middle-class Americans has been the loss of the American Dream. The number of jobs, especially good jobs, has declined dramatically, average wages have fallen, and benefits have declined since 1979 (Uchitelle, 1993). Many Americans have been forced to accept lower wages and part-time jobs. Permanent layoffs, retirees who lose their retirement benefits, and the closing of factories have created a sense of despair and anger among many. We have a large displaced homeless population, many of whom have dropped out of the ranks of the middle class. The sudden frustration associated with job loss has led to numerous incidents of violent outbursts.

One of the first incidents was the infamous mass murder at McDonald's in San Ysidro near San Diego, California, in 1984 (see Horvath, 1986). Huberty, a college-educated factory worker, had been laid off when the factory in his small Ohio town closed down permanently. Pursuing the American Dream, Huberty had invested in rental properties and had other investments. Nevertheless, joblessness created a sense of anger and frustration at the world that ultimately exploded in San Ysidro where he killed 21 people.

There have been a number of similar incidents involving angry postal workers and others who have experienced failure in a highly competitive system (Swickard, 1993; Koenig, 1993). These explosive acts, largely by white, middle-class failures, are the other side of the economic coin. Just as racial injustice produces violence among minority groups, economic injustice produces violence among those who assumed that they were immune from economic crisis.

Serial killing, too, appears to be a product of economic instability. The ability to kill repeatedly and escape detection is made possible by a society in which there are large numbers of displaced persons with no clear form of social identification. This anonymity makes the selection of vulnerable targets by serial killers possible. Henry Lee Lucas, who claimed at first to have killed several hundred persons, mostly female hitchhikers, did so while traveling the highways of America (Hickey, 1991:185–186). Convicted of only 10 homicides, Lucas has recanted his initial claims, but at least one investigator believes that 50 is a reasonable estimate (Hickey, 1991:186). Serial rapist Steven Judy was executed in 1981 for the rape and murder of a woman and the drowning of her three children, whom he had abducted from her disabled car on a highway in Indiana (*New York Times*, 1981a, 1981b). Judy was able to do so precisely because of the highly mobile and anonymous nature of our society. John Wayne Gacy, who resided in a working-class community in Chicago, was able to sexually assault dozens of young boys, murder them, and hide them in his basement without detection for several years (see Hickey, 1991:165–167). More recently, Jeffrey Dahmer, who maintained a residence in a transitional neighborhood in Milwaukee, admitted killing 17 young men and boys after drugging them during homosexual liaisons (Gelman, 1991; Mathews, 1992).

THE REPRODUCTION OF SOCIAL CONFLICT IN PRISON

In America, the production of violence is intimately linked to racial and ethnic conflict. During periods of economic and political crisis, we have seen overt manifestations of ethnic hostilities in racially motivated attacks. Some politicians have effectively used "wedge" issues to divide the electorate on racial and ethnic lines in order to win elections. For example, the campaign of Republican candidate George Bush in 1988 used the image of a black rapist, Willie Horton, who had raped a white woman during a furlough from a prison in the home state of the Democratic candidate Michael Dukakis, to gain votes from the white electorate.

In the 1960s, the civil rights movement created the opportunity for African Americans to question their subordinate status in American society and to seek to change it. In prison, this gave rise to organized resistance to the subordinate status that blacks had experienced at the hands of prison administrators and white inmates alike. The Black Muslims, also known as the Nation of Islam, had its origins in Detroit as early as the 1930s (Lincoln, 1961:10–11). But they did not really become a force in American society until they began to recruit heavily among black prisoners in the 1950s and

'60s (Pallas and Barber, 1973:243–248). The Muslims argued that "blacks as a group were victims of white society, that the miseries they faced were not the result of their own deficiencies" (Pallas and Barber, 1973:244). According to the original creed of the Muslims, all evil in the world was created by "blue-eyed devils," who used their power to dominate the nonwhite peoples of the world (Lincoln, 1961:75–80).

The Muslims told inmates that alcoholism, drug addiction, and criminality were a product of the evils of white society and the feelings of inadequacy that had been imposed on those of African descent who had had their true religion and true identities stripped away by the slavemasters. This message led to the conversion to Islam of large numbers of prisoners and to their rehabilitation in many cases. (Malcolm X was one of their most famous successes.) The additional appeal of the Muslims to black inmates was the evident success that this group had in reversing the hands-off doctrine of the courts. The power and effectiveness of the organization sent a clear message to African American inmates. They could overcome the historical racism of the prison system, and American society in general, by organizing to change prison conditions, and through this process gain self-respect.

Pallas and Barber (1973:246) argue that the Muslims became less militant over time and pursued a more separatist agenda, hoping to create a separate black nation in America. But it is clear that, even today, the Nation of Islam has retained a reputation for militancy among prison personnel. In addition, there has been a proliferation of Islamic groups in prison, including more conventional Shiite and Sunni sects whose beliefs are universal and nonracial.

The success of the Muslims may, in part, have created an incentive for prison reformers to ally themselves with increasingly politicized inmates in creating the prison movement of the late 1960s and early '70s. Many prisoners, especially blacks, defined themselves as "political prisoners," who were incarcerated because of the political and economic conditions of a society that produced both their criminality and their being caught and punished. The prison movement created a prisoners' union, organized work stoppages, and produced a manifesto declaring basic rights for prisoners (Irwin, 1980:110). This manifesto, or some derivative, often became a negotiating tool during prison strikes, demonstrations, or riots, as in the case of the Attica riot in 1971 (see Irwin, 1980:255–262). The ACLU (American Civil Liberties Union) founded the Prison Project in 1972, and the NAACP (National Association for the Advancement of Colored People) joined the fight for the civil rights of prisoners.

Although the successes of the Black Muslims contributed to the political consciousness of black prisoners (Pallas and Barber, 1973:246), others began to organize along less activist lines. Violent prison gangs first appeared in the California prison system in the late 1960s (Irwin, 1980:183–192). First, a group of urban Chicano prisoners organized the Mexican Mafia, which began to exploit less organized rural Chicanos and others. The other prisoners began to organize into defensive and retaliatory groups such as the Nuestra Familia (Hispanic), the Black Guerilla Family (black), and the Aryan Brotherhood (white). These four gangs have become the major prison gangs throughout America's prisons (Crouch and Marquart, 1989:204). Throughout the 1970s, most killings in the California prison system were attributable to the gangs (Crouch and Marquart, 1989:204). Some of these gangs began to exploit their control over members who were released from prison. The Nuestra Familia, for example, became active in promoting drug trafficking in northern California (see Lewis, 1980).

In Illinois, street gangs such as the Blackstone Rangers, a black group, and the Latin Kings, a Hispanic group, became active in the state's prisons (Irwin, 1980:191; Jacobs, 1977:158). Here, too, white prisoners organized defensively. In Texas, a small Hispanic group, the Texas Syndicate, had been around since the 1970s after developing among Hispanics of Texan origin in the California prison system to defend against the Chicano groups there. But, as the "authority vacuum" grew in the late 1970s and early 1980s in Texas, the Texas Syndicate grew in numbers and strength (Crouch and Marquart, 1989:206). The Aryan Brotherhood and Texas Mafia, both white groups, and the Mexican Mafia emerged as powerful gangs at the same time.

Throughout the history of the prison system, inmates have associated with others with whom they shared a common interest. Irwin (1980:58–60) described these as "tips and cliques," in the correctional institutions of the '60s and '70s. Tips were groups that shared common experiences, such as juvenile institutions, neighborhoods (homeboys), or criminal activities. Irwin describes cliques as smaller groups who interacted with·one another because of shared living arrangements and membership in a larger tip. By the 1980s, associating with homeboys became the major basis of group affiliation in American prisons. Of course, homeboys, because they come from the same neighborhoods and communities, usually share similar racial and ethnic backgrounds.

In the federal penitentiary at Leavenworth, geographical origin is a major source of gang affiliation. Earley (1992:91) describes "DC Blacks" as a the "largest single ethnic group" in Leavenworth. A major disturbance at Leavenworth in July 1992 involved gangs from two major "geographical regions," one reportedly from Washington, D.C. and the other from Los Angeles. At the time of the riot, a prison spokesperson suggested that the fighting that took place during a takeover of the auditorium and prison yard may have been caused by "overcrowding, racial trouble and gang violence," but the precise cause had yet to be determined (Hanna, 1992:3). One inmate was killed in a melee that involved about 300 prisoners.

In one of the first accounts of race relations in prison, Leo Carroll (1974) describes the emergence of racial conflicts in the late 1960s and early '70s after a period of relative peace from 1956 to 1968 at ECI ("Eastern Correctional Institution"). White editors of the prison newspaper were accused of racism when they refused to publish articles about newly emerging black consciousness. Conflict over control of prison social clubs ensued, and ultimately blacks were permitted to form their own Afro-American Society (Carroll, 1974:40). Carroll describes the institution as racially polarized from that point on.

One of the manifestations of the struggle for power between whites and blacks was rape. As in the outside world, rape is as much an expression of power and anger (by men against women) as it is sexual. In the prison world, where opportunities for heterosexual relations is virtually nil, homosexual acts are not infrequent. Under normal circumstances, as on the outside, most such contacts are consensual and involve many but not all prisoners. But homosexual rape, like heterosexual rape, is an expression of power and anger as much as it is sexual. For this reason, most prison rapes were interracial, and most of these involved groups of black assailants and a single white victim. In 1971, Carroll (1974:182) estimates that at least 75 percent of the rapes at ECI were black on white. Carroll attributed these rapes to black rage directed at dominant white institutions and the ability to exert symbolic control over a white victim who represented these institutions. On the other hand, Lockwood (1980:78) argues that sexual aggression by blacks against whites reinforces racist attitudes among white prisoners (also see Irwin, 1980:183).

Several later studies of prison rape described essentially the same interracial pattern (Lockwood, 1980:77–79; Bowker, 1980:7–10; Wooden and Parker, 1982:60). Wooden and Parker point out that consensual homosexual relations are predominantly intraracial. The irony is that most of the homosexual "punks" or "kids" are "turned out" forcibly by members of a different ethnic group. According to Carroll (1974:183–184), at ECI, a white inmate would be repeatedly assaulted by a group or groups of black inmates until a white convict offered to take him under his wing and protect him as long as he agreed to be his "kid," in a more or less exclusive and subservient homosexual relationship. This suggests that the pattern of sexual assault at ECI served the interests of the convicts, both white and black, who dominated the social life of the institution.

THE PRODUCTION OF THE
UNDERCLASS BY THE PRISON SYSTEM

There are two contrasting views of the nature of the American underclass. The first is that the underclass is a more or less permanent group stuck in the lowest stratum of the economic system. Produced by a "culture of poverty," the poor constitute a more or less permanent cadre of welfare-dependent, mostly minority group individuals who are ill-educated, untrained, and unsuited by temperament and lack of skills to participate in the industrial economy (Moore, 1985:1; Beverly and Stanback, 1986:24).

A second view takes the position that the culture of poverty thesis is essentially racist and classist in its assumptions (Moore, 1985:1; Beverly and Stanback, 1986:24). There is little evidence to support the idea that poverty and welfare dependency are transmitted from generation to generation (Wilson and Aponte, 1985:241–243). It is primarily the structure of the economy that determines economic opportunities and welfare dependency (Wilson and Aponte, 1985; Sanders, 1990).

This second approach views the underclass as a dynamic entity, one that includes many different kinds of nonproductive citizens whose life experiences have cast them out of the economic system. In addition to welfare families, this group includes the homeless, the seriously mentally ill, hustlers, winos, and habitual criminals. High levels of unemployment produced by economic recession create outcasts out of many individuals during hard times. But we must also understand that high rates of unemployment are endemic to our society. Thus, the underclass as a social position is a permanent fixture of our society, while the actual members of this underclass are being constantly produced and reproduced.

Very few of the members of the underclass were born into this status. Many, indeed, have experienced reasonably successful working-class or middle-class lifestyles at some point in their lives. Thus, the question becomes, *what are the mechanisms or processes by which productive or potentially productive citizens are transformed into social outcasts?* Once we understand that winos, addicts, and bums can be created by a society that degrades and humiliates its failures, leaving few options to return to conventionality, we can also begin to ask questions such as: How is it that society produces those groups who *appear* to be permanent members of the underclass? What role does the prison system play in producing the underclass?

As long as social and economic conditions do not change from generation to generation, the children of the underclass in one generation are likely to face the same conditions as their parents. If racism and the decay of the economic base remain problems in our inner cities, it is easy to see why racial minorities continue to be disproportionately represented among welfare and criminal populations.

The Role of the Jail in the Production of "Rabble": Winos, Addicts, and Bums

In his book on the American jail, John Irwin (1985) describes the process by which the jail system contributes to the production of "rabble": winos, addicts, and bums. Irwin points out that most people in city or county jails are either waiting for trial or have been convicted of minor offenses. Who is arrested and jailed and why? Irwin describes these individuals as "disreputables," individuals whose public behavior is unconventional or "offensive."

These disreputables include hustlers who sell small quantities of drugs, engage in unsophisticated swindles, or commit petty thefts such as rolling drunks, shoplifting, or burglarizing cars (Irwin, 1985:26). They also include skid-row drunks, released mental patients, junkies, and aliens. This last group is an unexpected category, yet the police treat those who speak and act differently in much the same way that they do other unconventional persons. Gay men were at one time treated as "rabble" and lived on the edge of legitimate society as they found themselves in and out of city jails. Today, with the gay rights movement and greater consciousness of the civil and political rights of homosexuals, there is effective pressure on police not to treat homosexuality as criminal, although police still find overt displays of a gay lifestyle as offensive.

Young black males may also get caught up in the criminal justice system because their behavior is viewed as offensive by police officers, although in many cases this is merely a first step toward further criminalization. This is especially true for junkies and a group that used to be called "corner boys" (see Liebow, 1967; Whyte, 1981). Hanging around and acting tough, inner-city kids are quickly labeled as troublemakers and may get pulled in by the police for minor offenses that might otherwise be ignored. Working-class whites, known in California as "low-riders," may find themselves in similar circumstances if they engage in behavior considered offensive to police officers and the community they represent, such as cruising noisily in a souped-up car. It is important to understand the way in which the jail contributes to the production of rabble because a major chunk of this group is likely to end up in prison, where they will be exposed to further violence.

The jail contributes to the creation of an underclass in four distinct stages: (1) disintegration, (2) disorientation, (3) degradation, and (4) preparation. During the *disintegration* stage, the new prisoner experiences several important losses, each anchoring his sense of who he is in the real world (Irwin, 1985:42–66). He loses his property, as his car may be towed and ultimately reclaimed by creditors, he loses his apartment, and his personal effects are temporarily removed and sometimes lost. He may also lose important social ties, not least of which is his job. Family and friends may disassociate themselves from someone who has been formerly considered "conventional."

For the inner-city youth, there is not much to lose since he owns little, pays no rent, and often is unemployed. But the jail experience further propels him, too, into the underclass because it diminishes whatever opportunity he had for employment before and reinforces the notion that he is indeed a propertyless individual in society who is likely to remain that way. It also means that ties to conventional others such as parents and preachers may become weakened, reducing the incentive to go "straight." The newly imprisoned individual also loses his capacity to "take care of business," that is, he loses control over his personal life. For the inner-city youth, ties to his family, wife or girlfriend, and children may be weakened, making it difficult to perform his expected roles as lover and father.

The experience of imprisonment leads to a sense of *disorientation* as the person's integrity and sense of self-worth is undermined (see Irwin, 1985:53–84). Subject to the indignities of close confinement in overcrowded cells, fear of sexual assault, and the powerlessness that comes from the regimentation and routines of those who run the jails, prisoners may be in a state of "shock." Of course, this is less likely to be the case as one has more experience in jail, but to some degree the loss of personal organization is inevitable for most people.

The disorientation experienced by being jailed is reinforced by the *degradation* rituals prisoners experience at every step of the way (see Irwin, 1985:67–84). Degradation means "loss of status" (i.e., *de-grade*), a consequence of the very fact of being jailed. But this is revealed, too, by the attitudes of those who treat them like "scum" and let them know it. Jailers are often the worst offenders because they must justify to themselves in some way the indignities that they subject their wards to. But even their defense lawyers do not treat them with respect, treating them as just another case number in a long series of cases handled each day. The net result of the disintegration, disorientation, and degradation process is the loss of commitment to conventional values and the society they represent.

Given the loss of commitment to conventionality, jail provides a psychological, sociological, and cultural environment that *prepares* the prisoner for participation in a variety of alternative lifestyles (see Irwin, 1985:85–100). Psychological preparation involves loss of conventional sensibilities concerning the senses, personal privacy, and appearance. One may also begin to think like a member of the "rabble" class, losing trust in others and respect for authority. Stealing and hoarding behavior in situations of scarcity are likely adaptations as well. This generalized preparation for rabble status is reinforced socially by association with others of similar background and experience. Here begins the specialization process, distinguishing bums and winos from addicts, tough guys from punks, and so on. And, finally, each grouping in jail has its own outlook on the world, a cultural perspective that lends legitimacy to what they have or are about to become.

For each category of ordinary rabble, a rationale or ideology provides an explanation for who they are and why they have become what they have become. For the mentally ill, the addict, the derelict, and the hustler, society has a set of available explanations for each of their failures. Most of these explanations tend to focus on the personal inadequacies and early traumatic experiences that may have caused these inadequacies.

What distinguishes those who are on their way to criminal status and life behind prison bars is, paradoxically, a more positive attitude. Those whom they encounter in jail reinforce their achievements, and when released on the street, they may become heroes to their peers since going to jail may become a badge of honor. In Chapter 8, we saw how those who rejected the therapeutic community in favor of returning to jail often had prior jail experience and displayed more self-confidence than those who chose to stay. In other words, although mortified by the jail experience, potential criminals are usually younger than ordinary rabble, have fewer commitments to conventional society in the first place, and less to lose. Although, like the others, their potential for reintegration in conventional society is reduced with each encounter with the criminal justice system, they experience support for their deviant conduct. This is especially true, it appears, if that conduct involves elements of aggression, a willingness to use force to pursue their ends.

A second group that is increasingly criminalized today are the petty hustlers who were caught up in the antidrug crusade of the 1980s and 1990s. With fewer opportunities to seek help in therapeutic environments, these petty drug dealers, who are usually users as well, find themselves at the victimized end of the stick once incarcerated in maximum security prisons.

The Role of the Prison in the Production of Violent Men: Convicts, Gangs, and Racial Politics

As we have seen, the production of the underclass begins in the city and county jails where prisoners lose their ties to conventional values and norms and begin to associate with those who support deviant or alternative lifestyles. As the accused felon makes his way from the local jail into the state or federal penitentiary, he is already prepared to some extent for the violent world he is about to enter. But his adaptations up to this point have been to *criminal lifestyles*, as thief, drug dealer, gangster, hustler, and so on. What he must learn to survive in prison is what it means to be a *convict*.

In an early work on the prison world, Irwin and Cressey (1962) described the inmate culture as a reflection of both the criminal subcultures that prisoners brought to the prison with them and the particular adaptive strategies individual prisoners used to survive in prison. The thief subculture was considered dominant, focusing on trust among thieves and outwitting or conning others. These attitudes supported general inmate solidarity while encouraging inmates to do their own time and find their own niche in the inmate world as "politicians," "merchants," or "gamblers." Outside the mainstream, yet clearly evident were "rapos," convicted of sexual offenses against children, and "snitches" (Irwin, 1980:13). Prison "toughs" were the precursors of today's convicts. They were "openly hostile to the prison administration, the conventional society, and most other prisoners and . . . displayed a readiness to employ violence against others" (Irwin, 1980:12–13).

Today, the dominant type of prisoner is the "convict" whose commitment to violence is essential to his survival in an increasingly violent world. No longer do street values matter. Consequently, the new prisoner may give up his preprison identity, which in many cases is criminalistic, in favor of prison identities that are no longer defined in the mercantilistic language and values of the professional thief. Instead, ethnic conflicts and rivalries dominant the self-conceptions and available adaptive strategies. The new convict is less likely to experience the disintegration and disorientation that the initiate experiences in jail. He has already gone through this process. But the degradation continues in terms of invasions of privacy—body cavity searches, shakedowns, checking personal correspondence for contraband, and so on—violating the individual's ability to maintain his personal integrity. The lack of control over his daily routines and relationships and the loss of ties to conventional society are reinforced. Consequently, for the long-term prisoner, the loss of conventional sensibilities and the acquisition of a more or less permanent criminal status are inevitable.

Irwin's three types of preparation, (1) psychological, (2) cultural, and (3) social, help us to understand the transformation of the inmate into the convict in the prison system. Psychologically, prisoners experience a great deal of anxiety and outright fear for their personal safety. No matter how well run an institution, no matter how carefully prison administrators attend to the legal requirement that they not put in place policies that permit inmates to victimize one another, these victimizations are inevitable. But even those who appear on the surface to be tough guys demonstrate that for many, this is a veneer. After all, even the most experienced soldiers feel fear in times of combat. Here, where combat is always a possibility, fear is something you must live with on a daily basis.

Cultural adaptation occurs when inmates learn the values associated with the *convict code*. These values constitute the cultural life of the American prison in the late twentieth century. First, there is the *commitment to violence* when faced with threats to oneself or those with whom one identifies. Second, there is *hostility toward the prison administration and conventional society*. Third, there is the demand for *loyalty to fellow convicts*. Fourth, *never show weakness*.

These values will be expressed in specific norms such as: (1) *snitches deserve to be killed*, (2) *fight to the death, if necessary, if you are threatened with sexual assault*, (3) *do not let anyone show you disrespect*, and (4) *never volunteer for prison programs*. These are all expressions of publicly held and legitimated norms that some convicts come to believe in and support, yet others may only give lip service to. For example, many prisoners may wish to pursue more education, but are less likely to do so today than in the past because it would appear that they were cooperating with the administration. In the past, prisoners were given incentives to participate in educational and other programs designed to improve their preparation for conventional roles in society. For example, completing a GED (high school equivalency diploma) might have earned credit toward parole. In today's climate of mandatory sentences and sentencing guidelines, these incentives are gone. The promise of early release provided a publicly acceptable excuse to participate in prison programs. But this is no longer true today.

Although there is a generalized convict identity that all prison inmates share, each is socialized today into different ethnic variants on the dominant theme. These variants constitute the third and final stage of the preparation process, the *social*. Prison life is organized largely in black, white, and Hispanic terms. Native Americans, relatively small in number in most prisons, have established their right to follow traditional religious practices and customs. Because group affiliation is important to survival in both an emotional and practical sense, many prisoners with some Native American background will become involved in the cultural and social life of traditional Native American practices.

For many of African American heritage, the existence of a variety of Muslim religious groups in prison provide a basis for adjustment to prison life. Useem and Kimball (1991:127, 135, 154, 174) make it clear that these are *not* prison gangs and these groups did *not* participate in the riots that have occurred in American prisons between 1971 and 1986. Moreover, federal guidelines for the management of prison gangs list the Black Muslims (Nation of Islam) among those groups that are *not* prison gangs (U.S. Department of Justice, 1991:2). Nevertheless, the Black Muslims, who undermined the hegemony of white authority and prison administrations in the 1960s, are still feared by many prison administrators. In New York State, the prison system does not hire imams "with political agendas, like that of black separatists," from the Nation of Islam (Clines, 1992:B2).

In Pennsylvania, correctional officers attributed the 1989 riot at Camp Hill Correctional Institution to the Fruit of Islam (see Senate Judiciary Committee, 1989; House Judiciary Committee, 1990). Lincoln (1961:14, 118) describes the Fruit of Islam as the "paramilitary" arm of the Black Muslims (also see Duke, 1989; Foxman and Boland, 1992). There was no evidence in the Pennsylvania House and Senate Judiciary Committees documents, however, to link the Fruit of Islam at Camp Hill with the Nation of Islam or any other Muslim group. In their report on the riot at Camp Hill to the National Institute of Justice, Useem, Camp, and Camp (1993:183) describe the Fruit of Islam as "a powerful inmate group who apparently engaged in aggravating rather than mitigating influences." According to this report, inmate leaders who negotiated with the superintendent of the prison were all members of the Fruit of Islam (Useem, Camp, and Camp, 1993:194).

In contrast, Irwin (1980:196–197) describes the Black Muslims as a "stabilizing force" who "do not follow the aggressive and rapacious patterns of the gangs," but may "assume leadership in periods of disorder." During the Attica riot in 1971, it was Black Muslim guards who kept the hostages from being harmed by other inmates (Useem and Kimball, 1991:34, 50).

The Aryan Brotherhood has become a notorious prison gang, largely because of the murders of two correctional officers by two members of the gang at the federal penitentiary in Marion, Illinois, which was considered the most secure prison in the country at the time (Earley, 1992:204). In both cases, the murders at Marion and the riot at Camp Hill, aggression was directed at representatives of authority and not other ethnic groups.

The ethnic basis of group affiliation in prison today is the dominant form of social organization. Whether or not these groups become active gangs, in the sense of organizing elicit activities or engaging in exploitive and violent relationships with other inmates, depends on a variety of conditions. Not all gang activity involves explicitly named gangs such as the Mexican Mafia. Some prison officials allege that religious groups may become fronts for gang activity. More precisely, any grouping in prison is likely to be used to the advantage of that group and for its self-defense. But these groups are considered gangs only when they (1) have a clear leadership structure, (2) are unified and well organized, and (3) pursue criminal activities as a group (see U.S. Department of Justice, 1991:2). These groupings, whether they constitute gangs or not, derive from racial and ethnic rivalries in the wider society and may, in turn, contribute to them. In this sense, these groups reflect the racial politics of the wider society.

THE IMPACT OF THE PRISON SYSTEM ON AMERICAN SOCIAL LIFE

Throughout this book, we have seen a number of ways in which the violent nature of American society is reproduced in its prison system. The nature of punishment in society reflects the nature of the society of which it is part (see Rusche and Kirchheimer, 1968; Foucault, 1979:3–31). But it is also the case that prisons, as part of society, cannot be understood in isolation from their impact on that society. The vast majority of prisoners are eventually released. The values and beliefs they have learned, the identities they have acquired and the roles they play, and the reliance on coercive means to solve problems affect the communities to which these prisoners return.

The Regulation of Surplus Labor

Throughout modern history there have been periods of economic and social crisis. In their book *Regulating the Poor,* Piven and Cloward (1971) argue that the welfare system has functioned mainly as a tool for regulating the poor. Threatened with unrest, political and economic elites have wisely provided for the support of the "surplus labor" population created by economic downturns. On occasion, this would occur in response to social unrest. At other times, social welfare legislation was enacted in anticipation of unrest and thus would prevent its occurrence.

In the 1960s, the Great Society programs proposed by Lyndon Johnson were a response to increasing pressure from the poor, especially African Americans, whose expectations for equal treatment under the law were being resisted by authorities, especially in the South. These programs were also designed to overcome the effects of past and present discrimination in employment and housing in the North. The frustrations that led to the riots of the 1960s were not alleviated by these social programs and conservative politicians, such as Richard Nixon, who took the opportunity to promote a "law and order" agenda as an alternative to welfare to address the concerns of the economically and politically disenfranchised. Thus, in the context of the American polity of the last 30 years or so, welfare and crime control have become alternative strategies for dealing with the surplus labor population in the United States.

Several studies (see Brenner, 1976; Greenberg, 1977; Wallace, 1981) have demonstrated that incarceration rates increase with increasing unemployment. In his study of incarceration trends in the 1970s, Wallace (1981) does not use official government unemployment statistics since they are misleading. Once a person gives up looking for work, he or she is no longer counted as "unemployed," so it is possible for large numbers of people to give up looking for work while the official unemployment statistics go down. When the total number of people working full-time compared with the total number of able-bodied adults in society goes down, we find that the incarceration rate, or number of people put in prison in each year, goes up. In other words, as the number of jobs in society decline, the number of people who go to prison increases. Moreover, the effect of unemployment on the incarceration rate is independent of the crime rate! The trends that Wallace observed in the 1970s have continued into the 1980s. The number of prisoners in state and federal prisoners doubled during the 1980s, the job base declined, and the crime rate was relatively stable.[2]

If the crime rate has not increased over the years, then how do we explain the increase in incarceration? Wallace (1981) has shown that welfare and incarceration are alternative mechanisms of social control in contemporary society. When the welfare system fails to provide a minimum of support and security for society, the state steps in with harsher measures. Furthermore, it appears that, historically, prisoners were going into prison at the same rate at which they came out. But when prisoners cannot make parole because they cannot find a suitable job on the outside, the prison population swells. As the number of job opportunities decline, the rate of release from prison slows down. In addition, there has been an increase in the number of parolees and probationers who have been sent to prison due to violations of their parole and probation conditions (Gilliard, 1993:7).

This situation has been aggravated over the past few years with mandatory sentencing, lengthening the average prison term. Almost half as many prisoners are released early on parole today than in the recent past, dropping from 72 percent in 1977 to 41 percent by 1990 (see Jankowski, 1991:5). About the same percentage, 40 percent, "maxed out" in 1990 (released at the expiration of their sentence or after completing the mandatory time required by law), compared with only 22 percent in 1977 (see Jankowski, 1991:5). But making things worse is that mandatory sentencing has led to the increased incarceration of first offenders who might have been put on probation in the past (U.S. Bureau of Justice Statistics, 1993:13). Moreover, many of these new admissions have committed drug-related offenses. The number of adult drug arrests doubled and the rate of incarceration of drug arrestees has quadrupled since 1977 (Gilliard, 1993:7–8). From 1986 to 1990, the rate of incarceration in the 75 largest urban courts in the United States remained stable for violent crime but increased by 25 percent for those convicted of drug trafficking (see Langan, 1993:7). In 1986, offenders sentenced for drug possession or trafficking for the first time comprised *one-third* (33%) of the nonviolent offenders sentenced to state prisons (Innes, 1988:5). By 1991, the proportion of nonviolent first offenders sentenced to state prisons for drug violations had *doubled* to 63 percent (see U.S. Bureau of Justice Statistics, 1993:13).

Who are these new prisoners? It is increasingly evident that young African American males, who have been most hurt by the economic and social policies of the past two decades, are filling up our prisons. As many as 48 percent of prisoners in state prisons are non-Hispanic blacks, although blacks comprise only about 12 percent of the population (U.S. Bureau of Justice Statistics, 1992a:3).[3] A recent study conducted by Jerome Miller's National Center on Insititutions and Alternatives reported that almost one out of four (23%) black men in their twenties are under the control of the criminal justice system on any given day, either in jail or prison or on probation or parole (Bencivenga, 1992). The U.S. Bureau of Justice Statistics (1993:5) reports that from 1986 through 1991 the number of black inmates serving time for drug-related offenses increased 447 percent, higher than the rate for Hispanics (324 percent) and four times greater than for whites (115 percent)! At the same time, the percentage of black and Hispanic inmates in prison for violent crimes went down.

The Antidrug Crusade

How have we managed to detect and punish more offenders than in the past? If the serious crime rate has not increased, where do these offenders come from? Why are they more likely to be young black males than in the past? What is the impact of this new pattern of enforcement on society, especially on inner-city ghetto youth? To answer these questions, we must turn to the drug wars and their impact on the prison population and its consequences for society.

The war on drugs has been one of the major vehicles of the anti-crime crusade for showing the effectiveness of tough law and order policies. Petty drug offenders are relatively easy to catch and prosecute. Without appreciably altering the flow of drug trafficking into a community, officers can produce high arrest statistics. For those who begin to build an arrest record, any future offense, although not serious by itself, may lead to harsher treatment by the courts since the past record is used as part of the sentencing decision. Since most street-level drug dealers are also users who sell drugs to feed their habits, the war on drugs criminalizes a large segment of the population, mostly poor and racial minorities, who in the past had been either ignored or placed in rehabilitation programs. Because many of these street dealers are young males, we see a greater number of minority males introduced to the criminal justice system relatively early in life.

Has the drug war reduced appreciably the flow of drugs into the United States? No. Has the overall consumption of drugs diminished? No. There is some evidence that there has been a change in the pattern of distribution and consumption of drugs, with declining usage in the middle class and an increase in the hard-core addict population among the poor. Why has the extent of drug usage worsened, if anything, in the inner cities? Recent rioting in Los Angeles demonstrates the level of frustration and anger inner-city residents feel at the lack of jobs in their communities and the hostility they experience from law enforcement.

John Hagedorn (1991) studied inner-city African American gang members who lived in Milwaukee between 1986 and 1990. Hagedorn showed that gang activity has changed dramatically over the years. In the past, inner-city gangs involved adolescents who engaged in a variety of criminal activities, including the distribution of drugs. As the gang members matured, they drifted from the "streets" into more conventional working-class lifestyles, getting a job, getting married, and raising a family. With the "deindustrialization" of the inner city, fewer opportunities for employment, and an educational system that is not meeting the needs of inner-city youth, these young black men delay entry into conventional society, continuing gang activity into their early twenties and beyond. And it is these gangs that have become the core of violent competition for control over drug trafficking in their communities. Just as Italian youth did during the 1920s and 1930s during the formation of the Italian American version of organized crime, which specialized in the distribution of alcohol to American consumers during Prohibition (see Whyte, 1981).

We see that difficult economic times have hit minority communities especially hard, creating greater incentives for participating in alternative, illegal economic enterprises. The demand for drugs is also great in such communities. At the same time, a crackdown on the drug trade disproportionately hits the street-level minority dealer and user. Keep in mind, too, that this population constitutes a major component of the surplus labor population. With policies that discourage welfare for the able-bodied male, incarceration has become the key mechanism for regulating this group.

Over the past twenty years or so, the prison system appears to have increasingly taken on a regulatory function in an economic system that is undergoing great difficulty. Increasing unemployment and underemployment has hit minority communities especially hard, leading to increasing involvement in organized criminal activity, especially involving drugs. The drug war has facilitated selective law enforcement directed at this surplus labor population, legitimating the incarceration of ever-increasing numbers of young black males.

Contemporary Inner-City Life: Violence and Values

One consequence of the selective enforcement of drug laws in minority communities has been to criminalize this population over time. By the late 1980s, young black males began to incorporate more and more violence in their daily lives. In fact, the homicide rate among young black males aged 14 through 24 rose dramatically from 1984 to 1991, while the homicide rate for all other groups remained stable during this period (Salholz, 1990:33; Eckholm, 1993; see note 2). According to a study by the Centers for Disease Control (see Salholz, 1990:33), from 1984 through 1988, most of this rise in the homicide rate among young black males, especially those between the ages of 15 and 19, was gun-related. While this rise in homicides can be explained by the increased availability of guns in the inner city and drug-related violence, it is also evident that violence has become generalized among young males in the inner city. The arrest rate for violent crimes in general, including assault, robbery, rape, and murder, for juveniles under the age of 18 increased 85 percent from 1987 through 1991, and the arrest rate for illegal weapons possession increased by 62 percent during the same period (Kantrowitz, 1993:43, 45).

In the early '90s, inner-city high schools are armed camps. About one-third (35%) of inner-city high school males carry firearms regularly or on occasion (Wright, Sheley, and Smith, 1992:85). Roughly 20 percent of the nation's high school youth carry weapons, often guns to school (Morganthau, 1992:25). New York City schools periodically report shootings in

school (see, for example, Kleinfield, 1992: Nordland, 1992). But this violence has been spreading even to America's smaller cities (Eckholm, 1993).
What is more, the most frequent explanation for gun possession among
these inner-city youth is the classic "frontier" rationale, "for protection." It
should not be surprising that the group most involved in this violence is also
the group that has been increasingly exposed to the criminal justice system
over the past two decades. Black youth are three times more likely than
whites to be arrested for weapons violations and six times more likely to be
the victims of homicide (Kantrowitz, 1993:45). In many ways, what we are
seeing today is the transformation of attitudes and behavior learned in the
prison system back onto the streets, creating a vicious cycle of violence from
the streets to the prison and back again.

One of the ways to demonstrate how prison life has influenced street life
is to show how the way in which prisoners have learned to adapt to the violent world of the prison has manifested itself in the language and behavior
of the streets. In his autobiography, Malcolm X describes the use of the
term "homeboy" to refer to someone from his hometown of Lansing,
Michigan, whom he met on the street in Boston in the 1940s (Malcolm X,
1965:39–55). In his 1960s study of a federal institution for drug addicts,
Tittle (1972:87) describes cliques of "homies" as "superficial reference
points" for only about 5 percent of the inmates. Today, the term "homeboy"
or "homey," which prisoners use to refer to others from their own neighborhood or community, has taken on greater significance. A homeboy is
someone you can trust because you share a common experience. Homeboys
will back you up if you are in trouble. The symbolic importance of the
homeboy reflects the importance of common social origin as the basis of
social organization in prison life today. By the late 1980s and early 1990s,
the terms "homeboy" and "homey" appeared in popular culture, first in rap
music, the expression of the frustrations of inner-city African American
males, and later in other mediums as well.[4]

An older example of the way prison life both reflects and contributes to
community life was the "prison 'dozens,' a verbal exchange exposing each
other's vulnerable points, most often related to homosexuality" (Irwin,
1980:7). The "dozens" originated in rural areas of the Old South before it
became part of the cultural life in the prisons of the 1930s and '40s (see
Berdie, 1947). By the 1960s, the dozens had become a game of verbal in-
sults in inner-city black ghettos, especially among the most "street-wise"
youth (Foster, 1974:227).[5]

One of the most interesting and unique adaptations from prison life to
the streets is what teenagers in New York City today call "props" (see Chapter 2, pp. 29–30). A prop is someone you hang out with, a close buddy who

will back you up if you get into trouble. In prison, two inmates who share a common background will provide mutual protection for one another.

In a recent shooting at Thomas Jefferson High School in Brooklyn, the fifteen-year-old assailant carried his gun to school along with 90 percent of the kids who "got guns or can get them" (Nordland, 1992:22). The fifteen-year-old shot and killed a sixteen-year-old who had been his crime partner in a mugging. The sixteen-year-old had done time and had called the fifteen-year-old a "rat" because he received probation. Since he had "called me a rat," the killer told the police, he thought the sixteen-year-old meant to kill him. It was "kill or be killed," the code of the prison convict! The victim was with his "inseparable buddy," his "prop," at the time of the shooting. The prop was also shot and killed (Nordland, 1992:22; Kleinfield, 1992:32).

The above example also illustrates the importance of the role of violence in defending oneself against attack by another. Just as the prison world has adopted its own version of the frontier culture and the self-defense attitudes that derive from it, the inner-city streets seem to have adopted that version from the prison world (Wright, Sheley, and Smith, 1992:88). But what has emerged in the late 1980s and 1990s is a particularly deadly version, one that seems to reflect the mores of the prison world rather than the traditional values of either African American or European American communities. Most high school students and incarcerated delinquents say that they carry weapons for "protection," but a substantial percentage of both groups, 10 percent and 14 percent respectively, say that people in their "crowd" carry guns to maintain "respect" (Wright, Sheley, and Smith, 1992:87). This reflects the world view of the hard-core convict. A white convict at Leavenworth expressed this view when he said, "As a child, I was taught not to be a stool pigeon. Don't tattletale on other kids. I was taught if someone hits you, you hit them back, and if they even think about hitting you again, you make them never want to see you again. That is what John Wayne always did and everyone in the country thought John Wayne was right" (Earley, 1992:181).

The Impact of the Contemporary Prison on Racial Politics

The prison system fosters racial division in a number of ways. First, the selective enforcement of the laws that places ever-increasing numbers of inner-city blacks into the prison system identifies blacks with criminality in the public mind, at least for the white public. The symbolism of a black Willie Horton raping a white woman used by the Republican presidential

campaign in 1988 still evokes the fears of white Americans of black male-
ness and sexuality that produced lynchings in the Old South. Second, it
contributes to the rage in the black community at both a white-dominated
society in general and at the criminal justice system in particular. This rage
was manifest in the racial violence that occurred during the Los Angeles riot
in 1992 following the acquittal of four police officers accused of beating
Rodney King (see, for example, *New York Times*, 1993).

But the racial politics within prison spills out into the public arena in
more sinister ways. As we have seen above, the cauldron of hate and violence in prison reproduces and magnifies the conflicts of the wider society.
We have seen the emergence of race and ethnicity as the dominant form of
social organization among prison inmates. This has produced a number of
different types of groups, from those that are strictly religious in orientation
to those that are active prison gangs at war with one another. The degree of
racial conflict varies over time and between prisons. But the very nature of
the prison system provides a breeding ground for racism and the ideological
beliefs that legitimate racial hatred.

Many groups that either originated in prisons or gained their strength
in prison promote racial supremacist doctrines. Still others, incarcerated because of their militancy on the outside, may find themselves in a world in
which kindred groups foster racial ideologies. The Black Guerilla Family
and the Aryan Brotherhood both originated in California prisons in the late
1960s as "racist cliques" (Irwin, 1980:191). The Aryan Brotherhood, which
originated as a self-defense organization for white prisoners who had become a minority in California prisons, eventually evolved a white supremacist doctrine (Ridgeway, 1990:91).

The basic philosophy of the Black Muslims is to use violence in self-
defense rather than to initiate violence (Irwin, 1980:69). Known for their
litigiousness in other states, the Black Muslims were closely monitored by
Texas officials, but they were "not particularly disruptive" (Crouch and
Marquart, 1989:205). But the doctrine of the Muslims is, nevertheless,
based on the "theory of black supremacy" (Lincoln, 1961:76).

A variety of neo-Nazi groups recruited white prisoners in the 1970s
(Irwin, 1980:185; Aho, 1990:60). By the 1980s, the Aryan Nations Church
(the Church of Jesus Christ Christian) had begun to recruit members from
the Aryan Brotherhood prison gang (Aho, 1990:61; Ridgeway, 1990:91).
Whereas the politics of some of the militant black prisoners in the late 1960s
and early '70s was primarily left-wing in character, the politics of white
prisoners today appears to be right-wing. Members of motorcycle gangs are
prime targets for recruitment into these right-wing groups since they share
many of their racial views and often display Nazi-like insignia (Watson,

1980:37). But the "military discipline and religious asceticism of the Aryan Nations Church" does not appeal to many who have enjoyed a more hedonistic lifestyle (Aho, 1990:61).

The promotion of racially oriented ideologies in prison provides a core of potential recruits for outside groups that share similar beliefs. To the extent that this racism is exported to the outside world, it reinforces and exacerbates divisions in the community at large. What we see today is the emergence of a coherent right-wing religious and social ideology for white prisoners just as such an ideology emerged for blacks in the 1960s. In both cases, they contribute to the production of racial hatred both inside and outside the prison system.

CONCLUSION

The social organization of prison life reflects and reproduces the social structure of the larger society and its cultural values. Social inequality based on race, class, or gender produces violence both in society and in prison. Racial inequality generates rage among its victims and a backlash by the white majority. Consequently, we should not be surprised to find that there is a long history of racial conflict in the American prison system.

The prison system controls the surplus population generated by a weak economy. The so-called underclass is a product of both joblessness and a criminal justice system that functions to regulate the poor when the welfare system fails to do so adequately. City and county jails are designed to control the disorganized and disruptive, whereas state and federal prisons control those who are more violent and deemed a "threat to social order" (Irwin, 1985:3). The antidrug crusade of the late 1980s has functioned to selectively enforce the law in the African American community, incarcerating young black males in ever-increasing numbers.

The prison system continues to grow, with the prison population doubling roughly every 10 years. With almost 900,000 prisoners in state and federal prisons and many more in city and county jails, the United States incarcerated a record 329 adults per 100,000 population at the end of 1992, up from 139 in 1980 (Gilliard, 1993:2). With an increase in the number of young black males under the supervision of the criminal justice system, we have seen the transmission of the violent values of the prison world to the streets. The availability of sophisticated weapons and the willingness to use deadly force to settle disputes has led to an increase in violence in inner-city communities.

There also have been increasing attempts on the part of radical right-wing groups to recruit white prisoners who share their racial beliefs. Consequently, the racial conflict that develops in prison has become a breeding ground for racial ideologies that divide Americans in the wider society.

NOTES

1. In his book *Confronting Crime: An American Challenge*, Elliott Currie (1985:143–180) provides an excellent summary of the basic research on the effects of economic and racial inequality on criminal violence.

2. See Chapter 7, p. 137 and notes 2 and 3, for a discussion of long-term trends in incarceration and crime rates. During the 1980s, violent crime rates continued to remain relatively stable, although the trend was generally downward for property crimes (U.S. Bureau of Justice Statistics, 1992b:4). The only serious upward trend was the age-specific increase in the homicide rate for young black males who were increasingly at risk in drug-related crimes involving increasingly sophisticated guns. The *New York Times* (Eckholm, 1993) reported statistics provided by James A. Fox and Glenn Pierce of Northeastern University, describing stable homicide rates from 1985 to 1991 for white males of all age groups, declining homicide rates for older black men (age 25 plus), and increasing rates for young black males aged 14 through 24. The Centers for Disease Control (Salholz, 1990:33) reported similar data for teenagers from 1984 through 1988. The risk of becoming the victim of homicide was stable for white males and for both white and black females. The risk of being murdered "almost doubled" for black males during the same period.

3. This represents an increase in the black population in prison during the antidrug crusade of the late 1980s. The U.S. Bureau of the Census (1990:187) reported Bureau of Justice Statistics data giving the black prison population as 46.9% as recently as 1986, but this included Hispanic prisoners of African descent. The more recent population data excludes Hispanic prisoners from the total. In 1990, 12% of the state prison population was of Hispanic origin.

4. Binder (1993:754) argues that between 1985 and 1990, rap music emerged as an expression of anger and defiance of authority among black youth. More recently, there has been a public outcry against so-called "gangster rap" for its more specifically violent themes. (See, for example, Staples, 1993.)

5. There is some evidence that the dozens was played by rural whites as well as blacks in the Old South (Dollard, 1939; Elton, 1950). By the 1960s, few inner-city youth knew the game by this name, except the "more sophisticated and street-wise" (Foster, 1974:227).

REFERENCES

Aho, James A. (1990). *The Politics of Righteousness: Idaho Christian Patriotism.* Seattle, WA: University of Washington Press.

Baron, Larry and Murray A. Straus (1987). "Four Theories of Rape: A Macrosociological Analysis," *Social Problems* 34:467–489.

Baumgartner, Mary Pat (1993). "Violent Networks: The Origins and Management of Domestic Conflict." Pp. 209–232 in *Aggression and Violence: Social Interactionist Perspectives,* edited by R. B. Felson and J. T. Tedeschi. Washington, DC: American Psychological Association.

Bencivenga, Jim (1992). "Prison Values Spill into Society," *Christian Science Monitor,* April 10:13.

Berdie, Ralph F. (1947). "Playing the Dozens," *Journal of Abnormal and Social Psychology* 42:120–121.

Beverly, Creigs C. and Howard J. Stanback (1986). "The Black Underclass: Theory and Reality," *The Black Scholar* 17:24–32.

Binder, Amy (1993). "Constructing Racial Rhetoric: Media Depictions of Harm in Heavy Metal and Rap Music," *American Sociological Review* 58:753–767.

Blau, Judith R. and Peter Blau (1982). "The Cost of Inequality: Metropolitan Structure and Violent Crime," *American Sociological Review* 47:114–129.

Blauner, Robert (1969). "Internal Colonialism and Ghetto Revolt," *Social Problems* 16:393–408.

Bowker, Lee H. (1980). *Prison Victimization.* New York: Elsevier.

Braithwaite, John (1979). *Inequality, Crime, and Public Policy.* London: Routledge and Kegan Paul.

Brenner, M. Harvey (1976). "Time Series Analysis: The Effects of the Economy on Criminal Behavior and the Administration of Criminal Justice." Pp. 25–68 in *Economic Crises and Crime.* Rome, Italy: United Nations Social Defense Research Institute.

Caputi, Jane (1989). "The Sexual Politics of Murder," *Gender and Society* 3:437–456.

Carroll, Leo (1974). *Hacks, Blacks, and Cons: Race Relations in a Maximum Security Prison.* Prospect Heights, IL: Waveland Press.

Clines, Francis X. (1992). "Prison Has the Body, but Allah Has the Spirit," *New York Times,* July 2:A1, B2.

Crouch, Ben M. and James W. Marquart (1989). *An Appeal to Justice: Litigated Reform of Texas Prisons.* Austin, TX: University of Texas Press.

Currie, Elliott (1985). *Confronting Crime: An American Challenge.* New York: Pantheon Books.

Dollard, John (1939). "The Dozens: The Dialect of Insult," *American Imago* 1:4–20.

Duke, Lynne (1989). "Big Demand for Drug Patrols Forces Muslims to Face Economics," *Washington Post,* February 12:B, 1:1.

Earley, Pete (1992). *The Hot House: Life Inside Leavenworth Penitentiary.* New York: Bantam Books.

Eckholm, Erik (1993). "Teen-Age Gangs Are Inflicting Lethal Violence on Small Cities," *New York Times,* January 31: 1, 1:2.

Elton, William (1950). "Playing the Dozens," *American Speech* 25: 230–233.

Foster, Herbert L. (1974). *Ribbin', Jivin', and Playin' the Dozens: The Unrecog-*

nized Dilemma of Inner-City Schools. Cambridge, MA: Ballinger.

Foucault, Michel (1979). *Discipline and Punish: The Birth of the Prison.* Translated by Alan Sheridan. New York: Vintage Books.

Foxman, Abraham and Mira Boland (1992). "Fruit of Islam on U.S. Tab?" *Washington Times,* August 19:F, 3:1.

Gelles, Richard J. and Murray A. Straus (1988). *Intimate Violence.* New York: Touchstone Books.

Gelman, David (1991). "The Secrets of Apt. 213," *Newsweek,* August 5:40–42.

Gilliard, Darrell K. (1993). *Prisoners in 1992.* Washington, DC: Bureau of Justice Statistics, U.S. Department of Justice.

Greenberg, David (1977). "The Dynamics of Oscillatory Punishment Processes," *Journal of Criminal Law and Criminology* 68:643–651.

Hagedorn, John M. (1991). "Gangs, Neighborhoods, and Public Policy," *Social Problems* 38:529–542.

Hanna, John (1992). "Inmates Restricted after Riots in Kansas," *Boston Globe,* July 7:3.

Hershey, Robert D. (1993). "Trade Gap Widened in April," *New York Times,* June 16: D1.

Hickey, Eric W. (1991). *Serial Murderers and Their Victims.* Pacific Grove, CA: Brooks/Cole.

Horvath, Imre (1986). *Acts of Violence.* Stamford, CT: Lightning Video.

House Judiciary Committee (1990). *HR 226: State Correctional Institution at Camp Hill.* Transcript of public hearing, March 7, Harrisburg, PA.

Innes, Christopher A. (1988). "Profile of State Prison Inmates, 1986," *Bureau of Justice Statistics Special Report.*

Washington, DC: U.S. Department of Justice.

Irwin, John (1980). *Prisons in Turmoil.* Boston, MA: Little, Brown.

Irwin, John (1985). *The Jail: Managing the Underclass in American Society.* Berkeley, CA: University of California Press.

Irwin, John and Donald R. Cressey (1962). "Thieves, Convicts, and the Inmate Culture," *Social Problems* 10:142–155.

Jacobs, James B. (1977). *Stateville: The Penitentiary in Mass Society.* Chicago, IL: University of Chicago Press.

Jankowski, Louis (1991). "Probation and Parole 1990," *Bureau of Justice Statistics Bulletin.* Washington, DC: U.S. Department of Justice.

Kantrowitz, Barbara (1993). "Wild in the Streets," *Newsweek,* August 2: 40–46.

Kleinfield, N. R. (1992). "The Fatal Vortex: Collision of 3 Lives in East New York," *New York Times,* March 1:1, 32.

Koenig, Robert L. (1993). "Postal Service Takes Hard Look at Policies," *St. Louis Post-Dispatch,* May 9: D6.

Krohn, Marvin D. (1976). "Inequality, Unemployment and Crime: A Cross-National Analysis," *Sociological Quarterly* 17:303–313.

Langan, Patrick A. (1993). "Felony Sentences in State Courts, 1990," *Bureau of Justice Statistics Bulletin.* Washington, DC: U.S. Department of Justice.

Lewis, George H. (1980). "Social Groupings in Organized Crime," *Deviant Behavior* 1:129–143.

Liebow, Elliot (1967). *Tally's Corner: A Study of Negro Streetcorner Men.* Boston, MA: Little, Brown.

Lincoln, C. Eric (1961). *The Black Muslims in America*. Boston: Beacon Press.

Lockwood, Daniel (1980). *Prison Sexual Violence*. New York: Elsevier.

Malcolm X (1965). *The Autobiography of Malcolm X*. New York: Ballantine Books.

Mathews, Tom (1992). "Secrets of a Serial Killer," *Newsweek,* February 3:44–49.

Messner, Steven F. (1980). "Income Inequality and Murder Rates: Some Cross-National Findings," *Comparative Social Research* 3:185–198.

Moore, Joan W. (1985). "Isolation and Stigmatization in the Development of an Underclass: The Case of Chicano Gangs in East Los Angeles," *Social Problems* 33:1–12.

Morganthau, Tom (1992). "It's Not Just New York," *Newsweek,* March 9:25–29.

New York Times (1981a). "Indiana Murderer Executed at Prison," *New York Times,* March 9:A1.

New York Times (1981b). "Murderer of Four Awaits Electric Chair in Indiana," *New York Times,* February 18:12.

New York Times (1992). "U.S. Is Bigger Debtor Nation," *New York Times,* July 4: A44.

New York Times (1993). "5 Blacks Dismissed from Jury Panel in Beating Case," *New York Times,* August 8:36.

Nordland, Rod (1992). "Deadly Lessons," *Newsweek,* March 9:22–24.

Pallas, John and Robert Barber (1973). "From Riot to Revolution." Pp. 237–261 in *The Politics of Punishment*, edited by Erik Olin Wright. New York: Harper & Row.

Piven, Frances Fox and Richard A. Cloward (1971). *Regulating the Poor*. New York: Pantheon Books.

Pleck, Elizabeth (1989). "Criminal Approaches to Family Violence." Pp. 19–58 in *Family Violence*, edited by L. Ohlin and M. Tonry. Chicago, IL: University of Chicago Press.

Ridgeway, James (1990). *Blood in the Face*. New York: Thunder's Mouth Press.

Rusche, Georg and Otto Kirchheimer (1968). *Punishment and Social Structure*. New York: Russell and Russell.

Salholz, Eloise (1990). "Short Lives, Bloody Deaths," *Newsweek,* December 17:33.

Sanders, Jimy M. (1990). "Public Transfers: Safety Net or Inducement into Poverty?" *Social Forces* 68:813–834.

Schwendinger, Julia R. and Herman Schwendinger (1981). "Rape, Sexual Inequality, and Levels of Violence," *Crime and Social Justice* 16:3–31.

Senate Judiciary Committee (1989). *Public Hearing on Recent Incidents at Pennsylvania State Correctional Institutions: Transcript of Proceedings,* November 27, Harrisburg, PA.

Sheinkman, Jack (1992). "How Washington Exports U.S. Jobs," *New York Times,* October 18:3, 3.

Staples, Brent (1993). "The Politics of Gangster Rap," *New York Times,* August 27:A, 28:1.

Swickard, Joe (1993). "A Crime for Our Time: 'Get Back at the Boss'," *Detroit News and Free Press,* May 8: A7.

Tittle, Charles R. (1972). *Society of Subordinates*. Bloomington, IN: Indiana University Press.

Uchitelle, Louis (1993). "Stanching the Loss of Good Jobs," *New York Times,* January 31:3, 1.

U.S. Bureau of the Census (1990). *Statistical Abstract of the United States, 1990* (110th ed.). Washington, DC: U.S. Government Printing Office.

U.S. Bureau of Justice Statistics (1992a). *Census of State and Federal Correctional Facilities, 1990.* Washington, DC: U.S. Government Printing Office.

U.S. Bureau of Justice Statistics (1992b). *Criminal Victimization in the United States, 1990.* Washington, DC: U.S. Department of Justice.

U.S. Bureau of Justice Statistics (1993). *Survey of State Prison Inmates, 1991.* Washington, DC: U.S. Department of Justice.

U.S. Department of Justice (1991). *Management Strategies in Disturbances and with Gangs/Disruptive Groups.* Washington, DC: U.S. Government Printing Office.

Useem, Bert, Camille Camp, and George Camp (1993). *Resolution of Prison Riots.* Report to the National Institute of Justice. Washington, DC: U.S. Department of Justice.

Useem, Bert and Peter Kimball (1991). *States of Siege: U.S. Riots 1971–1986.* New York: Oxford University Press.

Wallace, Don (1981). "The Political Economy of Incarceration Trends in Late U.S. Capitalism: 1971–1977," *Insurgent Sociologist* 10:59–66.

Watson, J. Mark (1980). "Outlaw Motorcyclists: An Outgrowth of Lower Class Cultural Concerns," *Deviant Behavior* 2:31–48.

Whyte, William Foote (1981). *Street Corner Society: The Social Structure of an Italian Slum.* Chicago, IL: University of Chicago Press.

Wilson, William J. and Robert Aponte (1985). "Urban Poverty," *Annual Review of Sociology* 11:231–258.

Wooden, Wayne S. and Jay Parker (1982). *Men Behind Bars: Sexual Exploitation in Prison.* New York: Plenum.

Wright, James D., Joseph F. Sheley, and M. Dwayne Smith (1992). "Kids, Guns, and Killing Fields," *Society* 30:84–89.

10

✳

Civilizing the
Prison World

R educing violence in prison will be difficult as long as the society
of which it is part is one of the most violent in the modern industrial world. To a great degree, the reduction of prison violence
depends on the reduction of violence in society as a whole. The origins of
social violence lie in the structural inequalities, both economic and racial,
that plague our society as a whole and in cultural traditions that expect violent responses in confrontations between young adult males.

As we have seen, racial and economic inequalities create the conditions
for assaultive behavior in society, which are then reproduced in prison. And
the frontier culture is reproduced in the values of inner-city males and in
the prison system in which a significant proportion come to reside at some
time in their lives. Since it is unlikely that American society as a whole is
going to change in the near future, the reduction of prison violence may be
limited to changes in policy that affect both whom we send to prison and
what we do with them once they are there.

MINIMIZING THE EFFECTS
OF STRUCTURAL INEQUALITY
ON PRISON VIOLENCE

Most assaults occur in maximum security penitentiaries, which house those who have committed the most violent crimes on the outside (Light, 1991:246). But it is not necessarily the most violent prior to incarceration who are the most violent while in prison. Although some studies suggest that those who have engaged in pre-incarceration violence tend to commit assaults while in prison (Skelton, 1969; Flanagan, 1983; Gaes and McGuire, 1985), others have found no association between preimprisonment violence and the likelihood of such violence while incarcerated (Adams, 1977; Cox, Paulus, and McCain, 1984).

Light (1990) explains these contrasting results by showing that it is the characteristics of the prisons themselves, which he calls *context effects*, that determine the level of violence in prison. Thus, maximum security prisons are more violent than minimum security prisons because they house more violent men, but the amount and severity of the violence in each prison will depend on characteristics such as the age composition of the inmates, the racial composition of officer and inmate populations, and so on. This is important because it shows that prison violence can be reduced by changing the way prisons are run (see DiIulio, 1989:129–130).

Light illustrates this point by showing that it is not necessarily younger prisoners who are more violent than older prisoners. But when younger prisoners are housed together, a more violent environmental context is created by the aggressive social norms associated with youth (Light, 1990:282). Officers, too, may expect younger inmates to be more rebellious in such an environment. For this reason, Light recommends that prisons distribute younger prisoners throughout the prison system rather than concentrating them in one location.

Similar responses to gang-related racial and ethnic violence has been a two-edged sword. Prison officials in California, Illinois, and Texas have isolated members of prison gangs by placing them in separate institutions (Irwin, 1980:190; National Institute of Corrections, 1991:10). But this practice serves to further legitimate and define those gangs. Although it is not possible for prison officials to ameliorate the racial and ethnic divisions of the wider society that create problems within the prison system, it may be possible to prevent and control the development of gang activity that is the source of much of the violence that occurs.

As a general rule, prevention of the formation of gangs should be a major concern for prison administrators. This may be accomplished by making it difficult for one group to monopolize valuable prison resources. One practice that appears to be employed in some prisons to alleviate racial tensions is to promote racial balance within the institution as a whole and within units in the institution (see Earley, 1992:46).[1] The purpose is to prevent one group from dominating another. This may be difficult to achieve in many maximum security state prisons where minority populations constitute a large majority. This practice also increases the risk of misclassifying prisoners in order to achieve racial balance.

MINIMIZING THE EFFECTS
OF FRONTIER VALUES
ON PRISON VIOLENCE

Long-term incarceration prevents habitual and dangerous offenders from committing crimes against society, at least while incarcerated. But it also increases the level of violence in society by reinforcing the frontier values needed to survive in a hostile world. More than 90 percent of those who are incarcerated are eventually released to society, often more dangerous than when they went in. Moreover, incarceration as state violence plays an important symbolic role in legitimating aggressive, "get tough" approaches to problem solving in general.

Although studies of the death penalty have had mixed results, Bowers and Pierce (1980) found that increases in homicides followed the use of the death penalty in New York State from 1907 through 1963. In their reanalysis of Ehrlich's (1975) study of the deterrent effect of capital punishment in the United States, Bowers and Pierce (1980; also see Bowers, 1984:303–335) also found that executions by the state, "legal homicide," harden public attitudes toward violence, leading to increases in the homicide rate. Several studies (Phillips, 1980; McFarland, 1983; Bailey and Peterson, 1989) have found short-term deterrence effects for well-publicized executions, but these effects disappear in the long run. Not only have studies comparing states with and without the death penalty revealed an absence of a deterrent effect, their findings are consistent with quite the opposite conclusion, that "abolitionist" states tend to have lower homicide rates than "retentionist" states (Bowers and Pierce, 1980:461). Today, Texas ranks first in the United States in total number of executions, although Louisiana ranks first on a per capita basis (Verhovek, 1993:6E). At the same time, Louisiana and Texas ranked first and second—16.9 and 15.3 per 100,000, respectively—in their homicide rates in 1991, both well above the national average of 9.8 (Federal Bureau of Investigation, 1992:13, 71, 76). The United States is the only Western democracy that has retained the death penalty, yet it has the highest homicide rate in the modern industrial world.

This adverse effect of the death penalty on homicide rates has been called the *brutalization effect* (Bowers and Pierce, 1980). The state's use of coercion plays an important symbolic role in society. By legitimating the use of violence to solve problems, whether through the death penalty or the "living death" that long-term incarceration involves, citizens become hardened to the use of violence to settle disputes in everyday life. They also become hardened to the realities of prison life.

Certainly, civilizing the American state would go a long way to civilizing the society as a whole. And a first step would be to abolish the death penalty. Justice Sandra Day O'Connor's majority opinion in *Hudson v. McMillian* (1992), the case that prohibits prison guards from using excessive force on prisoners, provides a clue to the future debate on the nature of punishment. For Justice O'Connor, "The Eighth Amendment's prohibition of cruel and unusual punishments 'draw[s] its meaning from the evolving standards of decency that mark the progress of a maturing society,' and so admits of few absolute limitations" (*Hudson v. McMillian*, 1992, citing *Rhodes v. Chapman*, 1981, and quoting *Trop v. Dulles*, 1958). What might have been permissible in the past may not be so in the future.

Another essential change in governmental policy that would play an important role in delegitimating violent responses to the solving of problems would be to begin to regulate gun possession, especially handguns, which are used both defensively and offensively in interpersonal conflicts and crimes (see Wright, Rossi, and Daly, 1983:154–174; Silberman, 1984:13; Kleck, 1991:41–45,101–152).[2] The evidence is mixed regarding the effectiveness of gun control legislation on the immediate reduction in the possession of guns (see Wright, Rossi, and Daly, 1983:273–309, for a review of the research). But it is instructive to compare American society with another, similar society with strict gun control laws, Canada. In Canada handguns are rarely available to those who do not have a legitimate need for them, and the homicide rate is especially low. Only 3 percent of Canadian households own handguns as compared with 24 percent of American households (Bilski, 1989:37). Moreover, legitimate owners of handguns and their Canadian representatives, the Shooting Federation of Canada (the Canadian equivalent of the National Rifle Association, the pro-gun lobby in the U.S.), have little difficulty with the strict gun laws in Canada (Bilski, 1989:37). Strict enforcement of gun control laws has made Canada a safer place, but it also generates more civilized attitudes toward violence. The same survey showed that Canadians viewed themselves as less aggressive and more tolerant than Americans.

Another way to reduce prison violence directly and at the same time contribute to the civilizing of both society and the prison system would be to eliminate overcrowding in prisons. Over the past twenty years or so, we have quadrupled the number of people in prison, creating what the courts have determined to be impermissible conditions in most state prison systems. A more sensible policy should restrict long-term incarceration to the most dangerous offenders and rely on community-based alternatives such as intensive probation for those who can benefit from such experiences.

Again, we can reduce the amount of state violence by reducing the extent and severity of criminal punishment, without losing the important symbolic role that punishment serves. Punishment serves an important deterrent function, but it is the certainty of punishment rather than its severity that plays a critical role for most crimes (Silberman, 1976). It is important to keep prisoners in contact with community life and the normative social controls this represents, so they are not subject exclusively to the coercive controls inherent in the prison system. The loss of contact with family and friends is strongly associated with commitment to the convict code and the violence associated with it (Silberman, 1992).

To accomplish the above purpose, we should use the *least restrictive environment* necessary to accomplish the goals of incarceration (see American Correctional Association, 1987:vii–viii; DiIulio, 1990:8). For example, the courts have recognized the necessity of solitary confinement to protect the general prison population or the prisoner himself, for the purpose of discipline, or to prevent escape (Krantz, 1988:193). But the U.S. Supreme Court has approved limitations on the use of solitary both in terms of duration and inhumane conditions (*Hutto v. Finney*, 1978). Moreover, some legal scholars have suggested that solitary confinement should only be used when no other means are available to accomplish the same purpose (Krantz, 1988:192). Prison sentences should be shorter for most prisoners, and longer for the most violent few. And more prisoners should be placed in community-based programs. Maximum security prisons should be relocated in the cities where most convicts live rather than in remote rural areas, enabling them to remain in contact with family and friends.

STAFF–INMATE RELATIONS

The prison is a total institution defined, in part, by the existence of two clearly defined oppositional groups whose interests are in conflict with one another (see McEwen, 1980; Light, 1991; Silberman, 1992). The central focus of this conflict is control over the basic goods and services necessary for the physical and emotional survival of the inmates. As in all total institutions, a subordinate population is subject to the regime of a dominant group that controls its daily routines twenty-four hours a day. Thus, the struggle for control over the "necessities" of life becomes, from the perspective of the inmate, a struggle over the expression of personal autonomy, resistance to authority, and the creation of informal social control mechanisms.

From the perspective of the correctional officer, the struggle for control of prison life is expressed through the assertion of their authority in ways that limit inmate autonomy, limit any expression of rebelliousness as a threat to that authority, and limit opportunities to control goods and services other than in ways that are officially authorized. For these reasons assaults on officers by inmates nearly always center around this struggle for control over the daily routines of inmates (Light, 1991). Whether planned or spontaneous, inmate assaults on officers occur in response to disputes arising out of attempts by officers to direct the movement of prisoners, inmate resistance to their authority, and attempts by officers to control the distribution of contraband such as drugs, weapons, or food (Light, 1991:255).

At Central prison, the single greatest factor linked to inmate assaultiveness directed at both staff and inmates was institutional alienation or "powerlessness." To the extent that inmates perceive that their fate is in the hands of others, inmates or staff, they are likely to respond, often spontaneously, in assaultive conduct in an attempt to assert some degree of control over their world and themselves. Hostility between staff and inmates is also a major source of assaultiveness in prison. Fellow inmates are an easier target than correctional officers, detection is less frequent, and punishment likely to be less severe. These frustrations are often taken out on someone of a different racial or ethnic background.

Several studies and reports indicate that assaults on officers are most likely to occur when disputes between officers and inmates take on a personal nature. Officers frequently see an inmate's resistance to their authority as a "personal affront" (Lombardo, 1981:91; Light, 1991:259). This, in turn, is likely to affect the way the officer treats an inmate. When the inmate begins to perceive that the officer is taking things "personally" rather than in the more general context of the prison itself, when the officer is perceived to be arbitrary in enforcing rules and distributing the goods of institutional life, the likelihood of a retaliatory action by the inmate increases (Earley, 1992:200).

One solution to the structural tensions in prison is to "empower" inmates in ways that do not create additional management problems for prison administrators. The empowerment process reduces inmate alienation and thus a major source of assaultiveness. In the 1970s, inmate councils not only created opportunities for greater participation in decision making but also an opportunity for inmate groups to enhance their power vis-à-vis the prison administration and in opposition to one another (Engel and Rothman, 1983). Another way to give inmates a greater sense of control over their own fate is to provide them access to the courts.

Access to lawyers has been shown to reduce the assaultiveness of inmates (Alpert, 1978; Silberman, 1991, 1992). Among those who show the most hostility are the so-called "jailhouse lawyers" who are actively pursuing their own legal cases without the assistance of counsel (Silberman, 1992). Although there is the risk that the pursuit of grievances through the courts may create short-term problems for prison administrators, in the long term, the courts have been a source of stability in providing guidance in the management of prisons. A responsive prison administration along with access to the justice system appears to reduce the alienation and assaultiveness of prisoners.

Still another way to reduce tensions in prison is to introduce third-party mediators into the prison setting (Silberman, 1988). Correctional counselors selected for their ability to communicate with inmates can be trained to negotiate and settle specific disputes among inmates. This is possible, of course, only in some sort of unit management system that permits staff to work closely with a small group of inmates.

For disputes concerning fundamental concerns such as rules and regulations, rights of prisoners, and complaints that are systematic in nature, an *ombudsman* can make suggestions concerning changes in policies and practices in the institution or in an entire prison system (see State of Minnesota, 1985). It is important that the ombudsman not have the power to enforce his or her recommendations since this would erode the authority of correctional staff. But the ability to gain objective insights regarding problems before they blow up in someone's face is important. When changes occur in response to inmate concerns, the level of alienation that contributes to hostility and aggression among inmates is reduced.[3] It is essential, too, that the ombudsman not be involved in the settlement of specific disputes.

One of the reasons that escapes and assaults were so infrequent during the rehabilitation era of the 1950s and early 1960s is that there was a level of cooperation between staff and inmates that had not occurred before or since (Irwin, 1980). Many staff members believed that it was possible to treat the emotional sources of criminal conduct. Later, as the civil rights movement began, some officials expressed an understanding of the plight of the poor and minorities, recognizing the need for job training and education in prison that had been unavailable on the outside. Inmates, too, believed that in prison they would receive help with their problems, emotional, social, or economic. In this environment of accommodation, inmates formed "tips and cliques" that were pluralistic in nature, including crime partners of different backgrounds, people with shared interests, and so on. It was always possible to find someone to mediate a dispute because there would be some overlapping group membership shared with both parties (Irwin, 1980:58–60).

Unfortunately, in today's prisons, inmates are so divided on racial and ethnic lines, you can only trust your "homeys." There are few opportunities for compromise and conciliation. Mediation works best when disputing parties share some common values and interests. It is the responsibility of the mediator to identify these common interests and provide a basis for negotiation. In prison, one such common basis is the fact of inmate status itself. To some degree this may be threatening to staff since effective mediation may promote greater inmate solidarity. But this is precisely why it should work to reduce alienation and assaultiveness by empowering inmates in ways that do not necessarily interfere with official authority. In fact, the most effective strategy on the part of prison administrators may be to select and train inmates in mediation techniques that promote the peaceful settlement of disputes. Correctional counselors at Central were especially effective mediators. Selected from among correctional officers who demonstrate an ability to get along with inmates without compromising their authority, correctional counselors are themselves natural mediators who could be used to identify, train, and monitor inmate mediators.

One of the major sources of tension in prison is created by changes in policies and procedures, which produce uncertainty regarding the interpretation and enforcement of rules and regulation. Certainly a high turnover rate among correctional officers is a source of potential staff–inmate conflict. Many prisons, including Central, rely on the rotation of guards from one post to another every three months or so. This is designed to prevent the corruption of authority that Sykes (1958:52–58) described at a maximum security prison in New Jersey in the 1950s. But this can also create uncertainty as a new cell block officer proceeds differently from the old one. One solution to this problem is to assign at least one officer on a fixed basis to one cell block. This officer should be selected because of his or her ability to get along with inmates without losing authority. Corruption is avoided because there are always new officers on the block, and arbitrariness is avoided because the nonrotating officer can act as an arbiter when necessary. This was the practice at Central where correctional counselors were assigned on a permanent basis to specific cell blocks or dormitory units.

Critical to avoidance of staff–inmate tensions that can erupt in violence is the fair and just enforcement of the rules and regulations and allocation of the goods and services of the institution. One reason why Central had a low incidence of assaults was that there was no evidence of bias in the enforcement of the regulations in any of the official disciplinary procedures. An examination of several years' worth of records indicated that, once charged with an offense, offenders were treated equally regardless of who they were. Although it was true, as many inmates claim, that the presumption of guilt was the operating norm—few inmates were found not guilty—it was also true that they were rarely, if ever, falsely accused by staff members. The most serious questions might arise when another inmate might have planted a weapon or contraband in the accused's belongings. But the staff were generally sensitive to such charges and made a good faith effort to determine whether they were credible.

Some Caveats Concerning the Empowerment of Prisoners

During the 1970s, in an attempt to appease prisoners' rights advocates' demand for "democratizing" the prison system, several prison systems introduced representative inmate councils. The New York State prison system did this in the wake of the Attica riot.[4] Although well intended, it appears that these councils contributed to the erosion of administrative controls and to the creation of the power vacuum that led to the evolution of prison gangs and racial strife. What reformers failed to recognize is that factional leadership would gain control over the inmate councils, creating a vehicle for further disputes and fragmentation of the prison population (Engel and Rothman, 1983). Carroll (1974:204–205) describes how white and black groups vied for control over the inmate council in a maximum security prison.

Whether there are well-organized prison gangs or not, the tendency to fragment along racial and ethnic lines is a given in today's prisons. At Central, social programs promoting public speaking, religious fellowship, community service, and cultural awareness were available to inmates to encourage self-expression and a sense of purpose. These sorts of programs, in principle, empower inmates in ways that do not conflict with prison authority. Nevertheless, there was a tendency for group membership here, too, to fragment along racial lines. Some groups were predominantly white or black, with token membership from the other group. Still another, a community service–oriented group, was fully integrated at the time of the study. On occasion, different factions within racial groups would try to dominate one of the social groups. The fact that these groups had to share resources—meeting rooms—created the need for some level of cooperation among inmates of different backgrounds. Prison staff continually monitored the group dynamics, a difficult process that required a good deal of skill. Hispanic prisoners were few in number and poorly organized and so were underrepresented in all the groups.

Another pitfall to avoid is the delegation to inmate leadership responsibility for the control of the distribution of the goods and services of the institution or discipline. This is the sort of situation that led to the abuses in the Arkansas and Texas prison systems in which trusties became all powerful. While the delegation of disciplinary authority to prisoners is clearly unconstitutional, the delegation of other responsibilities has been espoused in a number of settings. Advocates of the therapeutic community model, both in and out of prison, argue that inmates can only learn responsibility by being given the opportunity to express that responsibility. This may work in community-based settings where the line between staff and inmates is permeable, but such an approach in the prison world can only lead to disaster. As in the case of inmate councils, informal control mechanisms are likely to coopt the official distribution system, favoring inmate leadership and fostering racial strife over competition for control of scarce resources.

INMATE–INMATE RELATIONS

The current state of affairs in prison has left a fragmented inmate population competing for control over scarce resources. During the 1970s and early '80s, many prison officials lost control of the internal day-to-day management of the inmate population, leading to the development of prison gangs organized along racial and ethnic lines. The reasons for this loss of control are described in the preceding chapters. In the worst-case scenarios, correctional officers would consider certain cell blocks to be "no man's land" and essentially let them govern themselves.

At Central, prison gangs never developed because of the unit management system that was introduced in the mid-1970s in response to an increase in assaults and homicides and perceived racial tensions. To the extent that there are gang members present, they are often transfers from other institutions. Most of the gang members at Central were marginal at best, and many were in trouble with core members at other institutions. Although race and ethnicity was the basis of group affiliation and identification here as elsewhere, these groups did not evolve into prison gangs. Unlike prisoners elsewhere, inmates at Central do not report doing "gang time," but instead they "do [their] own time."

The unit management system is effective at reducing the level of violence for two reasons. First, case managers and correctional counselors are assigned to a cell block or dormitory unit for which they are responsible. In this way, they get to know the inmates, and the inmates get to know them. Thus, the depersonalization that comes from a more centralized management of prisoners is avoided. In other words, decentralized control structures are more effective at maintaining order. From the inmates' perspective, this is a more humane system in which their individual needs and concerns are more likely to be listened to. Disputes are less likely to arise because officers are able to gain compliance without having to resort to invoking their authority. Because someone is likely to know the inmate by name and can respond to him as an individual rather than as a number, problems of personal autonomy are less problematic. This does not imply that the prisoner always gets what he wants, but it does provide the opportunity for officers to explain their actions and for inmates to understand the constraints that affect inmate and officer alike. Officers and inmates do not become "friends," but it is interesting to observe the "friendliness" that can emerge out of such relations. Finally, oppositional inmate group structures are less likely to emerge.

Second, the unit management system is effective in reducing the level of violence when it relies on a classification system designed to separate aggressive from nonaggressive prisoners. The AIMS typology used at Central is effective in doing so. As we have seen, those who have histories of violence both inside and outside prison are labeled as "heavies" and placed in maximum security cell blocks. Heavies are likely to identify themselves as convicts and adhere to the convict code. Since gang structures emerge in situations where powerful inmates are able to exploit weaker inmates, the removal of potential leaders from the general prison population in advance of gang formation has been effective in preventing the sort of competitive structures that lead to high rates of violence. This sort of preventive strategy is far more effective and humane than the sort of approach used elsewhere to break up gang structures that have already formed by placing leaders in "maxi-maxi" segregation units or special prisons where inmates are locked up in small cells twenty-four hours a day, except for brief periods for showers, exercise, and to see visitors, "if they have any" (Pedersen, Shapiro, and McDaniel, 1988:261; CNN Morning News, 1993).

There is a risk of making false positive judgments regarding the dangerousness of prisoners in any classification system, including the AIMS typology. To meet the security needs of an institution, this risk is inevitable. It is better to be safe than sorry, from this perspective, in falsely identifying someone as dangerous who is not, than to let a dangerous person into the general population. At Central prison heavies are not, after all, in solitary confinement. They are housed in cell blocks, separated as much as possible from other prisoners, and monitored more closely by staff. Once someone who has been labeled as a heavy has demonstrated some responsibility, he may be housed in a more general area with other inmates who work in the prison factory.

But it is inevitable that whatever biases are built into the way we make judgments in our society, and race has historically been such a bias, that false positives concerning aggressiveness are likely to affect racial minorities, especially blacks, more than others. Because of the neighborhoods they live in, poor employment histories that reflect communities without an industrial base, and resulting unstable families, blacks are more likely to acquire criminal records at each stage of the criminal process. To the extent that the accumulation of a record of criminal convictions affects the labeling of prisoners once incarcerated, blacks are likely to be labeled as aggressive. The paradox is that it appears to be the *objective* nature of classification systems that reproduces societal biases by taking into account background factors and conviction records that reflect these biases.[5]

It would be a mistake to eliminate the unit management system or a classification system like the AIMS typology. This would be like throwing the baby out with the bath water. These systems are an effective means for reducing violence and creating a safer, more humane environment. But it is essential that prison administrators be sensitive to the ways in which the classification systems they use have built-in racial or other biases. With attention paid to eliminating those biases, a major source of tension and conflict can be eliminated. For example, employment history and family ties, factors used to predict aggressiveness, are likely to affect blacks more than whites. Yet the research findings on the effects of these factors are equivocal when it comes to predicting violence. The use of extralegal factors in the classification system should be avoided. On the other hand, evidence of violence in and out of prison should be taken into account. The use of multiracial panels should also be considered in both the construction and implementation of classification systems to avoid the appearance of bias in the assignment of institutional labels.

FOCUS ON THE LABELING PROCESS

The principal assumption of labeling theory is that the way in which society treats a person shapes who and what he or she becomes. Studies of adult criminality do not support the notion that punishment per se makes people more criminal, but there have been few systematic studies of the effects of long-term incarceration on the personality of the individual. There is a growing body of evidence that the societal reaction to juvenile delinquency does shape the delinquent identity and subsequent behavior of the adolescent (Harris, 1975; Farrington, 1977; Klemke, 1978; Horwitz and Wasserman, 1979; Bazemore, 1985; Ray and Down, 1986; Klein, 1986). Adolescence is a time of seeking and searching for one's place in the world. It is a time of uncertainty and vulnerability to defining experiences of all kinds. Thus, it is not surprising that juveniles, but not adults, are affected by involvement in the criminal justice system. For the most part, it appears that short-term incarceration for adults creates short-term changes in behavior, but in the long term, most adults return to their "suspended" preprison identities (Schmid and Jones, 1991).

Anecdotally, we know that many prison experiences are traumatic and transforming in nature. Being raped, or for that matter, participating in the rape of another, has a permanent effect on the way one views the world or oneself. Prisoners often describe the transforming experience that being a convict has on their view of life and themselves. Just as the POW undergoes a fundamental change in his personality while isolated from friends and family, so do long-term convicts whose isolation from conventional society makes the world of violence in prison the only world they know. From this experience, there develops the convict's view of the world that legitimates the violence pervading the American prison in the 1990s. People change under coercive regimes.

There are two distinct processes going on here. The first is tied directly to long-term incarceration itself. By isolating individuals from friends and family over a long period of time, the self-validation of old ways of being is gradually eroded. Increasingly one becomes dependent for one's very sense of reality on those with whom one interacts daily, monthly, yearly. Correctional officers become a source of hostility, alliances with fellow convicts become essential to survival, and rationalizations develop to "neutralize" one's values. These rationalizations may be supported by existing religious or political ideologies, which contribute to racial tensions in the prison population. Or one may join a prison gang—for life. Again, this is a more or less permanent commitment to a lifestyle generated in prison and taken onto the street once released.

The second process reflects a more narrow reaction to specific punishments received. The fact of labeling, whether through classification or the result of a disciplinary hearing, punishes the person by restricting his liberty in some form or other. Coupled with these restrictions is added surveillance, increasing the probability of detection and further sanctioning. This deviance amplification process reinforces a cycle of crime and punishment that furthers the individual's commitment to deviant lines of activity. Studies of adult criminality in the past may have failed to demonstrate a labeling effect because they asked the wrong question. For today's convicted criminal, the fact of conviction is less likely to have a transforming experience than the length and type of punishment he receives. Committed to the convict code, the contemporary prisoner comes to see himself as a "convict," characterized by his hatred for established authority, in or out of prison, and adapted to a violent lifestyle.

In order to minimize the deleterious effect of long-term incarceration, we must maintain the social integration of inmates by keeping them as close to their home communities as possible. We must also retain as many social (nonlegal) controls as possible on the behavior of inmates. By being close to their home communities, inmates can benefit from continuing contact with community leaders such as local ministers and teachers, among others. Where possible, work release and study release programs should be established. But this is only likely to occur if we incarcerate at a level that is rationally tied to effective penal policy and use short-term and community-based punishments more frequently. The deleterious effects of the labeling process may be unavoidable for those for whom long-term incarceration is still deemed necessary, the repeat violent offender and those who have engaged in the most destructive behavior. Moreover, by isolating the most dangerous prisoners from both society and other inmates, the increased surveillance may amplify their deviance as well. But this is a small percentage of the total number of those in prison today. Labeling effects may be impossible to avoid, but they should be restricted to a smaller proportion of those presently incarcerated.

PROFESSIONALIZING THE PRISON

In the past, the federal prison system has taken the lead in defining professional standards in corrections, both in anticipation of and in response to
court decisions (see U.S. Department of Justice, 1978:9, 14). This has been
especially true in the development of unit management as a control strategy
designed to prevent problems before they arise (see especially Toch, 1992).
In 1980, the U.S. Department of Justice (1981:preamble) responded to the
American Correctional Association's accreditation commission by establishing standards for federal prisons designed to promote "decent, humane and
safe prisons," further asserting that the federal Bureau of Prisons has "served
as a model for many state and local correctional agencies." Moreover, this
leadership has continued more recently in defining limits on the abuse of
authority by correctional officers. (See Chapter 6, p. 115.)

There have been two significant changes affecting the level of professionalism in prison administration over the past decade. The first has been
the development of rational procedures for the maintenance of security in
institutions. In 1982, federal correctional officers at Leavenworth penitentiary and military police officers at Fort Leavenworth began to cross-train
in disturbance control tactics employing more sophisticated techniques for
securing disruptive inmates and restoring order during disturbances (Federal
Prison System, 1992:1). This gave rise to the first SORT (Strategic Operations Response Team) teams. Following strict guidelines, and where possible
under routine conditions monitored by videocamera, each operation becomes a rational act based on a rational plan. Training of these officers at first
focused on physical fitness and tactics. More recently, SORT officers are
subject to annual written testing on procedures and undergo practical training in "disturbance control, building entry techniques, and various other
training maneuvers to enhance skills" (Federal Prison System, 1992:2).
Throughout this period SORT teams have participated in annual athletic
competitions, at first with local SWAT teams and later, prior to the establishment of mandatory SORT teams in all federal medium and maximum
security prisons in 1989, with other Bureau of Prisons SORT teams.

In the late 1980s, the National Institute of Corrections (1987:189–190)
established guidelines for state correctional Emergency Response Teams
similar to those for federal SORT teams. Although the Texas prison system
introduced the SORT concept under Procunier's reform administration in
1984, there is little evidence that these principles have been adopted on a
widespread basis. ERT units often enter into situations for which they have
not been specifically prepared or trained. Because they work together
closely and because they trust one another, they believe that they work well

together in emergency situations. But there appears to be little dissemination of the SORT concept in the early 1990s.

From an organizational perspective, we can see the increasing rationalism of the federal correctional bureaucracy, integrating prison administration as part of the wider rational-legal bureaucracy of the American governmental system. A symbol of the bureaucratization of the federal correctional system is the relatively large number of administrative personnel compared with the number of correctional officers working directly with prisoners. There is roughly one federal administrator for every seven or eight correctional officers, whereas there is one state administrator for every 25 correctional officers (see Bureau of Justice Statistics, 1992:61). In the current political climate, with concerns about the high cost of government, some might argue that this is typical government waste. But the management of a complex people-processing system requires the sort of administrative hierarchy that promotes the close supervision of line personnel. This cannot be done effectively when there are too few administrators responsible for the monitoring of the professional conduct of its employees.

The federal prison system also commits more of its resources to professional and technical support for its correctional officers than do the states (on average). This, too, requires the sort of coordination and administration that promotes bureaucracy in its best sense, an administration whose authority is "rational-legal" in nature. In 1990 (Bureau of Justice Statistics, 1992:61), the federal prison system had over 10,000 noncustodial employees, substantially more than the 7,055 correctional officers in the system. State prisons employed 162,532 correctional officers, which was more than double the 76,776 noncustodial employees in the state prisons. Professional and technical support alone constituted 27.3 percent of federal prison employees compared with only 12.0 percent of state corrections workers.

The second major development has been the increased willingness of the courts to intervene directly in defining the parameters of legality in prison administration. Because the initial intervention by the courts in the late '60s and early '70s, which ended the "hands-off" doctrine, defined what prison officials may *not* do rather than what they *must* do, a power vacuum occurred in prison administration that led to increased conflict and violence within prisons. Once prison administrators began to recognize that there was a new legalistic era in which the courts were willing to define the boundaries of acceptable prison policy, some administrators, especially those in the federal system, began to respond (see DiIulio, 1990:11).

The details of this transformation are spelled out in Chapter 6. But it is the *Hudson v. McMillian* case in 1992 that is a watershed here. An amicus brief was written on behalf of an inmate by Americans for Effective Law

Enforcement (1991), a group that usually defends officers against "frivolous suits filed by often bored and frequently malicious inmates" (1991:3). As an organization dedicated to the professional use of force by police and correctional officers, they distinguish between shoves and slaps, minor acts not intended to do serious harm but may be part of what is reasonably necessary to maintain order in prison, and unnecessary violence used to punish. It is the use of unregulated, unreasonable force to punish prisoners outside the rule of law to which this organization objects.

Similarly, the U.S. Department of Justice (1991) wrote an amicus brief on behalf of inmate Hudson stating that he was beaten "unnecessarily and wantonly" by Louisiana state correctional officers (1991:14). The central issue addressed by the Justice Department brief was that no matter how "insignificant" the injuries (Hudson did not require medical attention), beating a prisoner to teach him a lesson is cruel and unusual punishment and violates the Eighth Amendment (1991:1). The brief further states that "the United States has a general interest in ensuring that the law regarding violent conduct by law enforcement officials adequately protects the rights of citizens while taking into account the legitimate concerns of law enforcement officials" (1991:2). Moreover, the Justice Department has prosecuted state prison guards for similar conduct in the past. It is evident that the courts have stimulated self-examination among prison administrators regarding the parameters of the use of force. With the assistance of the courts, prison administrators are beginning to define these limits in a way that is consistent with effective management.

Because the above two developments promote the fair and effective use of force in the maintenance of order in prisons, and because these developments are consistent with the rational-legal bureaucracy that defines the democratic order of the United States generally, it is fair to describe the new era in corrections that is emerging in the 1990s as *legalistic* in nature. A consequence of this legalistic regime is the expectation that those who work within the system are as competent and professionally trained as possible. A manifestation of this new professionalism is the clear expectation for accountability through testing, competition, and monitoring.

CONCLUSION

This chapter has suggested a number of reforms necessary to reduce violence in the American prison. Some of these involve changes in society as whole. Greater economic and racial justice would go a long way toward solving both the crime problem and the prison problem. We must also consider civilizing the cultural values of American society by creating alternatives to the frontier traditions that promote violence in a number of contexts. This can be accomplished by promoting nonviolent approaches to settling disputes in everyday life at home, in school, and on the streets. But these are unlikely to occur in the short term, and something must be done now to deal with the potentially explosive conditions in American prisons.

Changes in sentencing policies rationally designed to promote more effective law enforcement and crime control are desirable. We need penal policies that are the least restrictive necessary to accomplish the goals of law enforcement and public safety. This means that fewer individuals need be placed in maximum security prisons, especially when their crimes are nonviolent or they are first offenders. Again, these changes are in the hands of politicians and not prison administrators. The real risks here are that community-based alternatives will not be treated as true alternatives but as devices for expanding the net of social (state) control, as in the past. Only when the prison population is significantly reduced as these alternatives are used will there be evidence that we are moving in the right direction.

It is certainly possible for prison administrators to pay greater attention to the deleterious effects of internal procedures that may exacerbate problems. Unit management is one of the most effective ways to prevent gang formation and reduce the alienation of inmates. The classification and separation of the more dangerous prisoners from others is an excellent goal, but it must be done in a way that is sensitive to the cultural diversity that exists in the inmate population. Ombudsmen and mediators will contribute to the empowerment of inmates and their reduced alienation but must not become vehicles for increased inmate–staff strife. There is always the risk that conflicts between two fundamentally different interest groups will be made worse. By relying on third parties, themselves representative of legitimate authority or part of the authority structure itself as in the case of correctional counselors, the needs of inmates can be met without threatening the authority of staff.

As in any reform, professionalism in bureaucratic settings could be taken to such extremes that it hampers effectiveness. The need for monitoring of use-of-force situations should not lead to paralysis, which is possible should each minor variation from accepted procedures lead to disciplinary action. On the other hand, it should always be possible to discipline officers who act in ways that violate an inmate's constitutional rights. The principal focus of professionalism should be on education regarding standards and expectations and training in specific use-of-force situations so that force will be employed in a rational and predictable manner.

NOTES

1. Some of the inmates in the study of Central prison claimed that this was also the case at Central. The proportion of blacks and whites who were maximum custody and maximum security were, in fact, similar (the differences were not statistically significant). This could also be taken as evidence of a nondiscriminatory policy whereby prisoners with histories of violence are placed in this maximum security prison regardless of racial background.

2. Kleck's research suggests that guns are frequently used successfully by victims or potential victims in self-defense or to prevent crime. One of the reasons that Americans find it necessary to defend themselves using handguns is because of the availability of handguns to those who use them to commit crimes. In prison, inmates say that they need weapons—shanks, or homemade knives—because other inmates have them and so they need them in self-defense. When the opportunity to possess a weapon is reduced through metal detectors and effective shakedowns, the need to possess a weapon for self-defense is reduced.

3. Interview and correspondence with a former Hawaii state prison adminstrator.

4. Interviews with a New York state official.

5. The AIMS classification system relies on both objective life history and subjective correctional adjustment criteria when classifying prisoners as aggressive. The latter does not appear to be a source of bias in the labeling process, as experienced personnel classified hard-core convicts at Central as aggressive regardless of their racial background.

REFERENCES

Adams, Thomas C. (1977). "Characteristics of State Prisoners Who Demonstrate Severe Adjustment Problems," *Journal of Clinical Psychology* 33:1100–1103.

Alpert, Geoffrey P. (1978). *The Legal Rights of Prisoners*. Lexington, MA: Lexington Books.

American Correctional Association (1987). *Guidelines for the Development of a Security Program*. Washington, DC: U.S. Department of Justice (National Institute of Corrections).

Americans for Effective Law Enforcement (1991). *Amicus Curiae, Hudson v. McMillian,* October Term No. 90-6531.

Bailey, William C. and Ruth D. Peterson (1989). "Murder and Capital Punishment: A Monthly Time-Series Analysis of Execution Publicity," *American Sociological Review* 54:722–743.

Bazemore, Gordon (1985). "Delinquent Reform and the Labeling Perspective," *Criminal Justice and Behavior* 12:131–169.

Bilski, Andrew (1989). "Portrait of Two Nations," *Maclean's,* July 3:36–51.

Bowers, William J. (1984). *Legal Homicide: Death as Punishment in America, 1864–1982*. Boston, MA: Northeastern University Press.

Bowers, William J. and Glenn L. Pierce (1980). "Deterrence or Brutalization: What Is the Effect of Executions?" *Crime and Delinquency* 26:453–484.

Bureau of Justice Statistics (1992). *Census of State and Federal Correctional Facilities, 1990.* Washington, DC: U.S. Government Printing Office.

Carroll, Leo (1974). *Hacks, Blacks, and Cons: Race Relations in a Maximum Security Prison.* Prospect Heights, IL: Waveland Press.

CNN Morning News (1993). "Class Action Filed Against Pelican Bay State Prison," August 16: Transcript #385, Segment #1.

Cox, Verne C., Paul B. Paulus, and Garvin McCain (1984). "Prison Crowding Research: The Relevance for Prison Housing Standards and a General Approach to Crowding Phenomena," *American Psychologist* 39:1148–1160.

DiIulio, John J., Jr. (1989). "Recovering the Public Management Variable: Lessons from Schools, Prisons, and Armies," *Public Administration Review* 48:127-133.

DiIulio, John J., Jr. (1990). "Prisons That Work," *Federal Prisons Journal* 1 (4):7–15.

Earley, Pete (1992). *The Hot House: Life Inside Leavenworth Prison.* New York: Bantam Books.

Ehrlich, Isaac (1975). "The Deterrent Effect of Capital Punishment: A Question of Life and Death," *American Economic Review* 65:397–417.

Engel, Kathleen and Stanley Rothman (1983). "Prison Violence and the Paradox of Reform," *The Public Interest* 73:91–105.

Farrington, David P. (1977). "The Effects of Public Labeling," *British Journal of Criminology* 17:112–125.

Federal Bureau of Investigation (1992). *Crime in United States–1991.* Washington, DC: U.S. Government Printing Office.

Federal Prison System (1992). "A Short History of SORT's," *Monday Morning Highlights,* May 18:1–2.

Flanagan, Timothy J. (1983). "Correlates of Institutional Misconduct Among State Prisoners," *Criminology* 21:29–39.

Gaes, Gerald G. and William J. McGuire (1985). "Prison Violence: The Contribution of Crowding Versus Other Determinants of Prison Assault Rates," *Journal of Research in Crime and Delinquency* 22:41–65.

Harris, Anthony R. (1975). "Imprisonment and the Expected Value of Criminal Choice: A Specification and Test of Aspects of the Labeling Perspective," *American Sociological Review* 40:71–87.

Horwitz, Allan and M. Wasserman (1979). "The Effect of Social Control on Delinquent Behavior," *Sociological Focus* 12:53–70.

Irwin, John (1980). *Prisons in Turmoil.* Boston, MA: Little, Brown.

Kleck, Gary (1991). *Point Blank: Guns and Violence in America.* New York: Aldine de Gruyter.

Klein, Malcolm W. (1986). "Labeling Theory and Delinquency Policy," *Criminal Justice and Behavior* 13:47–79.

Klemke, Lloyd W. (1978). "Does Apprehension for Shoplifting Amplify or Terminate Shoplifting Activity?" *Law and Society Review* 12:391–403.

Krantz, Sheldon (1988). *The Law of Corrections and Prisoners' Rights in a Nutshell* (3rd ed.). St. Paul, MN: West Publishing.

Light, Stephen C. (1990). "The Severity of Assaults on Prison Officers: A Contextual Study," *Social Science Quarterly* 71:267–284.

Light, Stephen C. (1991). "Assaults on Prison Officers: Interactional

Themes," *Justice Quarterly* 8:243–261.

Lombardo, Lucien X. (1981). *Guards Imprisoned: Correctional Officers at Work*. New York: Elsevier.

McEwen, C. A. (1980). "Continuities in the Study of Total and Nontotal Institutions," *Annual Review of Sociology* 6:143–185.

McFarland, Sam G. (1983). "Is Capital Punishment a Short-Term Deterrent to Homicide? A Study of the Effects of Four Recent American Executions," *Journal of Criminal Law and Criminology* 74:1014–1032.

National Institute of Corrections (1987). *Guidelines for the Development of a Security Program*. Washington, DC: U.S. Government Printing Office.

National Institute of Corrections (1991). *Management Strategies in Disturbances and with Gangs/Disruptive Groups*. Washington, DC: U.S. Government Printing Office.

Pedersen, Daniel, Daniel Shapiro, and Ann McDaniel (1988). "Inside America's Toughest Prison." Pp. 246–266 in *Order Under Law: Readings in Criminal Justice* (3rd ed.), edited by R. G. Culbertson and R. Weisheit. Prospect Heights, IL: Waveland Press.

Phillips, David P. (1980). "The Deterrent Effect of Capital Punishment: New Evidence on an Old Controversy," *American Journal of Sociology* 86:139–148.

Ray, Melvin C. and William R. Down (1986). "An Empirical Test of Labeling Theory Using Longitudinal Data," *Journal of Research in Crime and Delinquency* 23:169–194.

Schmid, Thomas J. and Richard S. Jones (1991). "Suspended Identity: Identity Transformation in a Maximum

Security Prison," *Symbolic Interaction* 14:415–432.

Silberman, Matthew (1976). "Toward a Theory of Criminal Deterrence," *American Sociological Review* 41:442–461.

Silberman, Matthew (1984). "Guns Don't Kill, People Kill," *Legal Studies Forum* 8:481–486.

Silberman, Matthew (1988). "Dispute Mediation in the American Prison: A New Approach to the Reduction of Violence," *Policy Studies Journal* 16:522–532.

Silberman, Matthew (1991). "Dispute Resolution in a Maximum Security Penitentiary." Pp. 104–120 in *Alternative Dispute Resolution in the Public Sector*, edited by Miriam K. Mills. Chicago, IL: Nelson-Hall.

Silberman, Matthew (1992). "Violence as Social Control in Prison." Pp. 77–97 in *Law and Conflict Management* (*Virginia Review of Sociology*, Vol. 1), edited by James Tucker. Greenwich, CT: JAI Press.

Skelton, W. Douglas (1969). "Prison Riot: Assaulters and Defenders," *Archives of General Psychiatry* 21:359–362.

State of Minnesota (1985). "Ombudsman for Corrections." Pp. 420–425 in *Correctional Institutions* (3rd ed.), edited by R. M. Carter, D. Glaser, and L. T. Wilkins. New York: Harper & Row.

Sykes, Gresham M. (1958). *The Society of Captives: A Study of a Maximum Security Prison*. Princeton, NJ: Princeton University Press.

Toch, Hans (1992). "Functional Unit Management," *Federal Prisons Journal* 2:15–19.

U.S. Department of Justice (1978). *Federal Prison System 1978*. Washington, DC: U.S. Department of Justice.

U.S. Department of Justice (1981). *Federal Standards for Prisons and Jails: December 16, 1980.* Washington, DC: U.S. Government Printing Office.

U.S. Department of Justice (1991). *Amicus Curiae, Hudson v. McMillian,* October Term No. 90-6531.

Verhovek, Sam H. (1993). "With Practice, Texas Is the Execution Leader," *New York Times,* September 5:E6.

Wright, James D., Peter H. Rossi, and Kathleen Daly (1983). *Under the Gun: Weapons, Crime, and Violence.* New York: Aldine.

CASES CITED

Hudson v. McMillian, 60 U.S. Law Week 4151 (Feb. 25, 1992).

Hutto v. Finney, 437 U.S. 678 (1978).

Rhodes v. Chapman, 452 U.S. 337 (1981).

Trop v. Dulles, 356 U.S. 86 (1958).

Index

Racism *(continued)*
  and labeling theory, 49,
    93–97, 104n, 105n,
    213–214, 220n
  prison influence on,
    194–196
  and regulation enforce-
    ment, 48–50
  and underclass, 181–182
Ramirez, John, 47, 94, 122
Rap music, 193, 197n
Rashke, Richard, 148
Ray, March B., 156
Ray, Melvin C., 88, 214
Raymond, Alan, 20, 35, 123
Raymond, Susan, 20, 35, 123
Reagan-Bush administrations,
  137
Reasons, Charles E., 118
Recoupling control systems,
  124
Regoli, R. M., 48, 94
Regulating the Poor (Piven and
  Cloward), 188
Rehabilitation philosophy
  demise of, 2, 30–31, 52,
    53, 62–63, 118–119, 131
  emergence of, 43, 62, 117,
    118
  programs, 30–32
Reiss, Albert J., 68
Religion
  and group affiliation, 29,
    45–46, 47
  prisoners' rights, 50–51,
    111, 186–187
  See also Black Muslims
Religious cults, 148
Remafedi, Gary, 57
Research, 4–7, 84
  measurement issues, 6–7,
    12–13n
  sampling issues, 5–6, 12n
  settings, 7–9
Rettig, Salomon, 83
Rhodes v. Chapman, 113, 115,
  116, 205
Ridgeway, James, 195
Ridlon, Florence V., 93
Rioting. *See* Prison distur-
  bances
Roebuck, Julian B., 34

Roles, 86–87
Rossi, Peter H., 66, 67, 70,
  205
Rothman, Stanley, 119, 126,
  208, 210
Rotter, Julian, 83–84, 159
Rucker, Lila, 138
Ruffin v. Commonwealth, 110
Ruiz v. Estelle, 43, 114, 119,
  121, 123, 126
Rusche, Georg, 188

Salholz, Eloise, 192, 197n
Samenow, Stanton E., 52, 101
Sanders, Jimy M., 181
Santa Fe Penitentiary, 63
Saxbe v. Washington Post Co.,
  111
Schein, Edgar H., 148, 169
Schmid, Thomas J., 15, 82,
  89, 214
Schneier, Inge, 169
Schwendinger, Herman, 174,
  176
Schwendinger, Julia R., 174,
  176
Scull, Andrew T., 132, 137
Seed, The, 135
Seeman, Melvin, 83
Self-defense attitudes, 37–38,
  69–70, 194
Self-help philosophy, 64, 68–
  69, 74–75, 134–135
Selltiz, Claire, 7
Senate Judiciary Committee,
  32, 64
Senna, Danzy, 57
Serial killing, 177
Sexual assault
  fear of, 15
  and gender inequality, 174,
    176
  and homicide, 26, 44,
    57–58
  and juvenile justice system,
    134
  and race/ethnicity, 56, 180
  and social control, 73–74
  of staff, 14, 56, 64
Shapiro, Daniel, 20, 122, 126,
  213
Shapp, Milton, 134

Sheinkman, Jack, 176
Sheley, Joseph F., 192, 194
Shinn, Larry D., 169
Silberman, Matthew, 33,
  51, 66, 67, 68, 120,
  126, 205, 206, 207,
  208
Situational aggression, 71–72
Skelton, W. Douglas, 203
Skinner, G. William, 148
Skovron, Sandra Evans, 1, 2,
  113, 114
Slavery, 66
Smith, M. Dwayne, 192, 194
Smith, W. Alan, 90, 125
Smothers, Ronald, 64
Snitching, 33–34, 63, 152
Social control
  and antidrug crusade, 190–
    192
  "Big House" era philoso-
    phy, 2, 61–62, 64, 117,
    142
  and community-based
    corrections, 137–138
  and compliance theory,
    81–83
  and law, 72–73
  regulation of labor,
    188–190
  and sexual assault, 73–74
  symbols of, 23–24
  See also Convict code
Social inequality, 173–184
  culture of poverty thesis,
    181
  and economic instability,
    176–177
  jail creation of, 182–184
  and law, 72–73
  and prison gangs, 177–180
  and production of violence,
    175–176
  structural origins, 174–177
  See also Race/ethnicity
Solitary confinement, 206
Special Operations Response
  Team (SORT), 20, 109,
  122–124, 216–217
Spohn, Cassia, 70
Staff
  abuse of power, 21–23, 43